Labor and the Progressive Movement
in New York State, 1897–1916

Labor and the Progressive Movement in New York State, 1897-1916

BY IRWIN YELLOWITZ

The City College of the City University of New York

Cornell University Press

Ithaca, New York

CORNELL UNIVERSITY PRESS

First published 1965

This work has been published with
the assistance of a grant from the
Ford Foundation

Library of Congress Catalog Card Number: 65-16500

PRINTED IN THE UNITED STATES OF AMERICA
BY VAIL-BALLOU PRESS, INC.

To my mother

Acknowledgments

IT is a pleasure to acknowledge the assistance of some of the people who have aided me during the preparation of this book. I should like to thank Professor Philip Taft of Brown University for his helpful criticism and encouragement. My thanks also go to the staff of the New York State School of Industrial and Labor Relations Library at Cornell University in Ithaca, New York, for several kindnesses which lightened the difficult task of working through the John B. Andrews Papers. Despite unexpected difficulties, Mrs. Bernice Linder consistently met my schedules in typing and retyping the manuscript. I am also indebted to the General Faculty Committee on Research of The City College for financial assistance which helped meet the costs of preparing the manuscript. My wife, Barbara, has been a constant source of encouragement and assistance, and to her I owe much more than I can ever acknowledge.

Contents

*Labor and the Progressive Movement
in New York State, 1897–1916*

I

Introduction

BETWEEN the conservative Mugwump reformers who moved into the right wing of Progressivism and the quasi-socialists who occupied its radical fringe there was politically a great distance. The supporters of the New Freedom attacked specific evils in the economy, especially those associated with the "interests," while the forces of the New Nationalism called for permanent government regulation of the economic heights rather than for attacks upon specified and supposedly temporary weaknesses. For the years 1910–1912 this difference has been examined thoroughly, even though it had greater meaning for the development of Progressivism in the states than in the presidential campaign of 1912.[1] However, other differences among Progressives are not always recognized. There were the Progressives who believed politics should be the vehicle for reform, and those who

[1] Herbert Margulies, "The Decline of Wisconsin Progressivism, 1911–1914," *Mid-America*, XXXIX (July 1957), 138–148; Ransom E. Noble, Jr., *New Jersey Progressivism before Wilson* (Princeton, 1946), pp. 122–127; George E. Mowry, *The California Progressives, 1900–1920* (Berkeley, 1951), pp. 161, 204–221. It should also be noted that recent studies have stressed the diversity of opinion within American business, and the hazards of generalizing for the entire group from the actions of some of its members. See Sidney Fine, *Laissez-Faire and the General Welfare State: A Study of Conflict in American Thought, 1865–1901* (Ann Arbor, Mich., 1956), p. 96; Robert Wiebe, "Business Disunity and the Progressive Movement, 1901–1914," *Mississippi Valley Historical Review*, XLIV (March 1958), 664–685; Robert P. Sharkey, *Money, Class and Party: An Economic Study of Civil War and Reconstruction* (Baltimore, 1959); and Stanley Coben, "Northeastern Business and Radical Reconstruction: A Re-examination," *Mississippi Valley Historical Review*, XLVI (June 1959), 67–90.

used reform as the vehicle for political preferment; there were the Progressives of the great stretches of the trans-Appalachian and trans-Mississippi West, who bore the heavy stamp of Populism, and who differed profoundly from the urban reformers in method and spirit as well as in program.[2] The Progressives who demanded social justice through the eradication of the evils of slum life, an end to the exploitation of female and child labor, the improvement of working conditions in stores and factories, and the abolition of excessive hours and inadequate wage structures, often had little in common with those who regarded the control of trusts, direct democracy, or effective public utilities commissions as the vital areas of reform. The social Progressives—who believed that social justice was the major objective for Progressivism—occupied a political position to the left within the reform movement as a whole, and the conservative wing of the movement usually offered little support to a program of labor and social welfare legislation.

The social Progressives stressed the importance of labor legislation in restoring justice to an economic order that still followed outdated slogans and forms.[3] Both employer and worker faced new problems which nineteenth-century individualism could not meet. Unregulated competition made a mockery of the virtues that the nineteenth century had associated with a free individual in a free economy. The scrupulous employer discovered that his humanity placed him at a disadvantage against the hordes of dishonorable businessmen. The weak and defenseless—children, women, and unskilled, unorganized men —became the victims of America's reliance on the formulas of the past. "To set limits to this competition, to establish standards in law which it cannot overcome, and thus to put an end to the

[2] See Russel B. Nye, *Midwestern Progressive Politics: A Historical Study of Its Origins and Development, 1870–1950* (East Lansing, Mich., 1951), and Paul W. Glad, "Bryan and the Urban Progressives," *Mid-America*, XXXIX (July 1957), 169–179.

[3] Henry Seager, *Social Insurance* (New York, 1910), Ch. 1.

process of exploitation are the meaning and purposes of *Labor Legislation*." [4]

To accomplish this aim, the social Progressives demanded permanent government intervention in certain important areas of the economy. They recognized that the American people still relied upon laissez-faire principles, but for them this only meant that the people's attitude must be changed. The social Progressives were convinced that "the fundamental conditions under which industry should be carried on, and labor performed, is, or should be, a prime function of the state." [5] They set out to persuade the nation that this principle must become operative if social injustice were not to be condoned under the guise of economic individualism.

Most of the social Progressives would have limited government intervention to alleviating the worst social and industrial evils. However, as the years passed the list of proscribed evils grew. By 1912 many social Progressives were demanding a complete program of government social reform, including minimum wage laws, workmen's compensation, health, accident and unemployment insurance, old age pensions, the abolition of child labor, the eight-hour day, and efficient, continuous enforcement of the labor laws. [6] Unlike those of the socialists, the aims of the social Progressives did not cross the theoretical boundaries of a capitalist system. [7] Their reforms were designed to strengthen American capitalism, not to destroy it.

The failure to recognize the heterogeneous nature of Progres-

[4] New York Branch, American Association for Labor Legislation, *Labor Legislation* (pamphlet, 1910), p. 3.

[5] William Willoughby in *American Labor Legislation Review* (American Association for Labor Legislation), IV (March 1914), 38.

[6] A fine presentation of the complete social Progressive program is in "Social Standards for Industry," a report prepared by the committee on standards of living and labor of the National Conference of Charities and Correction. See National Conference of Charities and Correction, *Proceedings*, 1912, pp. 376ff.

[7] Edward T. Devine, *Misery and Its Causes* (New York, 1909), pp. 120–121.

sivism leads to serious difficulties. The New Deal can become a mere adjunct of Progressivism if one concentrates on the advanced positions of the New Nationalism, especially as set forth in the Progressive Party platform of 1912.[8] Theodore Roosevelt had accepted an advanced social Progressive program for the social and industrial planks of the Bull Moose platform.[9] Even though the social Progressives thirsted for public discussion of their program, and even though they recognized that "social reform has the services of America's first publicity man and our ideas will become common currency," some reformers doubted Roosevelt's basic commitment to this program. "Just as defeat in Chicago has made him less of a politician and more amenable to real progressive influences so defeat this time in second place will deepen the liberalizing influences." [10] The campaign of 1912 marked a high point for the social Progressives, but by 1915 a conservative reaction in the states had stalled the drive for social reform. The New Deal program incorporated the social Progressives' demands of 1912, and much of the rest of the New Nationalism philosophy; but it also converted the program of one reform group, or the political platform of a third party, into a national program that could command popular support and become law. Many social Progressives had presented the concepts of positive government and significant social reform long before the New Deal,[11] but despite Theodore Roosevelt's temporary infatuation with their program, they had not convinced a

[8] See Andrew M. Scott, "The Progressive Era in Perspective," *The Journal of Politics*, XXI (Nov. 1959), 685–701.

[9] See Allen F. Davis, "The Social Workers and the Progressive Party, 1912–1916," *American Historical Review*, LXIX (April 1964), 671–688, for an excellent discussion of the role played by one prominent group of social Progressives in the campaign of 1912. Also see Josephine Goldmark, *Impatient Crusader: Florence Kelley's Life Story* (Urbana, Ill., 1953), pp. 139–140.

[10] Lillian Wald Papers (New York Public Library): Henry Moscowitz to Wald, Aug. 27, 1912.

[11] Sidney Fine in *Laissez-Faire and the General Welfare State*, pp. 167–369, points out that the call for the use of government as an agency for

majority of the Progressive movement, much less the nation as a whole.

Overemphasis on the reformers who demanded permanent government action erroneously suggests that the New Deal was the stepchild of Progressivism. It would be equally easy to demonstrate—so long as one selected conservative elements—that the Progressives had no interest whatever in continuous government intervention in the economy, and that the movement merely attempted to preserve a nineteenth-century economic system in the face of twentieth-century requirements. The true complexity of Progressivism is revealed only when the disparate elements of the reform group are viewed in relation to one another. For this purpose, studies of Progressivism in the states are indispensable.

Progressivism began in the cities and states of the nation. Small groups of citizens attacked the problems presented by industrialization, mass democracy, urbanization, and the decay of nineteenth-century values based on the individual and his free will. Progressivism steadily grew in the first decade of the twentieth century, expanding into new areas of interest, demanding new reforms, enrolling increased numbers of adherents, and, of course, leading to important struggles within the major parties. By the time the Progressive revolt assumed importance in Congress, many states had active reform movements, and political changes in the states had already occurred; by the time the Progressive spirit invaded the presidential campaign of 1912 it had already been distilled and defined in a series of battles in the states. An examination of the reform movements in the states and cities has begun, and in this study the author hopes to help demonstrate that Progressivism at the national level added little

---

social reform had become recognizable in the last quarter of the nineteenth century. The social Progressives were organized around this principle and made the concept an effective force for reform. The New Deal marked the general acceptance of extensive social reform through legislation.

that was new to the program, methods, or philosophy of the movement, although it did produce a program of federal legislation while contributing significant momentum for reform throughout the nation.[12]

Organized labor had a strong interest in the work of the Progressives, especially in those activities that were intended to provide social justice; yet the role of the labor movement in the reform forces has not been discussed very fully. Once again this gap in our knowledge of Progressivism is the result mainly of an overemphasis on the national labor movement and a consequent lack of attention to the state federations of labor, the city central labor councils, and the local unions.[13] Organized labor often played an important role in securing social reforms, and this was certainly true in New York. In an attempt to utilize its inchoate voting potential, the labor movement throughout the nation developed a series of complex procedures which reflected the basic ideology of American trade unionism; and labor organizations often cooperated with the social Progressives, although at other times they bitterly opposed the reformers. But little of this is evident from an examination of the A.F.L. and its work. Most labor legislation before the New Deal had to be confined to the

[12] George E. Mowry, *The Era of Theodore Roosevelt, 1900–1912* (New York, 1958), provides some discussion of Progressivism in the cities and states. More important is his *California Progressives.* For Wisconsin, see Robert Maxwell, *La Follette and the Rise of the Progressives in Wisconsin* (Madison, 1956); Margulies, *op. cit.,* and "Political Weaknesses in Wisconsin Progressivism, 1905–1908," *Mid–America,* XLI (July 1959), 154–172. Also of use are Noble, *New Jersey Progressivism;* Winston A. Flint, *The Progressive Movement in Vermont* (Washington, 1941), and Louis Geiger, *Joseph W. Folk of Missouri* (University of Missouri Studies, XXV, No. 2, 1953). Charles N. Glaab, "The Failure of North Dakota Progressivism," *Mid-America,* XXXIX (Oct. 1957), 195–209, and Nye, *Midwestern Progressivism,* are both helpful. Dewey W. Grantham, *Hoke Smith and the Politics of the New South* (Baton Rouge, La., 1958), presents some interesting information on the nature of Progressivism in Georgia.

[13] See Philip Taft, "Labor History and the Labor Issues of Today," *Proceedings of the American Philosophical Society,* CVI (Aug. 1962), 306–307.

6

states because of constitutional limitations, and it was thus at the state level that organized labor made its greatest contribution to the reform movements.

A study of the state labor movements reveals the struggle between small-town and big-city unions; between strong unions that controlled their trades and weak organizations that struggled to keep alive; and between those unionists who called for socialism in the future but demanded higher wages, shorter hours, and better working conditions for the present, and those labor leaders who focused their attention entirely on immediate gains. It is unfortunate that so little attention has been given to the state and local labor organizations, and especially to their connections with the middle-class reformers of the Progressive movement.[14] One aim of this study is to suggest the importance of this area of investigation, and it will carefully examine the relationship between the Progressives and organized labor in New York.

Events abroad had an important influence on American social Progressives. Since foreign states faced many of the same prob-

---

[14] See Clara M. Beyer, "History of Labor Legislation for Women in Three States," U.S. Department of Labor, Women's Bureau, *Bulletin* No. 66 (Washington, 1929), and Gerald D. Nash, "The Influence of Labor on State Policy, 1860–1920: The Experience of California," *The California Historical Society Quarterly*, XLII (Sept. 1963), 241–257. Two fine studies of the labor movement in California that shed some light on organized labor's political activities are Grace H. Stimson, *Rise of the Labor Movement in Los Angeles* (Berkeley, 1955), and Walton Bean, *Boss Ruef's San Francisco: The Story of the Union Labor Party, Big Business and the Graft Prosecutions* (Berkeley, 1952). Also valuable are Robert E. L. Knight, *Industrial Relations in the San Francisco Bay Area, 1900–1918* (Berkeley, 1960), and Melvyn Dubofsky, "New York City Labor in the Progressive Era, 1910–1918" (unpublished doctoral dissertation, University of Rochester, 1960). J. Joseph Huthmacher has tentatively suggested that Progressivism was not merely a middle-class movement, and he calls for recognition of the part played by the urban lower class and by organized labor in advancing the cause of Progressivism. See "Urban Liberalism and the Age of Reform," *Mississippi Valley Historical Review*, XLIX (Sept. 1962), 231–241.

lems that the social reformers hoped to eliminate in the United States, these Progressives attached a good deal of importance to contact with Europeans interested in reform and to close study of foreign conditions.

Britain and Germany established comprehensive programs of social insurance in an attempt to solve their persistent "labor question." Bismarck sponsored Germany's basic insurance codes in the 1880's; Britain did not organize a system of social insurance until the Liberal Party's reforms of 1906–1911, culminating in the National Insurance Act of 1911. Britain's insurance program included old age pensions, unemployment insurance, health insurance, and workmen's compensation for accidents.[15] Other nations had more modest programs, but by 1914 the principle of social insurance seemed well established in Europe.

Although some social Progressives favored social insurance, most American reformers emphasized the regulation of the labor of women and children, and the improvement of conditions of work in factories and home workrooms. Except for workmen's compensation, American states did not develop any sort of social insurance. Many European nations had developed their compensation systems before 1910. In the United States, thirty-one states passed workmen's compensation laws between 1911 and 1917, and these laws covered 75 per cent of American workers. Although the compensation laws differed in detail among the European nations, and among the American states, comparison in a general way is still possible. The extent of coverage, flexibility of administration, and rate of benefit in the laws of the American states, including those of New York, approached the

[15] For a complete discussion of German social insurance see William H. Dawson, *Social Insurance in Germany, 1883–1911* (London, 1912). American interest in the British National Insurance Act of 1911 was high. See the careful summaries and evaluations of the Act in Robert F. Foerster, "The British National Insurance Act," *Quarterly Journal of Economics*, XXVI (Feb. 1912), 275–312, and Edward Porritt, " The British National Insurance Act," *Political Science Quarterly*, XXVII (June 1912), 260–280.

standards established in Europe, although benefits in the United States usually were paid for a shorter period.[16]

Australia and New Zealand adopted a different approach. Between 1894 and 1912, New Zealand and the various states of Australia had all enacted arbitration or minimum wage laws. These statutes applied to the major industries, and sooner or later they all became compulsory. Although there were differences between arbitration boards and minimum wage boards, both made their decisions upon the crucial issue of wages. Strikes or lockouts were barred on any issue that fell within the jurisdiction of the boards. Australia began to develop this juridical approach to the labor problem after a bitter period of strikes in the early 1890's. Organized labor failed to win its demands, and the leadership concluded that more could be gained from arbitration than from direct action.[17] At first employers generally opposed the boards, but later most of them cooperated when it became clear that the wages set by the awards failed to keep up with prices. Besides, the use of the boards usually maintained industrial peace. "Indeed, the very machinery which by experiment had been devised to enforce fair and reasonable economic justice set limits to any rapid and far reaching working-class advance." [18]

But Australia and New Zealand did not experiment with other forms of labor legislation. Neither, for example, developed the sort of social insurance program contained in the British act of 1911. Australia did not regulate the working hours of men; New Zealand did. In both nations, however, the eight-hour working

[16] "Workmen's Compensation Laws of the United States and Foreign Countries," U.S. Department of Labor, Bureau of Labor Statistics, *Bulletin* No. 126 (Dec. 1913), 1–464, and No. 203 (Jan. 1917), 9–939; "Comparison of Workmen's Compensation Laws of the United States up to December 31, 1917," U.S. Department of Labor, Bureau of Labor Statistics, *Bulletin* No. 240 (May 1918), 5–101.

[17] Gordon Greenwood, ed., *Australia: A Social and Political History* (Sydney, 1955), pp. 202, 214.

[18] *Ibid.*, p. 254. Also see W. B. Sutch, *The Quest for Security in New Zealand* (London, 1942), pp. 90–91.

day was on its way to becoming standard. An American investigator declared that "self-help, organization and public agitation" secured the eight-hour day for Australian workers without the use of legislation.[19]

American states made no effort to enact the kind of legislation used in Australia or New Zealand. Both industry and organized labor in the United States successfully fought the suggestions from Progressive sources that compulsory arbitration could eliminate industrial strife. The social Progressives accepted the concept of a public interest in industrial affairs; but public opinion in the United States would accept this principle only for certain classes of "weak" employees, such as women and children, and thus the experience of the two Pacific nations failed to become a model for the United States.

European nations enacted laws to protect women and children, and to establish certain minimum safety and health standards for all workers in factories.[20] The United States kept pace with the major European states in this form of government regulation, much of which originated before 1900, although it became effective only in the present century, when the laws were recodified and extended, and their enforcement was taken seriously. All the Western European nations regulated the hours of women and children, and many American states had laws equally good—or bad—depending on one's point of view. Few

[19] Victor S. Clark, "Labor Conditions in Australia," U.S. Department of Commerce and Labor, Bureau of Labor, *Bulletin* X (1905), 169. This report and its companion, Victor S. Clark, "Labor Conditions in New Zealand," *Bulletin* VIII (1903), 1142–1311, provide a complete discussion of the arbitration and minimum wage boards.

[20] The exhaustive accounts by William Willoughby, "Foreign Labor Laws," United States, *Bulletin of the Department of Labor*, IV–VI (1899–1901), and C. W. A. Veditz, "Child-Labor Legislation in Europe," U.S. Department of Commerce and Labor, Bureau of Labor, *Bulletin* XXI (July 1910), 1–413, are extremely valuable. Also see Charles Pipkin, *The Idea of Social Justice: A Study of Legislation and Administration and the Labour Movement in England and France between 1900 and 1926* (New York, 1927).

statutes either here or abroad met the minimum requirements set up by the National Child Labor Committee of the United States. By 1914 only nine American states, including New York, had laws that met the Child Labor Committee's stipulation that there was to be no child labor under fourteen years of age (or sixteen in mines), no night work, a maximum eight-hour day for children between fourteen and sixteen, and an effective system for proving the ages of children.[21] In 1916 Congress passed a law incorporating these requirements for all businesses engaged in interstate commerce. However, this bill and a subsequent attempt to revise it both went down before the Supreme Court.

In 1909 the British established minimum wage boards for three "sweated" trades, and they added four more trades in 1913. Most of the workers concerned were women. In 1912 the British government also passed minimum wage legislation for the miners in order to end a disastrous national coal strike. Although such legislation had been recognized as a political necessity, the government clearly refused to accept the principle that the wages of adult men should be regulated by law. Twelve American states, not including New York, passed minimum wage legislation during the years 1912–1917, and these laws specifically limited the coverage to women and children.[22]

American and European practice also agreed concerning the regulation of the hours of adult men. The French and the British enacted an eight-hour day for their miners in 1905 and 1908 respectively. Some of the American states also limited hours in certain special trades. By 1921 fifteen states had regulated the hours of miners because of the extremely dangerous and unhealthful working conditions. However, the major mining

---

[21] Veditz, *op. cit.*, and *History of Labor in the United States*, Vol. 3 (New York, 1935), p. 438. Elizabeth Brandeis's discussion of American labor laws in this classic study is a basic reference tool for all work in this area.

[22] *History of Labor in the United States*, Vol. 3, pp. 501–519.

states, notably Pennsylvania, West Virginia, and Illinois, did not enact this legislation. By 1914 twenty-seven states, including New York, and the federal government had limited the hours of railroad workers as a safety measure.[23] The Adamson Act of 1916 gave the eight-hour day to American railroad workers, but this was a special case made necessary by political considerations, closely resembling the British concession to the miners in 1912. Neither the United States nor the European nations accepted government regulation of the hours worked by men as a matter of general policy.

Finally, in both Europe and the United States it had been agreed that government might establish standards for working conditions in factories so as to protect the health and safety of all employees. However, methods of enforcing these regulations differed. European governments provided an executive official with great discretionary authority to make new regulations, permit exceptions in special cases, revise rules as conditions changed, and set the exact requirements for different industries. In the United States the statutes attempted to cover all these possibilities, with the result that evasion, frequent amendment, and long court reviews were quite common. For this reason Wisconsin adopted the European practice for safety legislation when it organized the Industrial Commission in 1911. New York followed in 1913, and by 1915 six other states had the same system of enforcement for factory laws concerning safety and health. However, most American states had not accepted this principle before World War I.[24]

Despite the greater flexibility of their procedures, European nations had serious difficulty in enforcing their labor laws. Many American labor laws were completely worthless because of inefficient or nonexistent inspection procedures, and the social Progressives discovered that the European states could give little help in this area. Britain, France, Belgium, and Austria each had

[23] *Ibid.*, pp. 540–563.   [24] *Ibid.*, pp. 653–656.

an inadequate number of inspectors; Britain and Germany employed local officials to assist in inspection, and this practice led to the same variations in enforcement that had plagued American states when local health or police officials were given the responsibility; doctors and school officials often ignored provisions of the child labor laws in response to the pleas of parents that they needed whatever their children could earn; the courts regarded labor legislation with hostility, and where they did not emasculate enforcement through their interpretation of a law, they often weakened its effectiveness by suspending sentences for violators or by levying fines so low that conviction carried no real penalty for the offender; and labor unions often attacked the middle-class composition of the inspection force, asserting that this constituted discrimination against workers.[25]

Enforcement continued to be a serious problem for the American social Progressives. Politicians might respond temporarily to demands for reform, but the forces opposed to the laws were continually discovering new forms of evasion which proved hard to combat in the face of official inertia. When weaknesses that had appeared in enforcement called for new legislation, the public rarely responded to the less sensational task of refining the execution of the law as it had to the campaign that produced the original statutes. The courts, of course, stood beyond the immediate reach of the social reformers. Thus again and again the social Progressives saw their hard-won gains vitiated by ineffective enforcement.

American social reformers believed that in advanced capitalistic states industrial problems were universal, and that since the

[25] "Administration of Labor Laws and Factory Inspection in Certain European Countries," U.S. Department of Labor, Bureau of Labor Statistics, *Bulletin* No. 142 (Feb. 1914), p. 24; Veditz, *op. cit.*; and Victor S. Clark, "Woman and Child Wage-Earners in Great Britain," U.S. Department of Commerce and Labor, Bureau of Labor, *Bulletin* XVIII (Jan. 1909), 1–85.

problems were so often the same, the solutions might be expected to follow similar pathways. Although no two were exactly alike, nations were regarded as enough alike to allow a transfer of experience from one to another. Therefore, the reformers believed that the United States should avoid the mistakes of foreign nations and use their experience as a basis for a comprehensive and efficient system of labor law. However, American legislators paid little attention to this thesis.

The thesis came under attack from several quarters. Some of its opponents stressed the differences between conditions in the United States and in foreign nations. Victor S. Clark, who made several investigations of foreign labor laws for the United States Bureau of Labor, contended that the Australian experience could not be utilized in his own nation. Clark believed that since the United States exported manufactured goods and had to compete in foreign markets, wage regulation would be more difficult than in Australia, where this problem did not exist. Working conditions were about the same in Australia's two leading states, whereas in the United States the differences among the states were great, and Clark argued that the problem of competition among the industries of the various states would limit the effectiveness of state arbitration boards. In Australia there was no tradition barring the delegation of legislative power to arbitration or minimum wage boards, which would have been a serious problem in this country.[26] Clark did not deny the possible usefulness of arbitration procedures in Australia, but it was his belief that conditions in America precluded their success.

The Australian system also attracted the attention of the National Association of Manufacturers, which sent a special three-man committee to study Australia's industrial legislation. They reported that it was a total failure. And since it had failed among the homogeneous Australian population, they argued, it certainly would not succeed among the "heterogeneous masses of

[26] Clark, "Labor Conditions in Australia," pp. 159–160.

workers" in the United States.[27] Furthermore, the N.A.M.'s committee denied any value to the whole concept of government regulation, in whatever country. It was idiotic, in their opinion, to expect that government regulation could produce a more efficient economy and greater wealth than the freedoms of an unregulated capitalist system. Their condemnation of Australia's labor laws, which they labeled "State Socialism," was in fact complete.

Other opponents of foreign methods emphasized some particular genius or spirit of the American people which made foreign experience alien to the United States. The well-known investment banker Henry Clews believed that one hundred and thirty years of American history had placed "our system of government beyond the line of experimentation and raised it to such an elevation of recognition and respect, that it now ranks as the highest among all the nations." [28] In his opinion even postal savings banks, though admittedly successful in Britain, were unsuited for America. Clews finally concluded that "as a nation we have always been self-reliant and paddled our own canoe. We should remain so and make no concessions to foreign opinion, least of all to socialistic opinions, in the management of our public affairs." [29]

Samuel Gompers likewise believed that government regulation such as had been instituted in Australia should not be attempted in the United States. Strong trade unions would, in his opinion, secure all the gains that might be produced by legislation, and without placing American workers under the control of the middle-class members of government boards and agencies. Gompers concluded, "There is nothing in the system of govern-

[27] National Association of Manufacturers of the United States of America, *Report of the American Trade Commission on Industrial Conditions in Australasia* (New York, 1914), pp. 135–136.

[28] Henry Clews, *Financial, Economic and Miscellaneous Speeches and Essays* (New York, 1910), p. 277.

[29] *Ibid.*, p. 311.

mental regulation of industry as developed in New South Wales that is in conformity with the spirit or the genius of the people of the United States." [30]

Thus Americans tended to see in foreign experience whatever they wanted to see, and despite the social Progressives' hopes that the labor laws of other nations would provide many models for American statutes, opponents of reform discovered nothing abroad that required them to change their attitude.

As Samuel P. Hays has recently suggested, the local histories of an industrialized society can reveal the roots of social processes which more general studies fail to discover: "Local history, if purely factual and descriptive, advances knowledge in only a rudimentary fashion; but if local history can illuminate broad processes of social change concretely, then it adds a dimension unobtainable through an emphasis on top-level, na-tionwide personalities and events." [31] No two American states were alike, no two states met the same problems in exactly the same way; and thus New York could not be used as a basis for generalization about the precise situation in other states.[32] How-ever, the same political and social forces were at work in the various states, and a study of New York, conducted in line with Hays's suggestion, can identify these forces, suggest the areas of cooperation and disagreement between organized labor and or-ganized reformers, indicate the philosophy and methods of the reformers, and evaluate organized labor's political efforts. A study of the situation in New York can serve as a guide to what went on in other states, at the same time granting that no other area will duplicate it even though important and basic similarities will appear.

[30] Samuel Gompers, "Australasian Labor Regulation Schemes," *American Federationist*, XXII (April 1915), 263.

[31] Samuel P. Hays in his Foreword to Roy Lubove, *The Progressives and the Slums: Tenement House Reform in New York City, 1890–1917* (Pittsburgh, 1962), p. ix.

[32] See Beyer, *op. cit.*, Ch. 1.

Organized labor in New York was dominated by the business unionism of A.F.L. affiliates, with a bit of seasoning from socialist unions and unionists. It contained both immigrant and native workers. The legislative and political activities of the New York State Federation of Labor and the central labor councils in the cities resemble the actions of similar labor organizations in other industrial states. In New York, as in other states, the social Progressives cooperated with organized labor. Similar problems arose from this attempt to coordinate the work of middle-class reform organizations and trade unions. The social Progressive organizations in New York also had difficulty in defining their purposes, in selecting the most efficient methods, and in securing money and personnel. Problems of the same sort arose in other states. New York debated the same major reforms that were debated throughout the nation, and the successes—and failures —in the Empire State suggest the pattern elsewhere. The attempts to enforce the law produced the same serious problems in New York as in other areas. Finally, the New York electorate contained all shades of opinion, from rural and business conservatism on the right to the rigid Marxism of Daniel De Leon or the revisionism of Morris Hillquit and Meyer London on the left.

Thus New York is a useful area in which to examine the efforts of organized labor and of the social Progressives to win significant reforms, and to cooperate with one another. It also suggests important conclusions about the methods and effectiveness of political action by organized labor. It is to be hoped that there will be studies of Progressivism and the activities of organized labor in other states. Such work should add immeasurably to our understanding of reform in the early decades of the twentieth century.

II

The Legislative Forces
of Organized Labor

ORGANIZED labor was a permanent force for reform during the Progressive movement in the United States, demanding as it did a redefinition of important ideas in the American tradition as well as an increasing share of the national wealth for the worker. According to the American Federation of Labor's general policy, well organized, prudently managed trade unions would secure better hours, wages, and working conditions through concerted economic action; in practice, however, organized labor campaigned increasingly for labor reforms through legislation, particularly in the decade after 1906. The antistrike injunction and the inclusion of labor unions under the Sherman Anti-Trust Act had to be removed in order to free trade unions for efficient action. Organized labor devoted much of its legislative effort to these two purposes. State labor organizations also discovered that significant steps might be taken toward better working conditions through legislation, although the primary emphasis continued to be on economic action by trade unions.

Unlike many European labor movements, American organized labor generally was not attracted to socialism. In fact the American unions shared many of the middle-class ideas associated with conservatism. Samuel Gompers realized that the middle class in the United States was a state of mind as well as an economic category, and he understood that most of the workers in the A.F.L. were more interested in earning the status and benefits of the middle class in a capitalist society than in the possible rewards to the proletariat in a socialist system.[1] American workers had been influenced strongly by the well-publicized ideals of the middle class; furthermore, most of the A.F.L. members were skilled and semiskilled workers who could earn wages much above the subsistence level, especially in strongly organized trades. Other workers refused union membership because of the barrage of propaganda portraying organized labor as a dangerous foreign idea. Employers often reinforced this campaign with open opposition of their own.[2] This basic middle-class orientation of American organized labor is vital in understanding the policy of the A.F.L. and its affiliates.[3]

Organized labor claimed to represent the entire working force, but in 1910 it numbered only 5.5 per cent of the industrial workers. The unions enrolled 6.8 per cent of the men and .9 per cent of the women workers, and in only two industries, liquor distilling and brewing, did the membership rise to more than 40

[1] Moses Rischin, "From Gompers to Hillman: Labor Goes Middle Class," *The Antioch Review*, XIII (June 1953), 201.

[2] Theresa Malkiel, *The Diary of a Shirtwaist Striker* (New York, 1910), illustrates very well the workers' hostility to foreign ideas. The fictional diary was written to propagandize socialist dogma. It is interesting that the author depicts the working-class parents and fiancé of the native-born shirtwaist worker as opponents of her involvement with "anarchists." They also oppose the very ideas of unions and strikes for women.

[3] See William Z. Foster, *From Bryan to Stalin* (London, 1937), p. 44, and Anthony Bimba, *The History of the American Working Class* (New York, 1927), p. 192, for Marxist interpretations of the labor movement in the United States which accept the essentially bourgeois nature of the American worker. Writers as different as the radical Louis Adamic, in *Dynamite: The Story of Class Violence in America* (New York, 1934), pp. 194–195, and the cautious Louis S. Reed, in *The Labor Philosophy of Samuel Gompers* (Studies in History, Economics and Public Law Edited by the Faculty of Political Science of Columbia University, No. 327, New York, 1930), criticize the A.F.L. policies, but not the necessity for its basic conservatism. Selig Perlman and Philip Taft, *History of Labor in the United States, 1896–1932*, Vol. 4 (New York, 1935), p. 5, also regard the principle of conservatism as a necessity.

per cent of the total work force. In the skilled trades not more than 15 or 20 per cent of the workers belonged to labor organizations. Less than 10 per cent of the predominantly unskilled labor force in steel, oil, chemicals, and other mass-production industries were organized.[4] These figures for 1910 take into account the substantial rise in union membership during the 1897–1904 period. During the next twelve years union gains were slower because of determined opposition by employers.[5] Thus the A.F.L. represented only a small minority of the labor force.

Moreover, industrial workers in the United States did not compose a majority of the population. Industrial wage-earners comprised only 35.3 per cent of the work force in 1900, and only 38.2 per cent in 1910. The addition of lower-salaried workers and servants—whose interests did not always coincide with those of organized labor—increased the percentage of the work force that might be labeled "labor" to only 50 per cent.[6]

The numerical weakness of organized labor, the minority position of the industrial worker within the total work force, and the undoubted middle-class orientation of many organized and unorganized industrial workers all help to explain the conservative policies of the A.F.L. If organized labor were to avoid a direct attack by the middle classes and win their support for any part of the unions' program, it had to avoid an assault upon the principle of private property. Any radical move by the A.F.L. not only would excite immediate opposition among potential allies in the middle class, but might drive many workers from the union movement. Public apathy toward unionism

[4] Leo Wolman, "The Extent of Labor Organization in the United States in 1910," *Quarterly Journal of Economics*, XXX (May 1916), 499–500.

[5] Perlman and Taft, *History of Labor*, pp. 16ff. A.F.L. membership climbed from 447,000 in 1897 to 2,072,700 in 1904. The membership in 1916 was 2,772,700.

[6] Alvin H. Hansen, "Industrial Class Alignments in the United States," *Quarterly Publication of the American Statistical Association*, XVII (Dec. 1920), 420–421.

easily could become hostility, as the success of the open shop campaign of 1904–1908 demonstrated. Accordingly Gompers supported efforts to identify the A.F.L. with prominent persons whose support of unionism and the trade agreement would have a favorable influence on the public's attitude toward organized labor.[7] During the Progressive era the American labor movement was not a powerful, well established institution with a sizable membership, an adequate income, and a secure place within American society. Organized labor was a growing movement seeking the offensive, but cognizant of its handicaps. To make it a Goliath, when it was barely a David, is to misinterpret its character entirely.

It must also be recognized that the general prosperity of the Progressive era did not increase labor's real wages significantly. Despite the tremendous growth in profits, and a large increase in production, real wages in the years 1897–1915 remained stationary. Price rises swallowed up gains in money income.[8] Studies of living standards among unskilled workers in New York City indicated that wages were at a subsistence level, or below.[9] Widespread homework, the exploitation of child labor,

[7] Marguerite Green, *The National Civic Federation and the American Labor Movement, 1900–1925* (Washington, 1956), p. 117.

[8] Alvin H. Hansen, "Factors Affecting the Trend of Real Wages," *American Economic Review*, XV (March 1925), 40; Paul H. Douglas, *Real Wages in the United States, 1890–1926* (Boston, 1930), p. 232. Samuel Gompers vehemently denied the contention that real wages had fallen, or had remained stationary. In 1916, he argued that the conditions of American workers, including wages and hours, had improved more during the previous twelve years than they had in any other period or place in history. "If trade-unions can not secure an improvement in the condition of workers, they are a failure." See U.S. House of Representatives, Labor Committee, *Hearings on a Commission to Study Social Insurance and Unemployment*, April 6 and 11, 1916, p. 186; also pp. 43, 127–130, 139–150, 179–192, and 246–261. Gompers's argument receives support from Albert Rees, *Real Wages in Manufacturing, 1890–1914* (Princeton, 1961).

[9] Similar conditions existed in other urban labor centers. The studies concerning New York City include Robert C. Chapin, *The Standard of*

the rental of already overcrowded tenement rooms to lodgers, and long hours of work by women were the results.

Within New York this study will focus on the practical operations of the organizations involved rather than on propaganda pronouncements or theoretical aims and methods. One of the pioneer students of the American labor movement has noted that "history warrants the general statements that unions and especially unions that have lived and worked, have arisen mainly in direct response to the immediate needs and problems of specific working groups, and that they have developed characteristically by the trial-and-error method. . . . Unionists have been prone to act first and formulate theories afterwards." [10] It will be seen that the progressive organizations also were motivated more by the demands of the moment than by the niceties of theory.

In New York, as elsewhere, organized labor's attempts to push important reform legislation through the legislature were centered in state and city organizations rather than in the local unions. Under the name Workingmen's Assembly of the State of New York, the state labor body had originally been organized in 1865 to combat a proposed series of restrictive bills. [11] In 1888 a separate state A.F.L. organization was formed as a result of the struggle between the A.F.L. and the Knights of Labor. Unlike the Workingmen's Assembly, it did not permit the Knights of Labor's locals to affiliate. The Knights also established an exclusive state organization, thus producing a threefold

---

Living among Workingmen's Families in New York City (New York, 1909); Louise B. More, *Wage-Earners' Budgets: A Study of Standards and Cost of Living in New York City* (New York, 1907); and George E. Haynes, *The Negro at Work in New York City* (Studies in History, Economics and Public Law Edited by the Faculty of Political Science of Columbia University, No. 124, New York, 1912).

[10] Robert F. Hoxie, "Trade Unionism in the United States: General Character and Types," *Journal of Political Economy*, XXII (1914), 203–204.

[11] David Ellis, James Frost, Harold Syrett, and Henry Carman, *A Short History of New York State* (Ithaca, N.Y., 1957), p. 531.

division of organized labor's legislative forces. Although there was limited cooperation among these three organizations during the years that followed, serious disagreements also occurred, and lobbying by labor was handicapped severely as a result.[12]

The objectives of these three state organizations were the same: "To obtain the enactment of such measures by the state legislature as will be beneficial to us, and the repeal of all oppressive laws which now exist. . . . To use our utmost endeavors to impress upon the various divisions of workingmen the necessity of close and thorough organization, and of forming themselves into local unions wherever practicable." [13] Almost all the labor laws passed in these years concerned the regulation of the working conditions of women and children. Doubts about the constitutionality of state legislation for men prevented any significant action in this area. Several laws were enacted regarding working conditions in state employment and on public works projects; however, these measures were enforced so weakly and contained so many escape clauses and possible exemptions that they had little effect.[14]

In 1897 the increasing weakness of the Knights of Labor removed the main cause for the division of labor's legislative forces, and a proposal for the fusion of the three groups was made.[15] The Knights of Labor refused, but the other two organizations formed a new Workingmen's Federation of the State of New York, which held its first convention in 1898. In 1901 a split in the moribund Knights of Labor ended that or-

[12] H. L. Hurwitz, *Theodore Roosevelt and Labor in New York State, 1880–1900* (Studies in History, Economics and Public Law Edited by the Faculty of Political Science of Columbia University, No. 500, New York, 1943), pp. 32ff.

[13] From the Workingmen's Assembly Constitution as found in George G. Groat, *Trade Unions and the Law in New York* (New York, 1905), p. 18.

[14] Hurwitz, *Roosevelt and Labor*, pp. 47–48.

[15] *New York Times*, Jan. 25, 1897, p. 7. In 1910 the Workingmen's Federation changed its name to the New York State Federation of Labor. It had earlier affiliated with the A.F.L.

ganization's effectiveness within New York State.[16] The united labor movement now hoped it would have greater influence on the legislature.

The ultimate decision-making body in the Workingmen's Federation was its annual convention, but as in other unions the executive council held the real power because of its continuity and its power to adjust the resolutions of the convention to the needs of changing circumstances. The council determined the order in which bills recommended by the convention were to be presented to the legislature, and the amount of time and money each was to receive.[17] The Council might also "lay over" resolutions if the situation demanded,[18] and delegates regularly objected to the council's disregard of the convention's decisions.[19]

The actual management of the Federation's bills in the legislature was the responsibility of a legislative committee. In addition to its own lobbying activities, the committee supposedly coordinated and organized the efforts of all unions interested in any particular bill. However, unions and city central bodies continued to work for or against bills independently,[20] and the Federation never achieved its goal of becoming the sole representative of the labor interests in the state. Despite the Federation's claims that this multiplicity of labor lobbyists reduced the effectiveness of all, member organizations refused to give complete control over legislation to the state body—an example of the particularism which also was so prominent in the economic activities of the trade unions.

[16] *New York Evening Journal*, Jan. 8, 1901, p. 5.

[17] *Labor Legislative News*, Jan. 16, 1903, p. 1.

[18] Workingmen's Federation of the State of New York, *Official Proceedings*, Annual Convention, 1909, Secretary Bates's Report, p. 2. Several of the *Proceedings* were not paginated and thus references to them must be less precise.

[19] It was very difficult for delegates to discriminate between the council's inability to carry out resolutions of the convention and its intention not to do so.

[20] *The Saturday Critic*, March 28, 1898.

The Federation had an obligation to support the legislative work of member unions, but certainly not that of unaffiliated unions, although in practice it gave aid to both. It was believed that the Federation must support all bills concerning labor if it were to make good the claim that the state organization represented the interests of New York's trade unions. Nevertheless most of the work had to be done by the union, although the chairman of the legislative committee gave what assistance he could. This aid decreased as the years passed, and the number of bills handled by the legislative committee rose precipitously. Even before the merger in 1897, the officials demanded that fewer bills be presented to the legislature so that greater attention might be devoted to each. In 1902 the Federation's legislative committee managed twenty-seven bills; by 1908 the total had increased to seventy-eight despite repeated demands for fewer bills.[21] Under the aegis of the growing progressive spirit after 1910, the number of bills concerning labor rose to two hundred and fifty-eight in 1912,[22] and remained at approximately this figure until 1916. Local unions or members of the legislature sponsored many of these bills, and the legislative committee could not have functioned without somehow paring down the number. In practice, therefore, the executive council selected a few "preferred" measures to be supported actively; the remainder were aided by an appearance at the hearing or a statement in their favor. Since the committee chairmen who controlled labor bills during Republican administrations were usually opponents of organized labor, elected from upstate rural districts,[23] such weak lobbying for a nonpreferred measure almost inevitably meant that the bill would fail, unless another strong labor organization could campaign for it effectively.

Moreover, the problems of the legislative committee were

[21] Workingmen's Federation of the State of New York, *Proceedings*, 1908: Report of Legislative Chairman Fitzgerald.

[22] New York State Federation of Labor, *Proceedings*, 1912, p. 90.

[23] Workingmen's Federation of the State of New York, *Proceedings*, 1905: Report of Legislative Chairman Hooley.

compounded by a continuous lack of funds.[24] Until 1908 it did not even have its own office in Albany. Thus the legislative committee constituted one more step between the convention's resolutions and ultimate action. Its decisions on how to manage bills during the legislature's session had a critical effect on their final fate.

In the Federation's approach to the sponsorship of labor bills may be seen its fundamental method of lobbying. The first step was an effort to prove that organized labor in the state stood firmly for or against a proposed measure; thus the legislative committee would request that labor organizations send representatives to legislative hearings and address letters to individuals elected from their districts. The legislative committee would then claim to represent the united opinion of organized labor. The Federation could now threaten to retaliate at the next election if its wishes were not observed, since it spoke for the interests of a significant group of voters. The effectiveness of this basic policy was weakened, however, by three important factors: the Federation did not represent all unions, the threatened political retaliation defeated few enemies, and member organizations did not always respond to important calls for cooperation.

The first problem was perhaps the least serious of the three. The Federation never claimed more than one-third of the unions in New York as affiliates;[25] but since most of the large unions were members, the Federation did include a majority of the organized workers.[26] Only the Railroad Brotherhoods and the Bricklayers and Masons Union had no representation in the state body.[27] Even so, the small number of affiliated unions led op-

[24] *The Saturday Critic,* May 8, 1897; New York State Federation of Labor, *Proceedings,* 1912, p. 37.

[25] Only one-fifth of the unions in the state were affiliated in 1903. *New York Evening Journal,* Aug. 1, 1903, p. 11. One-third were affiliated in 1909. Workingmen's Federation of the State of New York, *Proceedings,* 1909: Secretary Bates's Report, p. 4.

[26] *New York Evening Journal,* Sept. 17, 1904, p. 9.

[27] Workingmen's Federation of the State of New York, *Proceedings,* 1905: President Pallas's Report.

ponents to attack the Federation's claim that it spoke for organized labor. Thus the officers continually called for increased membership.[28] After 1908 the A.F.L. ordered all its locals and central bodies to affiliate with proper state and city organizations, and this produced an intensive membership drive by the State Federation.[29] Although one hundred and thirty-five unions joined in 1910,[30] a large number continued to remain outside the Federation: the officers had to admit finally that the membership drive had not been a success.[31]

If the union voter had followed the political recommendations of the Federation, and if the member organizations had given full support, the membership problem would have been of little consequence. Organized labor's political action will be discussed fully in later chapters, and it need be said here only that the Federation's basic threat of retaliation lacked the support by voters necessary to make it effective. Furthermore, the Federation had no control over the actions of its affiliated organizations. Strong affiliates had no qualms about openly opposing the state body even concerning decisions by a Federation convention which should have bound all members.[32]

The major source of discord within the State Federation was the Central Federated Union of New York City (C.F.U.), the central body for Manhattan and the Bronx. The C.F.U. belonged to the Federation, and so did many of its member unions; however, the New York City unions often found their interests poorly represented. New York City always had a much greater number of unionists than the upstate areas—the margin varying

[28] Workingmen's Federation of the State of New York, *Proceedings*, 1904: Secretary Bates's and President Pallas's Reports.

[29] Workingmen's Federation of the State of New York, *Proceedings*, 1909: Secretary Bates's Report, p. 6.

[30] New York State Federation of Labor, *Proceedings*, 1910, p. 53.

[31] New York State Federation of Labor, *Proceedings*, 1911, p. 55.

[32] The Albany Central Federation of Labor was a strong supporter of the Federation, yet it repeatedly tabled requests from the state body for legislative aid. See *Official Record*, Aug. 1913, p. 1, and Dec. 1905, p. 1, for examples. The Federation's ability to command the active support of its affiliates was even less when politics was involved.

from 67,000 in 1902 to 318,000 in 1913 [33]—yet the method of representation in the Federation's convention gave a large majority of the delegates to the upstate unions. Each labor organization in the Federation was entitled to one delegate, regardless of its size; unions of three hundred or more members were permitted two delegates.[34] Since upstate New York always had smaller locals and a greater number of them,[35] though far fewer unionists, the New York City majority became a minority within the Federation.[36]

The upstate unions tended to be more conservative than the New York City organizations, primarily because public opinion in upstate cities and towns was decidedly less favorable to unionism as an institution. The C.F.U. compromised less on legislative issues, involved itself more in politics, and generally adopted less conservative positions than the Federation.[37] Unable to dominate the state body, as the membership figures indicated it should have done, the C.F.U. reserved to itself the privilege of independent action when it disagreed with the Federation's policy. Over the years, cooperation between the Federation and C.F.U. was the general rule, but on several of the most important issues, the state organization was embarrassed by open opposition from the C.F.U.

[33] George G. Groat, *An Introduction to the Study of Organized Labor in America* (New York, 1916), p. 128. For complete statistics on organized labor in New York, see the annual report of the New York Bureau of Labor Statistics. New York State figures show no peculiarity, and follow the general trend of A.F.L. membership.

[34] *Official Record*, Sept. 1900, p. 2.

[35] Groat, *Introduction to Organized Labor*, p. 128.

[36] From 1903 to 1916 the president of the Federation was always a New York City man, but the executive council and legislative committee were continually dominated by upstate leaders.

[37] On occasion critics would charge that there was a strong socialist group in the C.F.U. See *The Labor Advocate*, March 10, 1905, p. 5. There were socialist delegates in the C.F.U. after 1899, but they always constituted a small minority and never seriously influenced the central body's policies.

In 1906 the C.F.U. demanded the re-enactment of an 1899 law covering state and city public works projects, which had provided for an eight-hour day and the prevailing wage usually the equivalent of union rates in the better organized trades. The law had been declared unconstitutional in 1902, but an amendment to the state constitution had reversed the court decision. The New York commissioner of labor, P. Tecumseh Sherman, opposed re-enactment of the 1899 law because the penalties for violation had been so stiff that no court would convict.[38] Sherman called for a reduction of penalties and an exemption for new state roads. Lest the opposition of the labor commissioner kill the chances for any bill, the Federation supported his plan. The C.F.U., however, demanded that the old law be passed intact, and in February 1906 the Federation's executive council gave reluctant support to its re-enactment. However, the Federation reserved the right to choose another course of action should the C.F.U. bill not win quick approval.[39] Without actually attacking the New York City bill, the Federation then circulated an amended penalty clause. After much jockeying the legislature passed a compromise bill, which retained the strict penalties of the 1899 law but exempted new state roads.[40] During the struggle the C.F.U. openly attacked the Federation.[41] William Randolph Hearst, who was looking for the C.F.U.'s support as a candidate for governor in 1906, also began to criticize the Federation in his widely read newspapers. This development was considered serious enough to warrant Samuel Gompers's personal intercession, and he did stop further criticism of the state organization by Hearst.[42]

At the Federation's 1906 convention, in the following Sep-

[38] New York State Department of Labor, *Sixth Annual Report of the Department of Labor for the Twelve Months Ending September 30, 1906* (Albany, 1907), Vol. 1, pp. 70–72.

[39] Workingmen's Federation of the State of New York, *Proceedings*, 1906, p. 12.

[40] *Ibid.*, pp. 30–31.   [41] *New York Times*, March 12, 1906, p. 5.

[42] *American Federationist* (April 1906), pp. 230–231.

tember, the C.F.U. and its supporters ran a slate of officers in opposition to the incumbents, but were defeated for every office by a vote of about 105 to 65.[43] A resolution to endorse Hearst, who was now the Democratic candidate for governor, never even reached the floor because of upstate opposition.[44]

In 1911 a split developed between the C.F.U. and the State Federation over workmen's compensation. During the Progressive period, workmen's compensation was undoubtedly regarded as the most important issue by organized labor in New York. A compensation bill, limited to eight categories of "hazardous trades" in which it was compulsory, passed in 1910, but was declared unconstitutional in 1911.[45] Following the procedure used after the eight-hour law had been declared unconstitutional in 1902, organized labor launched the campaign for a constitutional amendment, which had to pass two successive legislatures and be approved by the people in a referendum. In the meantime the Federation supported a voluntary bill in 1912. Once again organized labor was divided, for the C.F.U. demanded a compulsory compensation bill, asserting that one could be framed which would not run into the roadblock of the 1911 decision. The executive council of the Federation called a special conference in February 1912 and attempted to work out a compromise; but when the C.F.U. refused to budge, the upstate-dominated conference supported the Federation's leaders by a vote of 30 to 13.[46] The New York City group refused to accept

[43] Workingmen's Federation of the State of New York, *Proceedings*, 1906, p. 54.

[44] *Official Record*, Nov. 1906, p. 2.

[45] *Ives v. South Buffalo Railway Company*, 201 N.Y. 271.

[46] New York State Federation of Labor, *Proceedings*, 1912, p. 36. Beginning with this convention, the State Federation stopped numbering the annual conventions from the formation of the Workingmen's Federation and began numbering from the establishment of the original Workingmen's Assembly in 1865. Thus the numbering of the conventions jumped from fifteenth in 1911 to forty-ninth in 1912.

the decision of the conference, and supported a separate compulsory compensation bill. Neither passed.[47]

In 1913 a new compensation bill sponsored by the State Federation met open opposition from several important New York City labor leaders.[48] At first the C.F.U. did nothing to aid the Federation, and although it finally supported the state body,[49] the assistance was hardly substantial. The Democratic majority in the legislature passed its own compensation bill—one opposed by the Federation. Only a veto by the Democratic governor, William Sulzer, who was feuding with Charles Murphy, the head of Tammany Hall and Democratic "boss" of the legislature, defeated the compensation bill.

When the Federation's convention met in 1913, it faced a second consecutive failure on compensation legislation, and a repetition of the discord within its ranks. The bitterness increased when its president, Daniel Harris, informed the convention that Tammany had assured him the Federation's workmen's compensation bill would be passed in 1913.[50] The opposition by some New York City labor leaders to the state body's measure, and their subsequent support of the Tammany bill, had given the Hall a chance to declare that its compensation proposal also enjoyed labor's support. These events led the convention to pass a constitutional amendment ejecting any individual or organization that did not support the state organization's decisions.[51] Shortly afterward the executive council expelled the only organization that had formally voted to oppose the Federation's compensation bill.[52] Thus the Federation used the only weapon it had—expulsion—in an effort to enforce discipline among its

[47] *New York Call*, March 2, 1912, p. 3.
[48] New York State Federation of Labor, *Proceedings*, 1913, p. 37.
[49] *New York Call*, April 19, 1913, p. 3.
[50] *New York Call*, May 15, 1913, p. 2.
[51] New York State Federation of Labor, *Proceedings*, 1913, pp. 136, 150.
[52] New York State Federation of Labor, *Proceedings*, 1914, p. 72.

affiliates; however, the state organization's essential lack of power was to become evident once more in 1916.

The organization expelled in 1913 was the United Board of Business Agents, a building trades organization; in 1916 the much more powerful C.F.U. again openly defied the Federation. It was not censured, however, for to have done so would have been to split the New York State labor movement.

In 1916 the Federation's executive council reluctantly supported a bill amending the state's limits on the hours of work for women. John Mitchell, the chairman of the New York State Industrial Commission, and John Lynch, one of its members, framed the bill, which would have permitted work above the legal limit of nine hours per day by women employees in canneries. The same exemption would apply to other industries whenever emergency breakdowns of machinery occurred.[53] Mitchell and Lynch were respected former labor leaders who had been suggested for their New York posts by the trade unions. Mitchell had a national reputation because of his successful leadership of the anthracite coal strike in 1902. He had headed the United Mine Workers for ten years before his replacement in 1908. Lynch was even better known in New York. Before his election in 1900 to the presidency of the International Typographical Union, he had led the Syracuse printers' local and the Syracuse Central Trades and Labor Assembly. Lynch resigned the presidency of the I.T.U. in 1914 to begin his work as a state commissioner.

Mitchell and Lynch contended that the new proposal did not weaken the protection for women, but the social Progressive organizations and the C.F.U. disagreed. The Federation felt compelled to support the two men because they were already under attack for alleged inefficiency. Since the two men were regarded as its nominees, the state organization would have

[53] *New York Call*, May 13, 1916, p. 1; *Legislative Labor News*, May 1916, p. 4.

suffered a loss of prestige if they failed to be reappointed to the Industrial Commission. Thus the details of the bill became less important than the necessity of protecting Lynch and Mitchell. The C.F.U., however, concluded that the reputation of the two well-known commissioners could withstand the loss of the bill, and despite a personal appearance by the two men, it voted 47 to 7 to oppose the state body's stand on the issue.[54] For the first time the Federation had attempted to formulate a joint program of labor legislation with the State Manufacturers Association and the Industrial Commission, and one delegate to the C.F.U. wondered whether the Federation's leaders were not becoming too friendly with nonlabor interests.[55] Even after the bill had been passed by the legislature, the C.F.U. continued to oppose it despite pressure from the Federation for support. Governor Charles Whitman ultimately vetoed it.

Thus the State Federation's quarrels with New York City labor organizations indicate the basic problem of the state body: that although it had to claim to represent all labor in the state in order to make its influence worth something in Albany, there was no guarantee that the member organizations would make this claim stick. The Federation clearly lacked the authority to enforce its assumption of pre-eminence. Without unanimity of opinion, organized labor might still split into contentious factions regardless of any theoretical unity.

The Federation also had to face the problem of opposition from unaffiliated labor organizations such as the Railroad Brotherhoods. On three key railroad bills, the Brotherhoods themselves were divided, the Engineers and Conductors opposing the Firemen and Trainmen. The Federation soon entered the dispute on the side of the latter. From 1902 until 1905 the Engineers and Conductors opposed a semimonthly pay bill, and an extension of a general employers' liability law specifically to railroads. The two Brotherhoods considered their pay high enough

[54] *New York Call*, May 11, 1916, p. 1.
[55] *New York Call*, May 13, 1916, p. 1.

to make the monthly pay system adequate, and believed that the increased costs resulting from an extension of the employers' liability law might be used as an argument against further wage increases.[56] In 1912 the same two Brotherhoods opposed a bill requiring the addition of extra trainmen on long-distance runs since it did not affect them and would only allow the companies to use higher costs as an argument in wage negotiations.[57] These craft disagreements further challenged the Federation's claim that it represented organized labor in New York State.

It should be stressed that the diverse elements within organized labor cooperated on the great majority of bills. Most of the proposals supported by the Federation fitted the interests of organized labor generally, and thus had the support of the affiliated organizations. The Brotherhoods also cooperated with the Federation on many measures,[58] and in 1915 they formed a committee to coordinate their own efforts in the face of a particularly fierce attack on the labor laws by the Legislature.

The campaign in 1915, against the proposed new state constitution, illustrates organized labor's capacity for united action. As the representative of the labor movement, the Federation submitted a program of changes to the constitutional convention; but when only two of its twenty-four proposals were accepted, organized labor fought against the new constitution.[59] Labor opinion agreed that the new document was certainly no better than the old—and might be worse. Trade union organizations of every sort cooperated under the direction of the State Federation. The state body prepared and issued several hundred thousand copies of a circular against the constitution. National unions, state councils, and city central bodies reprinted the same circular at their own expense, thereby greatly increasing the

[56] *The Labor Advocate*, March 24, 1904, p. 1.
[57] New York State Federation of Labor, *Proceedings*, 1913, p. 45.
[58] Workingmen's Federation of the State of New York, *Proceedings*, 1908: Secretary Bates's Report.
[59] *Legislative Labor News*, Oct. 1915, p. 4.

coverage. The C.F.U. and the joint conference of the Railroad Brotherhoods strongly supported the Federation.[60] The New York City campaign included local union meetings, and it was financed primarily by the unions involved. The Brooklyn Central Labor Union alone issued over 100,000 pieces of literature,[61] and the Albany Central Federation of Labor sent representatives to every local union meeting in the city to fight the proposed constitution.[62] The electorate decisively rejected the document in the November election, and although the labor campaign was not the prime reason for this outcome, it no doubt contributed significantly.

But usually the Federation did not receive such unequivocal and active support down to the local union level, although neither did it face active opposition from portions of organized labor. Rather, trade union organizations in New York permitted the Federation to represent organized labor so long as the state body's policies did not conflict with their own vital interests.

At times the legislative committees of the local central labor councils provided vital assistance to the Federation.[63] However, these same organizations could—and did—oppose the state body on other occasions. The Federation encouraged the formation of these local legislative committees because the basic threat of political retaliation could be made much more effective if labor representatives from the districts of wavering legislators worked actively for the bills of the state organization.[64] Under the Federation's control, widespread local support could be the most effective lobbying weapon of organized labor, yet these same local organizations could become centers for divisive activity.

The State Federation shared with all central labor bodies the

[60] *Ibid.*, Dec.. 1915.

[61] *New York Call*, Oct. 11, 1915, p. 1; Oct. 18, 1915, p. 5; Oct. 22, 1915, p. 2.

[62] *Official Record*, Oct. 1915, p. 1.

[63] *Ibid.*, March 1910, p. 1.

[64] Workingmen's Federation of the State of New York, *Proceedings*, 1899, p. 22; *Official Record*, Oct. 1900, p. 2.

two key problems of publicity and finances. The daily newspapers and popular magazines either ignored all but the most sensational labor news or presented a slanted—and usually hostile—view of organized labor's activities and policies.[65] To inform the worker of trade union policies and principles, in many cities the central labor councils attempted to support weekly or monthly newspapers devoted to labor news. Only a minority of these labor newspapers were actually published by the city central bodies. A greater number were issued by private publishers, who would provide space for the official announcements and news of labor organizations, and would adopt an editorial policy favoring unionism as an institution. In exchange the city central labor council designated the newspaper as its official organ.[66] A labor-owned newspaper was more desirable; but the failure of the workers to support the labor press made these ventures highly speculative, and city central bodies were reluctant to invest the large sums of money required.[67]

Some of the privately owned and edited labor newspapers continued to follow an independent course in politics, and this produced bitter disputes between organized labor and the supposedly pro-labor papers.[68] A city central body often ended its support of a newspaper that openly favored political candidates hostile to A.F.L. or State Federation policy. The editors often

[65] The *New York Times* offers one good example of this newspaper coverage. From 1897 to 1904 news of the C.F.U. meetings was printed regularly, but with an emphasis on disputes and personal conflicts within the organization. The reports had a tone of paternal forbearance, and in general tended to make the C.F.U. seem contentious and ridiculous. After 1904 the *Times* followed the general policy of other newspapers and reported only spectacular labor events, or labor's political activities when these agreed with its editorial policy. The State Federation was ignored throughout the period, and the *Times*'s editorials, like those of most newspapers, were thoroughly antiunion.

[66] *Utica Advocate*, Jan. 26, 1901, p. 1.

[67] See *The Saturday Critic*, Feb. 19, 1898, and New York State Federation of Labor, *Proceedings*, 1910, pp. 55–56, for lists of labor newspapers.

[68] See the *Utica Advocate* for Oct. 1900. The newspaper supported McKinley, whereas organized labor tended to favor Bryan.

refused to eliminate political endorsements, and it was frequently charged that they covered their deficits by payments from political machines in need of testimony that certain candidates were favorable to labor. Apathy among the workers and the independence of the editors doomed most of the labor press to a short life.

Bogus labor papers also were published. These claimed to represent organized labor, but they had no official endorsement and usually were issued as an adjunct to a political campaign.[69] The State Federation and local labor councils condemned such newspapers, but they continued to appear.

The Federation did not have an official newspaper until 1911, although beginning in 1903 it did make use of the privately owned *Labor Legislative News*. The editor supported the political policy of the Federation, and faithfully reported the state organization's legislative activities. In 1911 it became the official newspaper of the Federation under the title *Legislative Labor News*.

The C.F.U. did not endorse a newspaper until 1915, when it approved the *New York Call*, a socialist daily. The C.F.U. then asked the State Federation to help support the *Call*'s new bond issue. Fearful of setting a precedent that might lead to involvement with other labor newspapers, the Federation refused.[70] Moreover, the state organization was not pleased by the prospect of having unionism and socialism linked in the policy of a newspaper. The C.F.U. certainly was not socialist, and it recognized the dangers of endorsing the *Call*; but the differences in editorial policy were less important than the lure of an established publication, which would print official labor announcements and report labor news fully. It is thus obvious that organ-

[69] In some instances, labor newspapers vied with each other for readers. In 1905 *The Unionist, Knocker*, and *New York Union Printer* claimed to represent the interests of the printing trades in New York City.

[70] New York State Federation of Labor, *Proceedings*, 1916, p. 185. It is interesting to note that the *Call*'s reporter had been barred from the C.F.U.'s meetings in 1913 for alleged defamation and misrepresentation.

ized labor operated under a severe handicap: as compared with its opponents or with the Progressive societies, organized labor had little opportunity to present its views to the general public; and what was equally important, it had great difficulty in even reaching the masses within the labor movement.

Finances also presented a serious problem, for rarely was the income sufficient, or its sources desirable. From 1901 to 1903 the Federation operated at a deficit: the dues rate of one-third cent per capita was insufficient to meet the annual expenditure of from $2,000 to $3,000.[71] The Federation's convention did not approve the persistent demand of the officers for an increase in the per capita rate until 1905. The executive council had demanded that one cent per capita be the minimum figure for the new rate, but the convention set the dues at one-half cent per member.[72] This rate again failed to produce sufficient income, and the Federation had to continue the publication of an Official Book, crammed with advertising by local and statewide business concerns. The Official Book produced a sizable income, but was a most unsatisfactory source of revenue. Improper solicitation of advertisements was often hinted, and sometimes proved;[73] and the Federation's prestige was not enhanced by its dependence on advertising revenue supplied by business firms which often opposed organized labor in the legislature.

The increased legislative activities of 1912 and 1913, especially in connection with the workmen's compensation bills, once more left the Federation with a deficit and forced it to ask for contributions from organized labor. In 1913 the Federation's convention finally raised the per capita rate to the one-cent figure demanded by the officers in the much less active days of

[71] Workingmen's Federation of the State of New York, *Proceedings*, 1904: Secretary Bates's Report.

[72] Workingmen's Federation of the State of New York, *Proceedings*, 1905: President's and Secretary's Reports, and Resolutions of the Convention.

[73] Workingmen's Federation of the State of New York, *Proceedings*, 1904: Secretary Bates's Report.

1905.[74] This new rate, plus increased membership, put the organization back into the black.

These financial stringencies indicate the fundamental position of the State Federation in the labor movement. Organized labor primarily used the economic weapons of the trade union; the legislative activities of the Federation, although often important, were not the major interest. The unions thus refused to contribute any more to the support of their legislative organization than was absolutely necessary. This was especially true for the poorer and smaller unions, which had a difficult time even meeting their own expenses.

The shortage of funds limited the work of the State Federation and made it absolutely beholden to its members for their voluntary cooperation.[75] The Federation never had the money to carry out a large-scale program of political reward and punishment, and unless local unions and central labor councils contributed manpower and money, as in the 1915 constitutional campaign, the Federation's efforts were confined to the publication of a limited number of printed items, and to occasional visits by officers to different parts of the state. The Federation could not lead the labor movement of New York where it would not go voluntarily. In considering the reform activities of the Federation, and its cooperation with progressive societies, this essential relationship between the state organization and the other elements within organized labor must be borne in mind.

[74] New York State Federation of Labor, *Proceedings*, 1913, pp. 88, 150. The appeal for funds was addressed to all unions in the State, but only a minority (302) contributed even once; 83 answered the second appeal and 23 the third.

[75] A similar situation existed between the A.F.L. and its affiliates. See Philip Taft, *The A.F. of L. in the Time of Gompers* (New York, 1957).

III

The Social Progressive Societies

THE social Progressive movement cannot be studied in the works of a few influential writers, or through the activities of any one organization; it had no great theorist, and the social philosophy and activities of the reform organizations often differed substantially. Yet there was a basic common belief in the need for the improvement of working conditions and the establishment of social justice. This belief carried the social Progressives into a battle against all the conservative forces in a conservative nation. Despite disappointments and handicaps, this group of reformers added a dimension to Progressivism, and suggested a course for American reform which came to fruition during the New Deal.

The social Progressive movement included many elements, but two important types of organizations were peripheral at best. Various charitable groups had been active for many decades, and although they often supported specific reform measures, their focus was on the relief of individual need, not the removal of the causes which had produced such distress. Leaders of these organizations admitted that comprehensive social reform might eventually end the need for charity.[1] Under the influence of the social Progressives' ideas, leaders of the important Charity Organization Society in New York City organized a department for the improvement of social conditions, and they

[1] Social Reform Club of New York, Leaflet, March 1, 1898 (New York Public Library).

suggested that reform was an essential aim of social work.[2] In practice, however, the organized charities endorsed only bills that already had the approval of all the social Progressives, and that had gained a large measure of public support. Social reform was an adjunct to philanthropy, and the work of the charities was thus rather spotty. Moreover, the philanthropic organizations and the reformers occasionally came into open conflict. For example, during a period of high unemployment in 1914–1915, the charities in New York City killed a plan for giving immediate relief to those most in need through churches and trade unions, without the long wait made necessary by elaborate screening procedures.[3] There was a basic gap between the philanthropist and the reformer which theories of reform action and occasional cooperation could not bridge.

Civic reform groups, such as the Citizens Union, the Reform Club, and the City Club of New York, occasionally supported social reform measures which had gained significant popular support. These groups, however, had no real interest in the social Progressive movement, and they usually did not cooperate in the campaigns for social reform legislation.[4] The civic reformers continued the Mugwump tradition of the late nineteenth century, with its emphasis on honest, efficient government. They agreed with the social Progressives that since "most men were busy advancing their private interests, someone had to protect the interests of the community as a whole." [5] However, their main enemy was not social injustice but Tammany Hall.

[2] *Charities and The Commons*, XVII [Feb. 1907], 856; *Charities and The Commons*, XIX (Nov. 2, 1907), 948.

[3] *New York Times*, Dec. 31, 1914, p. 5. Also see Florence Kelley's attack on philanthropists and their lack of interest in the enforcement of child labor laws, National Conference of Charities and Correction, *Proceedings*, 1896, p. 162.

[4] City Club of New York, Papers (New York Public Library): Record of Activities, 1892–1922, indicates how slight the Club's interest was in campaigns for social reform.

[5] Lubove, *The Progressives and the Slums*, p. 90.

Within the ranks of the social Progressives proper, the consumers' leagues occupy a most important position. The original League was formed in 1891, in New York City, to help remedy the poor conditions under which women worked in department stores,[6] and quickly became interested in the general problem of women's working conditions. The New York City League attempted to bring about better conditions for female workers by first informing the public of the evils that existed in the manufacture of a garment, or in the staffing of a department store. The reformers then launched campaigns for the elimination of these bad conditions through legislation or direct consumer boycott of those businessmen who refused to reform themselves.[7]

Other such leagues soon appeared in the United States and Europe, and in 1898 a National Consumers' League was organized to carry on a specific aspect of the expanding work—the promotion of a label that would identify garments made under healthy and fair working conditions as determined by the League. A New York State Consumers' League began its work in 1901, and most of the important cities in the State had local leagues by 1908.[8] The cooperation among these national, state, and local leagues was close since their areas of interest were not mutually exclusive. The consumers' leagues did not believe in charity; instead they attempted to remove specific conditions which produced poverty, ill health, or the demoralization of the working woman.[9] They did not focus on the individual, but on

[6] Goldmark, *Impatient Crusader*, p. 52.

[7] Consumers' League of the City of New York, *Annual Report*, 1896, p. 10.

[8] See the two pamphlets, *Consumers' League of New York State* [1915], issued by the State League; and Consumers' League of the City of New York, *Historical Sketch of the Pioneer Consumers' Leagues* (1908), which outline the organization and activities of the New York State leagues.

[9] Consumers' League of the City of New York, *Annual Report*, 1909, p. 11.

42

the group, namely on that class of unorganized working women who upon investigation had been found to be suffering under poor laboring conditions and inadequate wages.

Women constituted 23 per cent of the working force in New York State in 1900, and 26.9 per cent in 1910. Only Massachusetts had a higher percentage of female workers.[10] New York's female labor force came from native and immigrant backgrounds, and was almost entirely unorganized. Although the consumers' leagues campaigned for the abolition of child labor and the passage of pure food laws, their chief interest was always in the improvement of working conditions for women.[11]

The consumers' leagues placed great reliance on legislative reform, which as the years passed became their most important and effective method.[12] Nevertheless, direct action by consumers was the distinctive method of the leagues, if not the most successful.[13] From the very first, the New York City League sought to enlist support for better working conditions in department stores by preparing a White List. To be on the List a store had to meet a series of requirements for a Fair House, including equal wages regardless of sex, a minimum wage of $6.00 per week for adult, experienced women workers, weekly payment of wages, hours no longer than from 8 A.M. to 6 P.M., three-quarters of an hour for lunch, a Saturday half holiday, one week's paid vacation in the summer, and no workers under fourteen years of age.[14] Consumers were to boycott the stores not

---

[10] Leo Wolman in Vol. 10, *History of the State of New York* (New York, 1933–1937), p. 70.

[11] Frederick Smith Hall, *Forty Years, 1902–1942: The Work of the New York Child Labor Committee* (New York, 1942), p. 68.

[12] Consumers' League of the City of New York, *The Consumers' League: The Why and the Wherefore* (pamphlet) [1919].

[13] J. Elliot Ross, *Consumers and Wage Earners* (New York, 1912), pp. 110–111.

[14] Consumers' League of the City of New York, *Annual Report*, 1897, p. 4.

appearing on the White List, since they did not meet these minimum standards of work. Volunteer workers conducted the frequent investigations necessary in order to designate Fair Houses.[15]

The effectiveness of the White List depended on the cooperation of the public, and the League was forced to admit that most consumers did not consider the conditions of work in choosing a store. One owner, in refusing to cooperate with the League, explained that "courteous treatment, low prices and a well selected stock are more attractive to the average shopper than the questionable honor of belonging to the Consumers' League and being compelled to buy only of stores that carry the seal of approval of the Consumers' League on their back." [16] By 1911 the failure of the White List to affect the business of the unlisted stores in New York City led to such backsliding by the approved shops that it had to be discontinued. Other New York State leagues attempted similar campaigns, but only in Buffalo and Syracuse was even limited success achieved.[17]

The relation of the social Progressives to organized labor constituted a major problem, for the labor movement also had an interest in social reform, and the activities of the reformers and organized labor frequently overlapped. Though both sought to aid the workers, this did not mean they would cooperate. An examination of the relation between organized labor and the social Progressive organizations will show the problems involved in cooperation, and indicate as well the significant differences in outlook among the reform societies.

In its early days, the New York City Consumers' League declared its support of unionism in unequivocal terms:

[15] Consumers' League of the City of New York, *Annual Report*, 1904, p. 11. There were 223 investigations of department stores in this year.

[16] Interview by H. C. F. Koch in the *Harlem Local Reporter and Bronx Chronicle*, June 11, 1898, as found in Consumers' League of New York, Papers (School of Industrial and Labor Relations, Cornell University).

[17] See Consumers' League of Buffalo, *Annual Report*, 1911, 1912; New York State Consumers' League, *Annual Report*, 1909, 1910–1913.

The improvement of the conditions of wage-earners should, where possible, be secured by the action of the wage-earners themselves associated for the purpose because they [the League] are convinced that such associated activity develops both the moral and intellectual nature of those who take part in it, and also that the advantages gained by self-effort are better appreciated and more lasting than those conferred in consequence of the exertions of others.[18]

Female employees of department stores were replaced easily, a situation which hampered effective organization among them. Thus an outside group like the League had to assist.[19]

In theory this remained the position of the New York City and national consumers' leagues, but in practice a much different attitude developed toward trade unionism. It first became evident in the leagues' reaction to strikes, either by established unions seeking better conditions, or by unorganized women demanding union recognition. The socially prominent perennial president of the New York City League, Mrs. Maud Nathan, indicated that the organization had never "sentimentally" supported unions, and often had refused aid to strikes, even among women workers.[20] The League intervened in only a few strikes, including the Troy starchers' strike in 1905, the shirtwaist strike in 1909, and the laundry workers' strike in New York City in 1912. In all three the conditions leading to the strike had been so bad that the workers had won public support, and even persons not connected with the social Progressive movement were active in attempts at a settlement. In none of these cases did the League support the principle of organization.[21]

[18] Consumers' League of the City of New York, *Annual Report*, 1895, p. 6.

[19] Josephine Shaw Lowell, *Consumers' Leagues* (Publications, The Christian Social Union, No. 46, Feb. 15, 1898), p. 30.

[20] Maud Nathan, *The Story of an Epoch Making Movement* (New York, 1926), pp. 59, 62.

[21] Consumers' League of the City of New York, *Annual Report*, 1905, p. 19; Consumers' League of the City of New York, *Annual Report*, 1909, p. 16.

In 1914 the secretary of the New York City League testified before the Factory Investigating Commission that a union among department store clerks would be "of assistance" in enforcing the labor law;[22] but the League took no real steps to encourage the embryonic union then at work.[23] In 1916 the New York City League enthusiastically supported a plan for using the organization as a central clearing house for violations of the labor law, which working women were reluctant to report for fear of losing their jobs. These working women would be affiliated with the League through a Junior Board composed of church, settlement, and girls' club groups.[24] The possibility that such an organization might hinder unionization was not discussed.

The consumers' leagues thus largely ignored the union movement. Their position was that the nonworking-class public, rather than unionization and collective agreements, would produce better working conditions for women. Instead of supporting self-help, the middle- and upper-class women who composed the leagues sought reforms in behalf of the working woman. The theory of 1895 was completely annihilated in practice, and legislation became the key to an improvement in working conditions.

The reaction of the Consumers' League of New York City to the garment industry protocol of 1910 clearly reveals its policy. Mrs. Nathan approved of the protocol because "it recognized that the public is a factor in these disputes, that our point of view is also to be considered on arbitration boards."[25] Subse-

[22] *New York Call,* June 13, 1914, p. 2.

[23] Women's Trade Union League of New York, Papers (New York State Department of Labor Library, New York City): Executive Board Minutes, June 19, 1913, pp. 2–3.

[24] Consumers' League of the City of New York, *Annual Report,* 1916, pp. 8–9; Consumers' League of the City of New York, *Laws Every Woman Worker Should Know* (pamphlet), 1918.

[25] Consumers' League of the City of New York, *Annual Report,* 1910, p. 13.

quently the League became the representative of the public on one of the boards. Thus the fundamental identification of the reformers in the League was not with the working woman but with the public—that is, with the middle class. The Consumers' League sought to improve conditions for workers, but by methods that left the interests of the middle class essentially intact. This social Progressive organization desired no radical shift in social power; it demanded only the correction of evils which, in many cases, were a shock to decency and which also might produce shoddy or disease-laden goods for the consumer. At all times, the middle and upper classes were to retain control of these reform activities, through the leadership of organizations such as the Consumers' League; for experience had proved that the interests of trade unions might not always coincide with those of the public.

The relation between the League and organized labor is further illustrated by the controversy over the National Consumers' League label, which was first issued in 1898. By 1906 the reformers had approved sixty-one manufacturers of ladies' underwear and white goods. To earn the label, a manufacturer had to obey all the factory laws of his state, permit none of his goods to be finished in tenements, allow no overtime without extra pay, and eliminate all child labor under the age of sixteen.

The fledgling International Ladies' Garment Workers' Union soon challenged the Consumers' League label. The Union asserted that its own label covered these industries, and it noted that the League's requirements for the label ignored wages and union recognition.[26] The League replied that it could appeal to persons who could not be reached by union labels, and that the League issued the label only where the I.L.G.W.U. had no unionized firms. Under pressure from the A.F.L., the reformers

[26] *Report and Proceedings of Fifth Annual Convention of the International Ladies' Garment Workers' Union*, 1904, President's Report, pp. 7–8.

finally agreed to withhold the label from any firm the Union declared unfair to organized labor.[27]

The National Consumers' League label was another attempt to substitute middle-class action for that of the trade unions in the improvement of working conditions. Although the I.L.G.W.U. was unable to organize the workers at that time, it objected to having middle- and upper-class reformers set the standards of work in any garment trade. In addition, the apathy of consumers and the active opposition of department stores destroyed the effectiveness of the label.[28] Some social Progressives criticized the National Consumers' League and supported the Union's position. One of them, the Reverend F. J. C. Moran, believed that no reform organization should attempt to guarantee conditions of work—be it by a White List or by a label—since by so doing it substituted middle-class efforts on behalf of the worker for united action by the workers themselves. That this was not a secure basis for reform, he argued, was proved by the failure of the leagues' campaigns for direct action by consumers. He called instead for support of union labels, and for the organization of workers.[29]

In 1910 the National Consumers' League began to endorse garment union labels, but it refused to abandon its own label until a protocol was signed that included public representation.[30] Unionization of the industry, without public participation, did not seem enough assurance that the principles embodied

---

[27] *Ibid.*, p. 7, and *Report and Proceedings of Sixth Annual Convention of the International Ladies' Garment Workers' Union*, 1905, Report of the General Secretary-Treasurer.

[28] Consumers' League of the City of New York, *Annual Report*, 1902, p. 19; and Consumers' League of the City of New York, *Annual Report*, 1914, p. 35.

[29] *Hammer and Pen* (Church Association for the Advancement of the Interests of Labor), March 1906, p. 131.

[30] Consumers' League of the City of New York, *Annual Report*, 1912, p. 17.

in the Consumers' League label would be protected. This basic distrust of union activity, and the insistence on the reformer's participation and control, through middle-class action on behalf of the working woman, were fundamental policies of the consumers' leagues.

The policy of the child labor committees closely paralleled the practice of the consumers' leagues. The formation of such a committee in New York in 1902 preceded the national organization by three years. After an investigation in 1902 had disclosed that child labor was widespread in New York despite state laws designed to limit it, the social Progressives responded by forming the New York Child Labor Committee, which quickly asserted leadership in the field of child labor reform.[31] The Committee also campaigned actively for reform in other major areas which interested the social Progressives, including the hours of work for women, working conditions in factories and stores, and the regulation of tenement manufacturing.

The Committee enjoyed cordial relations with organized labor. The trade unions had no interest in organizing juvenile workers, and fully supported the Committee's efforts to stop child labor. The exclusion of children from the labor force would open new jobs for adults and eliminate one form of low-wage competition. The Committee agreed with the basic belief of the Consumers' League that labor reform should be accomplished by middle-class pressure for legislation. Ideas of class had no place in social Progressive thinking, and organized labor's objection that the middle class might have interests of its own, which would reduce its ability to establish the fairest conditions for labor, was dismissed as a mere "special interest" statement.

The settlement houses gave considerable support to the social reform measures of the consumers' leagues and child labor com-

[31] See Consumers' League of the City of New York, *Annual Report,* 1903.

mittees. However, a fundamental difference in outlook placed the settlements in a distinctive position within the social Progressive movement. Like the organized charities, the settlements were primarily concerned with the individual. They sought to offset the advantages available to the middle classes by an intensive program of intellectual and recreational activities designed to help the underprivileged individual reach his fullest capacity.[32] The settlements supported legislation intended to improve the living and working conditions of the people whom they were hoping to uplift in other ways. Thus the settlements combined an interest in the individual with support of a program of social reform.

Although often friendly to unions,[33] the settlements provided little support for organized labor's economic activities. Instead, they favored the use of legislation to reform certain conditions detrimental to the fullest development of the underprivileged individual. Like the consumers' leagues and child labor committees, the settlements opposed a class analysis of society. Progress, they argued, was not to come through the recognition of class interests, or by compromises among the interest groups in society. They contended that "the interests of any class oppose the good of the State. Settlements should and largely do stand for the principle of social idealism, which opposes all class privileges that interfere with the development of the State as a whole." [34] These Progressives had identified themselves thoroughly with the concept of a classless public interest, and by this standard they tested the demands of groups representing more limited social units.

Unlike the consumers' leagues and child labor committees,

[32] Jane Addams, "The Functions of a Social Settlement," *The Annals of the American Academy of Political and Social Science*, XIII (May 1899), 323.

[33] University Settlement Society, *Annual Report*, 1901, pp. 46–47.

[34] Mary M. Kingsbury, "Women in New York Settlements," *Municipal Affairs*, III (Sept. 1898), 462.

other social Progressive organizations did not concern themselves mainly with working conditions for women and children.
Instead, they became interested in all aspects of labor reform.
The Social Reform Club of New York, founded in 1894, was
such an organization. The Club's original aim had been to permit
"men of leisure" to aid organized labor in the reform of unfortunate industrial conditions.[35] It not only cooperated with
organized labor, but also sought to have half of its membership
consist of workers, so that a true interaction between social
classes could take place.[36] Although the labor membership
never exceeded a third of the whole, the very idea of recogniz-
ing social classes, and of according labor equality of status, suggests differences in approach between the Club and the consumers' leagues. The Club's attempt to devote itself solely to
action led to a ban on any discussion of millennial programs such
as socialism.[37]

In its early statements, the Social Reform Club recognized
explicitly that cooperation between organized labor and its own
middle- and upper-class members was the basis for effective reform. The Club applauded unionism, and contended that "no
wage earner is doing his full duty if he fails to identify his own
interests with those of his fellow-workman. The obvious way to
make common cause with them is to join a trade union, and thus
secure a position from which to strengthen organized labor and
influence it for the better."[38] The Club aided several strikes
with financial contributions and with public statements favoring
the workers' cause.

In addition, the Club supported demands by organized labor,
which had never excited any enthusiasm in the consumers'

[35] Social Reform Club of New York, Leaflet, June 14, 1898, and *New York Evening Journal*, Jan. 14, 1897, p. 4.

[36] *New York Evening Journal*, Jan. 22, 1897, p. 6.

[37] Social Reform Club of New York, *Annual Report*, 1898, p. 2.

[38] Central Labor Union of New York, *Handbook*, 1897: statement by Ernest Crosby.

leagues. The increasing use of the injunction as a strikebreaking device produced sharp opposition from the A.F.L. A special report by a five-member committee of the Club also condemned the misuse of this legal procedure. The injunction had legitimate uses in the protection of property, but it should not become a weapon for breaking strikes. An injunction issued against the cigarmakers' strike in 1900 prohibited even peaceful picketing, and in the view of the Club made illegal the very weapons of trade unionism that had long been declared legal.[39] This injunction was later voided by a higher court. The Club also supported the A.F.L.'s contention that contempt-of-court cases arising from a violation of strike injunctions should be tried before a jury.[40]

The Club also sought to encourage the use of the union label. Its contention was that the public could support organized labor's efforts for better working conditions by buying labeled goods.[41] As part of its campaign for organized labor, the Club publicized the merits of trade unions. The influential and socially prominent members of the Club further aided unionism by bringing the positive features of the labor movement to the attention of middle- and upper-class persons who otherwise would have had no contact with organized labor nor any basis for understanding its principles. In recognition of these activities, the Workingmen's Federation of New York invited the Social Reform Club to attend its conventions as a fraternal delegate.[42]

Thus the Social Reform Club appeared to differ from the consumers' leagues and child labor committees. But despite its closer support of trade unionism, the Club refused to give full support to the activities of organized labor; and its reasons for withholding that aid indicate the limits of cooperation between middle- and upper-class reformers and the labor movement.

---

[39] *New York Evening Journal*, May 23, 1900, p. 8.
[40] *New York Evening Journal*, March 17, 1898, p. 8.
[41] Social Reform Club, *Union Label Leaflets*, 1897.
[42] *Report of the Proceedings of the Second Annual Convention of the Workingmen's Federation of the State of New York*, 1899, p. 8.

The strikes supported by the Club were mainly those in which the principle of unionism was at stake.[43] In other strikes, where the threat of violence by the union, charges of radicalism among the strikers, or the disruption of a vital public service led to active middle-class opposition, the Club withheld definite support, and instead suggested arbitration, even when it seemed clear that management would refuse to accept it.[44] The Club was not a completely homogeneous group, and though the left-wing members—many of whom had socialist sympathies—demanded consistent support of labor, the majority were of the opinion that the Club could not support all strikes.

One of the Club's statements said of the unions, "They may make the effort to improve the conditions solely in their own selfish interests, but the public will still be benefited." [45] Organized labor's own interests were not sufficient justification for middle-class aid, whether in support of the union label or of a strike. The Club included a large segment of organized labor's activities within the public interest, so that unionism and the attendant improvement in wages, hours, and working conditions were considered of benefit not only to the worker but also to the community as a whole. Support was thus possible as long as the demands of trade unions were judged to be beneficial to the public; but cooperation would collapse when for some reason, such as the possibility of violence or of radicalism, the efforts of the labor organization threatened some basic interest of the middle-class community. The Consumers' League and Child Labor Committee did not reach this point, for they demanded active control of reform by middle-class elements as well as the right to approve or disapprove activities that were directed by organized labor.

The Club's attitude toward the Seamen's Bill of 1898 is symp-

[43] Social Reform Club of New York, Card to membership, May 8, 1900 (New York Public Library).

[44] Social Reform Club of New York, Card to membership, Aug. 1, 1899, and *Annual Report*, 1900, pp. 11-12.

[45] Social Reform Club of New York, *Union Label Leaflets*, 1897.

tomatic of the problems inherent in its attitude toward organized labor. The A.F.L. supported a tough bill to improve conditions for American seamen, and the Club originally followed labor's lead. However, when the opposition of shipowners seemed to end all chances for the passage of a strong measure, the Club's lobbyists decided to work out a compromise. The owners were approached, and agreed not to oppose a new, weaker bill—but the labor forces held out for the original proposal. The Club's legislative committee then called on the entire membership to support its position. The committee chairman, in defending its action, interpreted the Club's position in relation to labor: "We have decided to stand for the principles and welfare of Organized Labor, but we have never decided to stand by all that it may do. Should we do this, we would become the auxiliary of Organized Labor, nothing more; our influence with other bodies, and therefore our power, would be lost." [46] A majority of the membership supported the committee.

This action indicated the basically middle-class orientation of the Club. It was pointed out by the minority that the membership now used its own judgment of labor's interests instead of relying on that of labor itself. In practice, the Club's policy increasingly stressed cooperation when the reformers' interests dictated it, but not wholehearted support of the responsible leaders of the labor movement—a policy which organized labor naturally refused to accept.

As might be expected, the Social Reform Club was also active in other major areas that interested the social Progressives. It worked for the passage of reform legislation at Albany, publicized reform views at its meetings, and sought to cooperate with other reform groups. However, its major emphasis continued to be aid to organized labor: tenement reform, the end of child labor, and municipal ownership of gas plants, for example, were judged to be in the best interests of the worker.

---

[46] Social Reform Club of New York, Leaflet, June 14, 1898. The debate extended from the meeting of May 31, 1898. See Leaflet for that date.

The American Association for Labor Legislation, founded nationally in 1906 and in New York in 1907, was among the most influential of the social Progressive societies. Like the Social Reform Club, it took an interest in all areas of labor reform, and was concerned with the problem of the relations to be established with organized labor. Unlike the Club, the A.A.L.L. did not assert that it existed to support organized labor. Instead, its aim was "to encourage the study of labor conditions in the United States with a view to promoting desirable labor legislation."[47] The Association did not concern itself "with questions of open or closed shops, with strikes or lockouts, with the boycott or the blacklist."[48] Thus the troublesome problem of the union label on the A.A.L.L.'s printed matter was met by the use of both union and nonunion shops.[49] Although the social Progressives in the Association frequently praised trade unionism and called for its acceptance as an American institution, the organization itself offered no aid to the economic activities of organized labor.

Many influential labor leaders joined the Association between 1907 and 1915, but their role in its activities was small. The reformers sought more significant support for their legislative program from organized labor, but without much success.[50] Trade-union leaders realized that the Association basically shared the attitude of the social Progressives toward social reform, and many within the A.F.L. doubted whether progress could be achieved through middle-class intervention on behalf of organized labor.

The A.A.L.L. had an important contingent of college professors in its ranks, among whom Henry Seager of Columbia

[47] John B. Andrews Papers (School of Industrial and Labor Relations, Cornell University): Andrews to Roland B. Woodward, June 15, 1915. Andrews was secretary of the American Association for Labor Legislation, and played an important role in the formulation of its policies and programs.

[48] Andrews to Henry Seager, Andrews Papers, Dec. 26, 1911.

[49] Andrews to Henry Farnum, Andrews Papers, June 26, 1909.

[50] Paul Kennaday to Samuel Gompers, Andrews Papers, Nov. 11, 1911.

University typified the new Progressive spirit on American campuses. He was three times president of the Association. With John Commons, Richard Ely, Henry Farnum, and William Willoughby, among others, he believed that the social scientist should also be a social reformer, and that scholarship should enter into the service of society. Seager believed in trade unions, and in the union shop. It was also his opinion that employers must likewise organize and then bargain collectively with the unions. Organized labor's actions were to be judged by the courts on the basis of "whether its rules and policies have due regard for the interests of the community." [51] Thus the interests of the middle class, as represented in the "community," clearly became the judge of labor's actions. Although the Association supported unionism, it always stressed reform by legislation where organized labor was weak, primarily among the unskilled.[52] However, as years passed, the Association proposed legislative reform for all workers, organized or not. A majority of the A.F.L.'s leadership opposed this extension of legislative reform into areas the trade union considered its own responsibility.

Union opposition to legislative reform was stated clearly by Gompers in 1915, although it had always existed in the A.F.L. The labor movement, Gompers wrote, "undertakes to secure from government, both state and nation, the enactment of laws for the accomplishment of such things as working people can not secure or enforce themselves." [53] Reforms by the state ended labor's right to determine its own conditions of work through its own organizations. It placed the workers' interests in the hands of the government, and opposition thus became a breach of law. "Is human nature so constituted that the workers

[51] Henry R. Seager, *Labor and Other Economic Essays* (New York, 1931), p. 51.

[52] American Association for Labor Legislation, *Proceedings of First Annual Meeting* (Madison, Wis.), 1907, p. 88.

[53] *American Federationist*, Feb. 1915, p. 114.

can trust matters affecting their real liberty in the hands of 'disinterested' outsiders?" [54] Gompers thought not, and he demanded reform by union action, even if it took longer to accomplish; whereas the reformers thought disinterested outsiders could be trusted, and saw no reason why workers should suffer under poor conditions—which might be remedied by legislation —while awaiting some successful organization campaign in the future.[55] Gompers's acceptance of the idea of competing social classes found little favor among social Progressives, who preferred a classless concept of the public interest.

The Association constantly added new measures to its reform program, and although only a few of the proposals were accepted by the state legislatures during the Progressive era, almost the entire program became law as part of the New Deal.

The Association called on the nation to face its responsibility for industrial conditions, and to legislate all necessary reforms. These included minimum wage boards for men and women, since "the economic interest of society" required a living wage.[56] Once again, labor reform did not benefit the worker alone, and this was a basic reason for the reformer's interest. The Association also supported workmen's compensation in preference to the wasteful system of employers' liability, under which the injured worker had to sue the employer, prove some degree of negligence by the latter, and establish that there had been no contributory negligence of his own. Very few workers collected damages under the employers' liability laws, and much of the award, where there was one, went to lawyers.[57] The A.A.L.L. favored compulsory health insurance for all workers with an income of less than $1,200 per year—which meant most

[54] *Ibid.*, p. 176.

[55] *American Labor Legislation Review*, VI (March 1916), 92–95.

[56] Seager, *Essays*, p. 212. See the full discussion, pp. 202–212.

[57] See the statement presented by Miles Dawson before the United States Commission on Employers' Liability and Workmen's Compensation, *Hearings Before the . . . Commission*, 2 vols. (Washington, 1911), pp. 240–257.

of them. Unemployment relief proposals included public works, effective state employment agencies, and unemployment insurance.[58] In addition, the A.A.L.L. supported all the campaigns for prohibition of child labor, the regulation of women's hours and working conditions, the prevention of industrial accidents and diseases, a postal savings system, and extended popular education. This was a comprehensive program of labor reform, much beyond what the public or organized labor would accept, and generally in advance of the social Progressive movement as well.

The Association's program did not end with legislative interference in industrial affairs. State compensation commissions, industrial boards, and minimum wage boards, with varying degrees of quasi-legislative power, were to enforce the law and insure its effectiveness.

The Association prepared its recommendations on the basis of "scientific" investigation by experts.[59] In this respect the Association shared in the trend among social Progressive societies toward increasingly intricate studies by skilled investigators.

Several studies have emphasized the importance of churchmen and religious groups in the development of the social reform movement in industrial America. The social gospel was the response of one segment of American Protestantism to the challenge of a modern industrial society. It sought to reform society in the image of Christian love, and in pursuit of this goal it supported various reform measures which alleviated some of the obvious evils of the industrial system. Some of the social-gospel clergymen denied that reform could regenerate society, and these turned to Christian Socialism. Most of the rest remained within the Progressive movement. Reform-minded clergymen supported the trade unions because organized labor also opposed the entrenched power of capital; but the clerical reformers had

[58] *American Labor Legislation Review*, V (June 1915), 174.
[59] Andrews to Stiles P. Jones, Andrews Papers, Feb. 5, 1914.

little patience with the assertive and contentious methods of the labor movement.[60] They advocated arbitration as the best means of insuring industrial peace and protecting the public interest; and they agreed with their lay counterparts in accepting legislation, under the direction of the social Progressives, as the method of reform.

The churches and trade unions had become antagonistic during the final quarter of the nineteenth century because the religious bodies failed to support organized labor. Conservative control of the churches was not broken during the Progressive period, and the advocates of the social gospel were always a minority. Trade unions and church organizations usually had a perfunctory relationship, and this often meant only a labor supper or labor sermon once a year. The influence of the social gospel upon the union movement was small before 1896,[61] and notwithstanding the claim that the social gospel had grown in importance during the Progressive period,[62] there was little effective support of social reform by Protestant organizations in New York State.

Although such individual clergymen as W. D. P. Bliss or F. J. C. Moran were prominent among New York's social reformers, the social Progressive movement was definitely lay-directed and financed.[63] At best, the social gospel affected the attitudes of

[60] The leading work on the intellectual development of the movement is Charles H. Hopkins, *The Rise of the Social Gospel in American Protestantism, 1865–1915* (Yale Studies in Religious Education, No. 14, New Haven, 1940).

[61] Henry May, *Protestant Churches and Industrial America* (New York, 1949), p. 216.

[62] Aaron I. Abell, *The Urban Impact on American Protestantism, 1865–1900* (Cambridge, Mass., 1943), pp. 246–255.

[63] It is interesting to note that both men had strong ties to Christian Socialism although they worked within the Progressive movement. Bliss had organized the Christian Socialist Union in 1889, and ten years later headed the National Social Reform Union, which attempted to campaign for social reform throughout the nation. It did not achieve any significant results but did point the way for later social Progressive groups.

individual Progressives.[64] Many of the social-reform leaders had been subject to strong religious influences, and all were familiar with the writings of the leading advocates of the social gospel. Through this avenue the social gospel may have helped develop a favorable attitude toward reform, which would then have been implemented through lay organizations. On the other hand, Lillian Wald noted that many settlement workers had no "formal manifestation of religious belief" and that there was much "skepticism of a personal Deity." [65] The conservatism of the church hierarchies undoubtedly alienated many of the idealistic young people who staffed the settlements and worked in the social Progressive organizations.

The influence of the Roman Catholic Church upon the American labor movement and upon social Progressivism has also been discussed, notably in two recent works.[66] Although social reform activities by Catholic laymen increased considerably during the Progressive period, and despite the reform work of several well-known Catholic clerics, the hierarchy took little interest in social Progressivism.[67] My investigation suggests that the influence of Catholic organizations upon the course of social reform in New York was slight. The only religious organization to work continuously for social reform, and to exert any observable effect, was the Church Association for the Advancement of the Interests of Labor (C.A.I.L.)—an Episcopalian group.[68] The organization never had the strength or influence

[64] May, *Protestant Churches*, pp. 223–227. One unidentified member of the A.A.L.L. "sent us a brief letter stating that he believed our Association was ushering in the kingdom of God about as rapidly as any organization he could see around him, and that he therefore enclosed draft for $882." Andrews to Henry Farnum, Andrews Papers, April 11, 1911.

[65] Wald to Mr. Scherer, Wald Papers (copy undated but probably July 1908).

[66] Marc Karson, *American Labor Unions and Politics, 1900–1918* (Carbondale, Ill., 1958), Ch. 9; Aaron I. Abell, *American Catholicism and Social Action: A Search for Social Justice, 1865–1950* (New York, 1960).

[67] Abell, *American Catholicism*, pp. 119–186.

[68] C.A.I.L.'s membership included lay Episcopalians and clergymen.

of the lay groups, and by 1908 it was practically bankrupt.

C.A.I.L. had been organized in New York City in 1887, and by 1897 it had branches and members throughout the nation. From his observation of working conditions, Bishop Henry Potter of the Protestant Episcopal Church had concluded in 1887 "that no Christian man can be innocently indifferent to the interests of working men and women." C.A.I.L. was the result of the Bishop's subsequent effort to put this sentiment into practice,[69] and it always had a Christian Socialist tinge.[70]

Although C.A.I.L. added many bishops as vice presidents, it never received official support from the convention of the Episcopal Church. A Joint Commission on the Relations of Capital and Labor, formed by the Church in 1901, offered to serve as an arbitrator, but received no requests. The convention supported child labor restrictions, a half holiday on Saturday, and rest on Sunday, but went no further toward formulating a social reform program, despite the work of C.A.I.L.[71]

The activities of C.A.I.L. continued without official assistance from the Church, and its year-by-year development presents a curious mixture of attitudes and policies. C.A.I.L. wholeheartedly supported the social Progressives' legislative efforts, and cooperated closely with the consumers' leagues on several occasions. It became a leader in the movement for the abolition of all manufacturing in tenements.[72] It also supported the middle-class reformers' demand for the arbitration of labor disputes, arguing repeatedly that only compulsory arbitration of all strikes could end industrial chaos.[73] Its journal attacked the boycott as an unjust means, even though directed against an acknowledged

[69] George A. Stevens, *New York Typographical Union No. 6* (Albany, 1913), pp. 608–609.

[70] *Hammer and Pen.* The official declaration of principles is found on the last page of every issue.

[71] Spencer Miller, Jr., and Joseph F. Fletcher, *The Church and Industry* (New York, 1930), pp. 64–75, 111–115.

[72] *Hammer and Pen*, July 1905, p. 65.

[73] *Hammer and Pen*, Dec. 1898, p. 2, and Aug. 1899, p. 58, are two examples out of many.

evil—the kind of retaliation forbidden by Christ.[74] C.A.I.L. also criticized the truculence of many trade unions, and offered the suggestion that the unions publish a special labor paper to further industrial understanding.[75] The chairman of C.A.I.L.'s Organized Labor Committee, upset by a scandal in the New York City labor movement, concluded that "Organized Labor, like Organized Capital, is fraught with tremendous possibilities for evil." Both, he said, could combine to plunder "the unorganized public." [76] In all these instances, the organization followed the general attitude of the social Progressives toward labor and social reform.

At the same time, however, C.A.I.L. cooperated fully with organized labor. Like the Social Reform Club and the A.A.L.L., it favored the principle of unionism, but unlike the lay groups C.A.I.L. continuously supported organized labor's attempts to organize. Despite its insistence on the principle of compulsory arbitration, the organization supported strikes more persistently than any of the social Progressive societies previously discussed. It publicized the strikers' cause in its journal and in church meetings, and contributed small amounts to the strike funds. C.A.I.L.'s support of trade unionism is typified by the Reverend W. D. P. Bliss's quip, "I believe that if Jesus Christ were here now he would be a member of the Carpenters' Union." [77]

In the dispute between the National Consumers' League and the I.L.G.W.U. over the League's label, C.A.I.L. favored the Union, and its statements so aroused the ire of Florence Kelley, the secretary of the National Consumers' League, that she threatened legal action against the church group.[78] C.A.I.L. consistently attacked padrone labor, not only because of the poor conditions under which the immigrant workers lived and labored, but because this form of employment threatened trade union-

[74] *Hammer and Pen*, Oct. 1899, p. 69.
[75] *Hammer and Pen*, July 1901, p. 234.
[76] *Hammer and Pen*, Oct. 1903, p. 156.
[77] *The Saturday Critic*, May 29, 1897, p. 2.
[78] *Hammer and Pen*, March 1904, p. 21.

ism.[79] The misuse of the injunction in strikes was criticized, and C.A.I.L. supported the futile efforts of the Workingmen's Federation to win relief through legislation.[80] Like the Social Reform Club, the church group participated in the conventions of the Workingmen's Federation as a fraternal delegate, and despite occasional differences over specific bills, it consistently aided labor's efforts in the legislature. Finally, at the very time when the campaign for the open shop attacked a basic policy of organized labor, C.A.I.L. publicly offered support for the closed shop.[81]

C.A.I.L. recognized the unions as allies of the middle class in an effort to regenerate society, and it thus supported the efforts of organized labor to maintain or strengthen its position. It viewed the relation as a partnership, and the labor forces as open to criticism when wrong; but unlike the consumers' leagues, or even the Social Reform Club, the church group did not establish the interest of the middle class as the standard and then expect labor to measure up to it. C.A.I.L. favored the social Progressives' plans to correct the weaknesses of capitalism; but the Christian Socialist influence made the organization less fearful than most Progressives that reform might lead to some reorganization of the capitalist society, and thus more tolerant of forces independent of the middle class, such as the trade union movement.

The social Progressive organization most closely connected with the labor movement was the Women's Trade Union League (W.T.U.L.). The national organization was founded in 1903, one year before the New York branch. The W.T.U.L.'s membership and aims differed substantially from those of other reform groups. The fundamental purpose was not to legislate reform for the working class, but to stimulate organization among working women. These trade unions could then win re-

[79] *Hammer and Pen*, Feb. 1900, pp. 102–103; June 1900, p. 138.
[80] *Hammer and Pen*, Sept. 1901, p. 251.
[81] *Hammer and Pen*, June 1904, p. 48.

forms through economic action.[82] This was the basic position of the A.F.L. concerning labor reform, and although Gompers had doubts whether any group not wholly within the union movement should be permitted to assist in organization, or whether such efforts could have any success,[83] the A.F.L. agreed to aid the League's efforts by permitting W.T.U.L. personnel to act as organizers, and by contributing money to support these activities.

The executive boards of the national organization, and all branches, had to have a majority of women trade unionists. The remainder of the membership was composed of middle-class reformers, similar in their origin and background to members of other social Progressive societies. These nonunionist members, or "allies," exerted a persuasive influence upon the course of affairs even though they were rarely a majority of the membership.[84] The allies assumed office and committee assignments, for which the working girl did not have time, and soon they controlled the actual day-by-day operation of the organization. In addition, the greater part of the League's funds came from the well-to-do allies.[85]

Despite the primary aim of assisting in the formation of trade unions for women, the National W.T.U.L. soon also developed a legislative program. Like the labor movement, it supposedly

[82] From the Constitution of the National Women's Trade Union League as found in *The Union Labor Advocate*, January 1908.

[83] Gladys Boone, *The Women's Trade Union Leagues in Great Britain and the United States* (New York, 1942), p. 84.

[84] The allies temporarily outnumbered the unionists in the New York Women's Trade Union League during 1910 and 1911. The shirtwaist strike of 1909 had publicized working conditions in the garment trades, and produced a burst of middle-class support for the unionization of women workers. The membership of the New York League reflected this by a sharp increase in the number of allies. Other branches of the Women's Trade Union League, however, continued to have large unionist majorities. See National Women's Trade Union League, *Proceedings, Third Biennial Convention*, 1911, pp. 17–18, 32–33.

[85] See Women's Trade Union League of New York, *Annual Report*, 1906–1907, 1907–1908, for the leading contributors.

regarded legislation as only a supplement to action by the trade unions. However, a serious conflict soon appeared within the W.T.U.L., between those committed wholeheartedly to the traditional A.F.L. position and those who saw little chance for real and immediate reform in the slight gains made through the League's efforts at organization. This second group was attracted by the methods of the other social Progressive societies.

Mary Dreier, an influential and socially prominent ally member of the New York League, clearly stated the original view of the W.T.U.L. on the relation between organization and legislation: "Yet while we make laws, let us not forget the more important work of organization, for we know that the greatest power to enforce labor laws is trade unions, and a strong trade union can demand better conditions and shorter hours than the law will allow, and then, too, we get education and power through organization, which we do not get through law." [86] Although an Interstate League Conference in 1908 called for expanded organizational activities, the increasing influence of social Progressivism throughout the nation focused attention on the possibility of legislative action, and in 1909 the National League issued its first legislative program. Subsequent national conventions of the W.T.U.L. increased the legislative demands, and minimum wage boards for women soon became a basic objective.[87] In 1911 the New York League also set up a legislative committee to lobby in Albany.[88]

When the reformers' demand for minimum wage boards began to attract attention, the A.F.L.'s leadership opened fire upon it. The New York League thus found itself in a quandary. In 1914 the desirability of minimum wage boards came before

[86] National Women's Trade Union League, *Report of Interstate Conference Held September 26–28, 1908 in New York*, p. 6.

[87] National Women's Trade Union League, *Proceedings, Fourth Biennial Convention*, 1913, p. 28, and *Proceedings, Third Biennial Convention*, 1911, p. 42.

[88] Women's Trade Union League of New York, *Annual Report*, 1910–1911, p. 16.

the New York League's executive board, where it was defeated by a vote of four to six. The Board then voted six to two, with two abstentions, that it did not consider the time "opportune" to agitate for minimum wage boards for women.[89] Clearly this vote did not signify opposition to the principle of labor reform through legislation, but only meant that at the time the New York League would not risk a rupture with the A.F.L. over the issue.

In 1915 the New York League once more faced the issue after the national convention of the W.T.U.L. had again demanded minimum wage boards for women. The New York League avoided the issue by approving the entire report of the New York delegation to the convention, which included support of the convention's stand on wage boards.[90] By considering the report as a whole, the specific issue was submerged in a general approval of the convention's work.

The stoutest defender of the organizational view and the A.F.L. was the secretary of the New York League, Helen Marot, who feared that support of the reformers' activities would lead to an eventual split with the A.F.L. and that if this occurred the W.T.U.L. would lose the very reason for its existence, to become just another of the social Progressive organizations. The League, she believed, had power and purpose only because of its distinctive connection with organized labor: to jeopardize that relationship would be to kill the Women's Trade Union League.[91] Miss Marot had a strong influence upon the national and New York leagues, but despite her activities the trend was definitely toward a greater acceptance of legislative reform.

Despite the struggle over the relative merits of legislation and

[89] Women's Trade Union League of New York, Papers: Executive Board Minutes, Nov. 24, 1914, p. 2.
[90] Women's Trade Union League of New York, Papers: Minutes of League Meeting, Oct. 4, 1915, p. 4.
[91] Women's Trade Union League of New York, Papers: Secretary's Monthly Report, April 27, 1911.

organization, the W.T.U.L. never adopted the Consumers' League's reliance on reform by law, nor did it ever abandon its close support of the labor movement. The New York League followed the State Federation of Labor's lead on almost every major legislative issue, providing more consistent support than could be expected from other social Progressive organizations. The New York League's refusal to campaign for minimum wage boards isolated it from the rest of the social Progressive movement. At other times the New York League also refused to cooperate with other social reform societies because their activities had provoked the criticism of organized labor.[92]

The New York League contributed materially to the success of several important strikes, and in the shirtwaist strike of 1909 it was a crucial factor in the victory of the strikers. Despite the League's denial of leadership,[93] the record indicates that it contributed sizably to the strike fund. Even more important, however, was the involvement of the League's socialite members in picket duty. This evoked widespread publicity and sympathy for the strikers, especially when these women of position attacked the pro-management actions of the police. The publicity brought about by the involvement of the League changed a poorly organized, unnoticed garment industry dispute into a general strike of all shirtwaist workers, with the whole range of social Progressive organizations providing aid. This middle-class support was instrumental in the strikers' final victory.

Although the New York League played no such important role again, it did contribute money and volunteers to many other strikes in succeeding years. In the white goods strike of 1913 the money contributed by the New York League matched the International Ladies' Garment Workers' Union's financial aid to its striking local. The League also aided the cloakmakers in 1916,

[92] Women's Trade Union League of New York, Papers: Minutes, League Meeting, Dec. 6, 1915, p. 4.

[93] Women's Trade Union League of New York, Annual Report, 1909–1910, p. 11.

even though the union was almost entirely composed of men.[94]

Yet in the years after 1910, the relations between organized labor and the New York W.T.U.L. became increasingly strained because of a basic shift in the policy of the League. The leaders of the New York W.T.U.L. had originally limited their role in organizational work to assistance, with no attempt at control. In 1906 the executive board explained that the League's function was "to assist trade unions to help themselves, instead of doing their work for them or assuming their responsibilities" [95] Helen Marot, two years later, stressed that the League sought to aid in organizing women, and she attacked those male unionists who interpreted aid to mean substitution of themselves for women as leaders of newly formed unions.[96] However, the New York League had to face the practical problem that many of the unions in the garment industry were highly unstable, and that much of its own organizational work would have to be done in these trades because of the great number of women employed.

Following the successful shirtwaist strike of 1909, the New York W.T.U.L. increasingly ignored these earlier promises of assistance only, and demanded a new role in the union movement. In 1910 the New York League received a gift of $10,000 for the purpose of establishing a permanent strike fund. This new wealth required a new policy if the strike fund were not to disappear in the numerous garment strikes which occurred each year. In the shirtwaist strike of 1909, the League and several central labor bodies had been given places on the strike committee in order to ensure their active support. Using this as a precedent, the New York League decided to withhold all substantial financial aid to

[94] Women's Trade Union League of New York, *Annual Report*, 1916–1917, p. 19; and *New York Call*, July 22, 1916, p. 1.

[95] Women's Trade Union League of New York, Papers: Executive Board Minutes, Oct. 11, 1906.

[96] Women's Trade Union League of New York, Papers: Secretary's Monthly Report, Nov. 26, 1907, p. 6.

strikers unless it were represented on the strike committee.[97]

The New York League also called on the garment unions to become more stable if they expected assistance. Helen Marot declared that the radical background of the leaders, many of whom were recent immigrants from Czarist Russia, often produced this instability. These men substituted "fine phrases or idealist sentiments" for "business methods," and although considerable excitement could be generated, the unions fell apart under the first serious strain.[98] Another prominent figure in the New York League, Leonora O'Reilly, believed that a major aim of the League had to be the education of workers in the methods of unionism. This would ensure the stability of future organizations.[99] Thus the call for a change in the methods used by garment unions, plus a demand for representation on all strike committees, changed the relationship between the League and the unions.

The International Ladies' Garment Workers' Union had gained in stability and prestige by 1910. Like the New York W.T.U.L., the Union now began to insist on a greater degree of control over the activities of the garment industry locals. Frequent strikes by poorly prepared locals would deplete the Union's funds, and hurt its reputation.[100]

Despite this agreement on the need for greater stability in the garment trade locals, the I.L.G.W.U. did not intend to share any of its authority with the New York League. In 1911 both the Union and the League agreed that another shirtwaist strike was unwise, but in 1912 the two organizations differed on the

[97] Women's Trade Union League of New York, Papers: Executive Board Minutes, Sept. 26, 1912, p. 4, and Oct. 22, 1914, p. 4. The National League at its 1909 Convention also had demanded this policy.

[98] Women's Trade Union League of New York, Papers: Secretary's Monthly Report, May 13, 1911.

[99] Women's Trade Union League of New York, Papers: Executive Board Minutes, Jan. 14, 1914.

[100] Report and Proceedings, Eleventh Convention of the International Ladies' Garment Workers' Union, 1912, pp. 15–17.

wisdom of a general strike in the white goods trade. The New York W.T.U.L. at first opposed the strike; when the I.L.G.W.U. sponsored it, the League refused to give aid until it received representation on the strike committee.[101] The Union opposed this interference in its affairs. After much haggling, the League finally agreed to support this strike without representation, but it did not revise its policy of demanding a voice in the conduct of future strikes.

In 1911 the New York League interfered in the elections for the executive committee of the waistmakers' local.[102] The incumbent executive committee won, however, and relations became quite strained. In 1912 a fledgling union of retail clerks sought to organize the department store workers in New York City, and the New York League supported the effort. However, by June 1913 the League's insistence on a voice in policy led to a rupture with the same union.[103]

Thus the New York League discovered it could not remain a mere adjunct to the union movement as it had originally planned to do. Instead, increasing interference by the organization—with its important group of middle-class leaders—had led to strife. Trade unions opposed interference in areas they considered their responsibility, even from a strongly pro-labor society such as the Women's Trade Union League; they were even more wary of efforts by less congenial social Progressive organizations to eliminate the workers' problems through extensive government action.

[101] Women's Trade Union League of New York, Papers: Executive Board Minutes, Sept. 26, 1912, p. 4.

[102] Women's Trade Union League of New York, Papers: Executive Board Minutes, April 27, 1911.

[103] Women's Trade Union League of New York, Papers: Executive Board Minutes, May 22, 1913; June 19, 1913.

IV

Membership, Methods, and Problems

of the Social Progressives

ALTHOUGH increasing public support provided the impetus for social Progressive legislation, most of the reform organizations depended upon a small group of wealthy patricians, professional men, and social workers for their financial support and leadership. Wealthy women, including some from New York City society, were indispensable to the financing and staffing of the Consumers' League.[1] There was only one labor member on the governing board of the National Child Labor Committee in 1905, and by 1907 his name had disappeared. The Committee's leading members included many wealthy men from business and banking, as well as professional men and social workers.[2] The New York Women's Trade Union League had substantial support from wealthy contributors. Mary Dreier, who led the League until 1913, and made vital contributions to it thereafter, came from a wealthy, socially established family; many of the other "allies" were also women of leisure.[3] During the shirtwaist strike of 1909, several of the League's most active workers were socially prominent young women from Vassar College. Some of

[1] *New York Evening Journal*, Dec. 12, 1898, p. 6. Also see the annual reports of the New York City League.

[2] National Child Labor Committee, *Leaflets*, Nos. 1 and 9.

[3] Women's Trade Union League of New York, *Annual Report*, 1906–1907, p. 14; 1907–1908, p. 15; Stevens, *Typographical Union*, p. 612.

these women continued their support during the years that followed. The Social Reform Club increasingly filled its ranks from among the rich and prominent despite its original aim of enrolling a large working-class membership.[4] The influence of this group weakened the Club's support of organized labor.

DUES AND CONTRIBUTIONS PAID TO THE AMERICAN
ASSOCIATION FOR LABOR LEGISLATION IN 1912
ACCORDING TO AMOUNT

Amount	Number of members contributing this amount	Total contributed at this amount
$ 3	1,420	$4,260
5	697	3,485
10	77	770
15	5	75
20	2	40
25	36	900
30	1	30
75	1	75
100	10	1,000
250	5	1,250
1,000	2	2,000
2,500	1	2,500
3,000	2	6,000
5,000	1	5,000
	2,260	$27,385

The American Association for Labor Legislation also steadily courted the rich. The Association's big contributors included John D. Rockefeller; Elbert Gary of the United States Steel Corporation; Felix Warburg, a leading banker and philanthro-

[4] *New York Evening Journal*, April 13, 1900, p. 3.

pist; Mrs. Madeline Astor; V. Everitt Macy, who also contributed large sums to philanthropies and other social Progressive organizations; and Miss Anne Morgan, the daughter of the financier.[5] The table above indicates how important a few large contributions were to the Association.[6] Thus of 2,260 members who contributed $27,385 in dues and gifts, only twenty-one gave sums of $100 or more; but they supplied $17,750, or 65 per cent of the Association's funds.

The interest of the wealthy in the social Progressive organizations appears to be a continuation of their previous support of philanthropic activities. The settlement houses, with their emphasis on the development of the individual, received heavy financial support from the rich.[7] The consumers' leagues and child labor committees stressed that the aim of their reform programs was to protect the underprivileged in the community—the poor or helpless who often came to the philanthropist's attention through the established charities. The social Progressives offered the hope that selected reform of the worst evils in the industrial system would help alleviate the need for continued charity, and strengthen the fiber of the nation by eliminating the self-abasement associated with asking for charitable help. This program thus presented a rosy alternative to some of those who supported other philanthropic enterprises without threatening private property or the stability of the social order.

However, the social Progressive organizations never received

---

[5] Financial matters occupied much of the executive committee's time. See the Andrews Papers. Items of special interest concerning large contributions include Andrews to Anne Morgan, Dec. 15, 1911; Andrews to John D. Rockefeller, March 20, 1912, May 5, 1913, and Nov. 26, 1915; W. S. Richardson (Rockefeller's secretary) to Andrews, Jan. 7, 1916; Andrews to John M. Glenn of the Russell Sage Foundation, June 19, 1914; Andrews to Felix Warburg, May 11, 1915; and Warburg to Andrews, July 22, 1915.

[6] Financial statement, American Association for Labor Legislation, Andrews Papers, Oct. 1, 1912.

[7] See the annual reports of the University Settlement House for the names and contributions of wealthy supporters.

as many large contributions as did the charities, settlements, or civic clubs. In New York the City Club and the University Settlement House always had larger receipts than any of the purely social reform organizations. A series of contributions by the wealthy banker and philanthropist Jacob Schiff illustrate the point: Schiff contributed $100,000 to establish a rural nursing program, and $50,000 to aid poor persons in New York City who had been hard hit by the upsurge of unemployment in 1914 and 1915, but only $1,000 to *The Survey*, a leading journal of social Progressive opinion.[8] The objectives of the social Progressives had less appeal to most of the chief contributors than did the more conservative action through the charity or settlement.

Despite the need for funds, the reformers made it clear that generous contributors could not expect to control policy. Paul Kellogg, editor of *The Survey*, expressed very well the attitude of the social Progressive societies when he was negotiating for a large contribution:

Obviously I should not be accepting your gift on the basis of holding or of undertaking to continue to hold any given editorial position. On the other hand, you will be entirely free to discontinue it any time because you broke with an editorial position or for any other reason.

Dealing with a field in which controversial issues are many and strongly felt, obviously we could not, if we wanted to, attempt to take any given editorial position to which all of our cooperating contributors would subscribe; or to take all positions which any given contributor would endorse.[9]

As their activities expanded, the social Progressives discovered that their revenues were insufficient, and many programs had to be limited or abandoned. Deficits appeared in years of exceptional activity, such as the agitation for the Federal Child Labor Bill in 1914 or the battle of the American Association for Labor

[8] Wald to Julius Rosenwald, Oct. 29, 1913; form letter sent by Wald, March 23, 1915; Paul Kellogg to Wald, Nov. 8, 1916. Wald Papers.

[9] Paul Kellogg to Jacob Schiff, Wald Papers, Sept. 15, 1916.

Legislation for workmen's compensation in 1913. The A.A.L.L. made special financial appeals to the membership, but the deficit continued.[10] After many special appeals, in 1908 C.A.I.L. had to discontinue its journal because of lack of funds. The Social Reform Club experienced increasing financial difficulties in the years after 1900, and by 1903 it had ceased to be an effective force in the social Progressive ranks.[11] The National Women's Trade Union League never had adequate funds,[12] and its magazine, *Life and Labor,* was able to continue publication only because a few of the richer allies subsidized it.[13] The Consumers' League of New York City complained constantly that vital programs were being abandoned or delayed because of a shortage of money. Only the remarkable dynamism of the National Consumers' League's perennial secretary, Florence Kelley, allowed that organization to exert influence so out of proportion to its financial resources or size. As Miss Kelley put it, "Where would we be if I waited for funds?"[14]

The various societies competed with each other for money, and the national and state units of the same organization sometimes quarreled over it. The American Association for Labor Legislation had joint finance and membership committees composed of two representatives of the national society and five members of the local branch. These committees tried to coordinate policy and eliminate controversy. However, attempts by the A.A.L.L. to increase its contributions from the Chicago area produced opposition from the Illinois branch. The campaign nevertheless continued, since "each cause must stand for its own

[10] *American Labor Legislation Review,* IV (March 1914), 147–148; Andrews to Charles E. Ozanne, Andrews Papers, Dec. 19, 1914.

[11] See Social Reform Club of New York, Leaflet, Dec. 3, 1901; Leaflet, Nov. 24, 1902; Card to membership, Sept. 29, 1903.

[12] Mary Dreier, *Margaret Dreier Robins: Her Life, Letters and Work* (New York, 1950), p. 35.

[13] *Life and Labor* (National Women's Trade Union League), V (Feb. 1915), 35; and National Women's Trade Union League, *Proceedings, Fifth Biennial Convention,* 1915, p. 12.

[14] Goldmark, *Impatient Crusader,* p. 57.

merits in a big city." [15] The New York branch and the
A.A.L.L. made a joint appeal for funds after protracted negotiations concerning the distribution of receipts and the division of
expenses. The appeal was hardly worth the effort, for it produced only $114.61.[16] Just as in organized labor's central
bodies, in the social Progressive organizations a lack of funds
proved a serious barrier to effective action.

The membership of the social Progressive organizations fluc-
tuated with the fortunes of the Progressive movement both in
the nation and in New York. After 1906 membership figures in
New York rose as the election of Governor Hughes stimulated
calls for social as well as political reform. The membership of the
national social Progressive organizations increased after 1908 as
the growth of political Progressivism spurred interest in the
organizations already laboring for social reform. After 1914, the
effects of the business recession of 1914–1915—which were
blamed in part on the reforms of previous years—the increased
attention to foreign events, and the discouraging decline of the
Progressive Party tended to reduce membership totals, and only
the Child Labor Committee, which was fighting for the passage
of the first Federal Child Labor Bill, maintained its strength.

The membership of the social Progressive organizations was
never very large. The National Child Labor Committee enrolled
8,733 members in 1914, and this was the high mark for any of
the reform societies. The A.A.L.L.'s highest membership total for
the period was 3,348 in 1913, and the New York Women's
Trade Union League did not exceed its 1912 total of 670 during
the Progressive years.[17] Unlike organized labor, the social Pro-

---

[15] Andrews to Charles M. Cabot, Andrews Papers, May 22, 1911.

[16] Charles R. Henderson to Andrews, Andrews Papers, Jan. 31, 1914.
Also see Henderson to Andrews, Jan. 24, 1914, and Andrews to Henderson, Jan. 28, 1914. Andrews Papers.

[17] For membership figures, see annual report of the secretary of the
National Child Labor Committee in *The Child Labor Bulletin* (National
Child Labor Committee); the report of the secretary of the A.A.L.L. in
American Labor Legislation Review, and the annual reports of the Wom-
en's Trade Union League of New York.

gressives did not use the number of potential voters included in their membership as the basis of their political strength. Instead, the reformers constituted the advance guard of social reform thinking, and after educating the public they claimed to represent unorganized public opinion.[18]

All of the societies used the services of volunteer workers, but as the scope of their activities enlarged, the reformers had to rely increasingly on a paid, full-time executive secretary and paid clerical help. Also, the specialized investigations that were demanded by the reformers as evidence of bad conditions soon went beyond the competence of untrained volunteers; and after 1909 paid social workers did most of these investigations for the social Progressive organizations. In general, the regular activities of the organizations were performed by a small staff of paid employees, while the general membership made up the governing boards, did some of the committee work, and paid the expenses. The trend away from volunteer work by untrained members, and the employment of permanent staffs and experts on social work, indicate the increased sophistication and widened scope of the social Progressives' activities.

Only a small part of the membership did more than pay their yearly dues or make more generous contributions to their favorite organizations. Helen Marot wrote in 1911, "It's a lucky organization which can boast that it has thirty members who give strong and active service."[19] The New York Women's Trade Union League must have been unlucky, for Miss Marot did not have her thirty volunteers. A small group of interested members dominated the governing boards and committees of all the social Progressive groups. These active workers made much of the policy for the organizations, and it was then ratified at the monthly open meetings. A national organization also faced the problem that its leaders were scattered, so that informal consul-

[18] See John Graham Brooks, *The Consumers' League* (pamphlet), 1900, pp. 31–32, for one good example of this basic attitude.

[19] Women's Trade Union League of New York, *Bulletin*, Vol. I, No. 2 (March 1911), p. 2.

tation often replaced formal committee meetings.[20] The social Progressive movement thus depended upon an exceedingly small number of volunteer workers and paid employees, who gained political influence by rallying public opinion to their support.[21]

With so many organizations working for social reform, overlapping and cross purposes became a serious problem. In 1901 the work of the reform societies was described as a species of guerrilla warfare.[22] As Mrs. Maud Nathan, president of the New York City Consumers' League, commented a decade later, "The Consumers' League welcomes all honest efforts in this direction [industrial reform] and merely pleads for cooperation, so that there be no unnecessary waste of energy, time or money. The same efficiency that we bespeak for industry should be carried on in social agencies. The goals should be kept in mind rather than any diverging paths." [23]

The difficulties and confusion arose from the differences in approach among the reform societies, and from the refusal of leaders to subordinate their ideas—and their predominance within an organization—to the discipline and compromise necessary for a joint effort. The difference in opinion between C.A.I.L. and the National Consumers' League over the Consumers' League label has already been mentioned. Similarly, the New York Women's Trade Union League on several occasions refused to cooperate with other reform groups less favorable to organized labor.[24] During the strike of the ladies' tailors in

[20] Henry Farnum to Andrews, Andrews Papers, Nov. 13, 1910.
[21] As Owen Lovejoy, secretary of the National Child Labor Committee, put it, "If the legislature finds that a majority of the people of the state want child labor laws, the legislature will want it too." *The Child Labor Bulletin*, II (May 1913), 169.
[22] The League for Political Education, *Yearbook* (1902), p. 72.
[23] Consumers' League of the City of New York, *Annual Report*, 1912, p. 18. Also see New York Women's Trade Union League, Legislative Committee to Andrews, Andrews Papers, Jan. 24, 1911.
[24] See New York Women's Trade Union League, Papers: Secretary's Monthly Report, Feb. 25, 1912.

1898, the Social Reform Club and C.A.I.L. asked the New York City Consumers' League to assist in the formation of a cooperative shop which would employ the striking workers and thus aid their cause.[25] After some indications of support, the League finally refused, insisting that it was not convinced that the strikers' cause was just.[26] Instead, the League proposed arbitration, and the plan collapsed.

There were several attempts to integrate the social reform organizations into a unified reform council, but these never made much progress. In 1900 W. D. P. Bliss sponsored a City Reform Federation in New York City, "to be composed of representatives of labor unions, social reform and other progressive associations in the City." [27] The City Reform Federation was to be a nonpartisan alliance of all reform forces, which would not hesitate to enter politics if that were necessary to achieve its program. Bliss believed that the elevation of the worker was the goal of reform, and his proposed organization was to secure aid "from the man of Progressive thought" for organized labor's reform efforts without subordinating the labor representatives within middle-class organizations.[28] Despite early support from the social Progressives, Bliss's plan never was accepted, and the organization had the power only to recommend action on specific bills to the member societies.[29] The City Reform Federation never had any influence, since the reformers refused to accept the limited role of merely assisting organized labor.

A year later a new Council for Civic Cooperation was formed, from which organized labor was excluded. Thirty-one organizations joined, but this new council once again had the power only to advise on effective cooperation; [30] and by 1903 it had dwindled

---

[25] *Hammer and Pen*, Dec. 1898, p. 4.

[26] Social Reform Club of New York, Leaflet, Nov. 1, 1898.

[27] *New York Evening Journal*, Dec. 3, 1900, p. 7.

[28] *New York Evening Journal*, Dec. 7, 1900, p.8.

[29] *New York Evening Journal*, Jan. 15, 1901, p. 9.

[30] The League for Political Education, *Yearbook* (1902), pp. 73–74.

to two meetings a year, and a membership of "some fifteen or sixteen societies."[31]

A formal union of reform forces did not occur until 1918, when the Women's Joint Legislative Conference was formed at the request of the State Federation of Labor. This organization limited its activities to the support of labor legislation for women, toward which its lobbyists directed a united effort during sessions of the legislature. The Women's Joint Legislative Conference received the support of many social Progressive groups,[32] and it succeeded precisely because it confined its attention to one area of social reform activity where substantial unanimity of opinion already existed. Thus in reality the organization only formalized cooperation that already had occurred. As early as 1910 the American Association for Labor Legislation had suggested cooperation among the reform societies working for a reduction of hours for women.[33] In 1912 the same organization proposed a committee on women's work to capitalize on the unanimity among the reformers, and to eliminate overlapping and wasted effort.[34] However, the A.A.L.L. soon became involved in other reform activities, and the proposal languished until it was successfully revived by the State Federation of Labor in 1918.

These failures in the effort for formal cooperation do not mean that the reform groups never worked together; it indicates, though, that the cooperation was informal, limited, and temporary. Throughout the period, the social Progressive socie-

[31] "New York Council for Civic Cooperation," *Charities*, X (Jan. 31, 1903), 113.

[32] Elizabeth Faulkner Baker, *Protective Labor Legislation with Special Reference to Women in the State of New York* (Studies in History, Economics and Public Law Edited by the Faculty of Political Science of Columbia University, Whole No. 259, New York, 1925), p. 172. An eight-hour day for women, and minimum wage boards for women, were the primary objectives of the organization.

[33] Andrews to Florence Kelley, Andrews Papers, Dec. 21, 1910.

[34] *American Labor Legislation Review*, II (Jan. 1912), 169.

ties worked together on specific pieces of legislation. There was no loss of organizational independence, but similarity of purpose led to cooperation. Although most social Progressive societies supported a great variety of reforms, a degree of specialization developed as different organizations took the lead in promoting certain measures.[35] The newly formed New York Child Labor Committee headed the drive for a stronger child labor law in 1903, and the New York City Consumers' League took command of the efforts to pass a fifty-four-hour week for women in 1912. Similarly, the social Progressive societies increasingly cooperated in sponsoring investigations by professional social workers who had to be paid.

Most important, however, in overcoming the independence of the various organizations was the interlocking of social Progressive leaders within them. Throughout the Progressive period, the consumers' leagues and child labor committees had a substantial interlocking of leaders at the national and branch levels. Undoubtedly the similarity in purpose and philosophy attracted the same persons to both societies; but even where differences in method and aim existed, important individuals provided bridges among the organizations. Thus in 1900 over one-third of the governing board of the New York City Consumers' League were members of the Social Reform Club. Many leaders of the New York branch of the A.A.L.L. were active in other social reform organizations. Even the New York Women's Trade Union League recruited members from other reform societies despite its closer ties with organized labor. The professional social workers who entered the reform movement in increasing numbers often belonged to more than one organization.

Many social Progressive organizations had their offices in the "so-called Charities Building" in New York City. When Charles Spahr of *The Outlook*, a magazine which had its office in the same building, looked in one day at the Assembly Hall, he saw

[35] See Andrews to Mary Van Kleeck, Jan. 28, 1911, and Andrews to John Commons, Nov. 25, 1910. Andrews Papers.

Edward Devine, head of the Charity Organization Society and a leader in tenement house reform and in the campaign against tuberculosis; Lawrence Veiller, best known for his work for tenement house reform, although he was interested in other reforms as well; Samuel McCune Lindsay and Owen Lovejoy of the National Child Labor Committee; George Hall of the New York Child Labor Committee; Florence Kelley and others from the national and New York consumers' leagues; and Arthur and Paul Kellogg of the *Charities* magazine. " 'Ah,' exclaimed Charles Spahr genially, 'what's this bunch call itself today?' In point of fact, this was a meeting of the new American Association for Labor Legislation which John R. Commons had come from Wisconsin to introduce in New York." [36]

Thus the social Progressives developed a cooperation based on personal contact rather than organizational union. Where differences among the reform groups existed, the interlocking of membership did little to stimulate cooperation; but in areas of general agreement, the close ties among the societies' leaders helped make formal unity of organization less necessary. A ubiquitous social Progressive like Florence Kelley, who held membership in the A.A.L.L., the Child Labor Committee, and the Social Reform Club, among others, who directed the National Consumers' League, and who kept in close touch by correspondence and personal contact with other social reform leaders, is a conspicuous example of this interlocking.

The social Progressives admitted the unpopularity of their activities, but they believed that this was the very reason their work must continue.[37] The societies stood well in advance of public opinion, and their major aim was to persuade the public to accept their views. Mrs. Nathan concisely described the social Progressive method as, first, careful and thorough investigation; second, publicity for the facts; and then a "creating of public opinion concerning them" that would lead to the enactment of

[36] Goldmark, *Impatient Crusader*, pp. 68–69.

[37] *The Independent* (Binghamton), Oct. 7, 1899, p. 3, and Mary E. Dreier, *Margaret Dreier Robins*, pp. 22–23.

laws.[38] The social reformer had to educate, and often "create" public pressure for reform where it did not exist. This was discouraging work, for often the social Progressives despaired of "enlisting the cooperation of the great unthinking, ignorant public." Frequent failures suggested that a majority of the voters were neither informed nor interested.[39] To stimulate a public demand for reform, in the face of conservative control of the press and the American tradition of individualism, was the basic problem of social Progressivism.

The Progressives, in general, envisaged the public as an undifferentiated, classless body which would act as umpire among contending special interests in the spirit of fair play.[40] The public might be exploited by the special interests, especially the trusts, and thus the people had an obligation to use government powers judiciously for their own protection. A Progressive writer explained that "if the arteries of government are freed from impurities; if a majority of the people are given the opportunity to express themselves clearly and easily, no class legislation will result and . . . the best interests of all will be conserved." [41] The Progressives firmly believed that if the public were given fuller control over the legislative process by initiative, referendum, recall, and direct primaries and elections, it would eventually, after appropriate education, realize the necessity and humanity of the Progressive reforms and provide the pressure to enact them. Even though the Progressives' "public" really meant the middle class, and even though it was not as impartial as they believed, these concepts were very important to the reform movement itself. The social Progressives needed the

[38] Consumers' League of the City of New York, *Annual Report*, 1914, p. 12.

[39] Paul Kennaday to Frank Morrison, Andrews Papers, Sept. 8, 1911. Also Mary Dreier to Wald, Wald Papers, Nov. 15, 1915.

[40] John R. Commons, *Labor and Administration* (New York, 1913), pp. 72, 82.

[41] Benjamin P. DeWitt, *The Progressive Movement: A Non-Partisan, Comprehensive Discussion of Current Tendencies in American Politics* (New York, 1915), p. 92.

stoutest public support since their reforms ran so strongly against American traditions.

The social reformers adopted several basic devices in their attempt to educate the public. The direct appeal to the consumer never achieved much success; the consumers' leagues discovered that the attraction of low prices and the convenience of late hours or specific services, such as delivery of gifts on Christmas morning, had more appeal to the public than the unfair working conditions that might accompany them. Despite the use of the White Lists, the label, leaflets, picture postcards calling for early Christmas shopping, advertisements in theater programs and newspapers, posters in private schools and clubs, street banners and speeches before organizations of every kind, the campaigns of the consumers' leagues had little real success when they clashed with the interests of the consumer. Such use of direct appeals never spread widely through the social reform movement, although organized labor continued to emphasize the union labels.

The social Progressives' basic method was to publicize investigations undertaken by the societies or by government agencies. Simply worded leaflets described the most deplorable conditions discovered by these inquiries and suggested a specific piece of legislation that would help eliminate the evil. Photographs were used extensively to show the stunted children and broken women produced by the excesses of the industrial system. The reformers employed cartoons, graphs, and all manner of illustrative materials to capture the reader's interest. The use of these illustrative materials became a characteristic of the social Progressives' method.

The reformers hoped to convert large portions of the public by the emotional repetition of a simple set of facts, and the constant demand for social action. The approach was not dispassionate and reasoned, but partisan and humanitarian: it stressed the tragedies of individuals, not principles of economics or politics. The Child Labor Committee pioneered in the use of such material, but other organizations also developed emotionally charged literature of their own.[42]

In their campaigns, the social Progressives emphasized two separate arguments. First, they reiterated the inhumanity of the industrial or social evil and appealed to the public's sentiments of compassion and revulsion. Yet this was often not enough, since compassion does not necessarily bring action. Thus much of the social Progressives' literature also attempted to tie the industrial evils directly to the self-interest of the middle class. Tenement-made clothing meant not only pitifully low wages for the laborer, but also the possibility of contagion for the consumer should any of the workers have had a communicable disease; excessive hours meant not only fatigue and poor health for the child or woman, but danger to the vitality and strength of the nation because of the physical and moral weakening of the family; low wages led directly to the growth of vice and crime, which might easily affect the middle-class community, and low wages necessitated higher taxes to support courts, prisons, hospitals, clinics, and sanatoria; industrial degradation bred resentment among the working class, which if not relieved might lead to the development of radicalism. Over and over, the dual appeal to the basic humanity among men and to the self-interest of the middle class came before the public through speeches, leaflets, books, articles, magazines, conferences of reformers, and the published accounts of all manner of investigations in the journals of the reform organizations.

[42] The social Progressives also sought to win educated opinion by the familiar method of reasoned, often erudite, argument. *The Child Labor Bulletin* and the Proceedings of the Annual Conferences of the Child Labor Committee contain examples of this material aimed at a smaller but individually more influential group. The A.A.L.L. is an exception to the trend in the social Progressives' method of propaganda. With a large group of professors among its leaders, the A.A.L.L. placed more emphasis on erudite discussion than on popular propaganda, although leaflets were also part of its program of publicity. For examples, see the *American Labor Legislation Review*.

This educational campaign was the basis for legislative success, fot it built up the necessary support among the voters. However, the reformers often found that their publicity alone did not arouse sufficient public pressure to force reforms over the concerted opposition of conservative forces. Mrs. Nathan noted that "public opinion is not easily aroused. A terrible disaster will do more for reform than much constant work, especially where the evils are not monstrous, but only unnecessary." [43] Such climactic events did occur. The evils the reformers campaigned against periodically came to public view in tragedies such as the Triangle Fire of 1911, in which 145 women lost their lives. This calamity occurred because of the weaknesses of the Factory Code and poor enforcement of the existing laws. The excitement of an event like the shirtwaist strike of 1909 could arouse a lethargic public, and such colorful leaders as Theodore Roosevelt and Governor Charles Evans Hughes aided social reform immeasurably by bringing the entire issue of reform into the headlines.

The social Progressives sought to convey the impression in their lobbying that the public had been aroused in favor of the projected law and that the reformers therefore represented the people. The greater the unanimity among social Progressives, the greater their insistence that the public was truly behind the reformers' campaign. Thus the societies attempted to have as many as possible of their members, from the widest possible variety of organizations, attend the legislative hearings. In addition, the public was asked to write directly to the legislators, in order to convince the individual assemblyman or state senator that support for reform existed in *his* district.[44] Unlike organized labor, the social reformers did not threaten political re-

[43] Consumers' League of the City of New York, *Annual Report,* 1901, p. 15.

[44] "Recommendations to the Plan and Scope Committee in Regard to the Future Work of the Club," March 10, 1904, p. 4, Lawrence Veiller Papers (Microfilm, Columbia University).

taliation, although the social Progressives' campaign did carry the implicit threat that opposition to the aroused force of public opinion would wreck the career of the politician.

Just as their opponents did, the social Progressives attempted to use private influence whenever it seemed necessary. Owen Lovejoy suggested that to pass a bill and see that it was enforced, one must not only have a committee that was strong numerically, but also "get a number of leading citizens from different sections of the state, men and women who will have influence with their legislators, so that when the bill comes up and some man proceeds to oppose the bill you will be able to telegraph to that man's chief constituent, and ask him to stimulate his representative a little and get him on the right side." [45] Unfortunately for the reformers, their opponents often had the better of the battle in applying private pressure, and thus the social Progressives had to rely mainly upon the force of public opinon.

Almost every major reform passed in New York State during the Progressive period was attacked soon afterward by a series of weakening amendments. Against these the reformers had to battle constantly, and they were handicapped by the public's lack of interest following the passage of a Progressive measure. The struggle of the social Progressives for effective reform thus did not end with the passage of legislation—it only entered a new phase.

[45] *The Child Labor Bulletin*, II (May 1913), 169. The attempt to use Jacob Riis's influence with Governor Theodore Roosevelt of New York to secure the post of chief factory inspector for Florence Kelley failed. See Florence Kelley to Wald, Jan. 24, 1899; Jane Addams to Wald, Feb. 18, 1899; and other correspondence between Addams and Wald during 1899. Wald Papers. Also interesting are Wald to Mortimer Schiff, April 2, 1906; Louis Marshall to Wald, April 5, 1906; and Pauline Goldmark to Wald, April 10, 1906. Wald Papers.

V

Organized Labor and the Social Progressives: Areas of Cooperation

THE campaigns for social reform in New York State exhibit no one pattern. Close cooperation among all reform organizations marked some of the battles for legislation, whereas at other times the reformers split among themselves, or opposed the demands of organized labor. The social Progressive societies and the central labor bodies led, prodded, and cajoled the fickle and often indifferent public; and the relations among these reform groups were a significant factor in the final success or failure of any campaign.

One of the major concerns of the social Progressives was child labor. No other issue attracted so much attention, both nationally and at the state level, and by 1916 the reform forces could claim substantial gains. In New York the foundations of child labor legislation had been laid in the last fifteen years of the nineteenth century. By 1900 New York law set a ten-hour day as the maximum for children fourteen to sixteen years of age; prohibited children under fourteen from working in factories and stores; and required a minimum attendance of eighty days per year in school.[1] The Knights of Labor and philanthropic societies such as The Society for the Prevention of Cruelty to Children took the lead in promoting this legislation.[2] However, the nineteenth-century laws on child labor soon proved to be

[1] *History of Labor in the United States*, Vol. 3, pp. 404–413.
[2] *Ibid.*, pp. 404, 435.

ineffective because of loopholes and lax enforcement.[3] In 1903 the social reformers and organized labor attacked these weaknesses and made the laws more effective.

Before 1903 a parent's affidavit had been acceptable as proof of a child's age. Experience proved that parents who needed the proceeds of child labor would not hesitate to add a few months —or years—to a child's age. After 1903 documentary evidence of age became necessary. The educational requirement had merely ordered eighty days of attendance at school; the reformers raised the minimum requirement to 130 days per year, and demanded that children achieve a basic competence in reading and writing before being discharged into the labor force as supposedly qualified citizens. Work during the summer vacation had been permitted before 1903 for children under fourteen, but this now was prohibited. The temptation to continue the job into the school year had often proved stronger than the attraction of the classroom. Finally, the nine-hour day replaced the old ten-hour limit, and children who carried on certain street trades, such as newsboys, came under the law for the first time. In this program, the emphasis was not on sweeping changes in the basic structure of the child labor laws, but on stricter enforcement and wider coverage.

The campaign for the amendments of 1903 illustrates three major features of a successful social reform campaign in New York during the Progressive period. First, there was cooperation between organized labor and the social Progressives; second, public opinion rallied to the support of the reformers; and finally, the social Progressives themselves cooperated effectively.

A contemporary work on social reform in New York gave prime credit for the laws of 1903 to the social Progressive movement. Labor's role was concisely summarized:

Assistance and cooperation came from various trade unions, to a certain extent, but their aid was inclined to be perfunctory. The

[3] New York Child Labor Committee, *Child Labor—Factories and Stores* (pamphlet), New York, 1903.

unions took little real interest in the movement and did little efficient work. They were used by the Child Labor Committee to distribute as their own, the circulars gotten out by the committee, stating the results of its investigations and its appeals for new legislation. In this way, the committee was enabled to reach a class who are always inclined to be suspicious of appeals coming from philanthropists of the "upper class." This was about the extent of the active participation of the trade unions in the movement, although it was endorsed by the Central Federated Union of New York City, which appointed a special committee to assist in the campaign, and by organized labor in general.[4]

Without doubt the social Progressives did take the lead during the campaign for the amendments, and their publicity was vital in awakening the public's interest. The Workingmen's Federation knew that an investigation by the social Progressives and the Central Federated Union of New York City in 1902 had disclosed widespread evasion of the laws, and that a Child Labor Committee was being formed to demand reforms from the 1903 legislature; yet the Federation's executive council did not place child labor legislation on its preferred list of bills for 1903.[5] Organized labor in New York City played a more important role, however.

In 1902 the University Settlement demanded an investigation of child labor conditions, and this investigation subsequently led to the formation by the aroused reformers of the Child Labor Committee. The Central Federated Union of New York City cooperated with the Settlement from the earliest stages of the investigation, and shared in the demands for reform legislation.[6] The reformers led the campaign for the amendments before the legislature, but the Central Federated Union took an active if

[4] Fred R. Fairchild, "The Factory Legislation of the State of New York," *Publications of the American Economic Association*, Third Series, VI, No. 4 (Nov. 1905), 86.

[5] *New York Evening Journal*, Jan. 14, 1903, p. 9.

[6] *New York Evening Journal*, July 14, 1902, p. 5; July 21, 1902, p. 7.

less publicized role. When the campaign reached its climax in March 1903, the C.F.U. wrote to other central bodies asking for their cooperation in the final effort.[7] Samuel Gompers already had appeared at the hearings to add the prestige of the A.F.L. to the Workingmen's Federation support of the amendments.[8]

The Central Federated Union followed the leadership of the Child Labor Committee once it had been formed; [9] for this group of prominent social Progressives and philanthropists took command of the reformers' efforts as well. Organized labor thus became part of a united effort to put through the amendments. The effective cooperation between the reformers and organized labor was a vital factor in producing such quick success. It would thus seem that the campaign of 1903 was a united effort of all reform forces, and although the social Progressives directed the battle through the Child Labor Committee and contributed most of the money used in the campaign, organized labor in New York City actively supported the movement from its inception, and played its part in rousing working-class opinion in favor of the amendments.

The reformers generally agreed that their efforts to gain public support for child labor reform were an overwhelming success. The Consumers' League of New York City declared that "the agitation for this legislation received the unqualified support of the public, and in Albany the bills were designated as the most popular of all introduced at the session." [10] C.A.I.L. noted that all portions of the public and not only the middle class, had been deeply stirred.[11] The contrast between the scattered demands for child labor reform before 1902 and the solid news-

[7] *Official Record*, April 1903, p. 1.

[8] *Labor Legislative News*, March 6, 1903, p. 1.

[9] *Labor Legislative News*, Feb. 6, 1903, p. 1; *New York Times*, Feb. 23, 1903, p. 12.

[10] Consumers' League of the City of New York, *Annual Report*, 1903, p. 29.

[11] *Hammer and Pen*, April 1903, p. 109.

paper support for the amendments of 1903 indicates how successful the reform forces were.[12] Governor Benjamin Odell aided the campaign, and so did the New York Department of Labor.[13] Thus within one year, investigation and agitation by reform forces had enlisted the support of key conservatives and awakened the public outcry necessary to overcome the opposition of business interests. By early 1903 the Child Labor Committee did in fact represent the public, and thus its program passed the legislature without serious difficulty. By following the social Progressives' program—Investigate, Educate, and Legislate—the reformers had aroused dormant public opinion and had channeled it into an early victory.

At the very time when attempts to bring about formal unity among the social Progressives were a miserable failure,[14] the child labor campaign produced a significant degree of informal cooperation among the social reform organizations. Many of the leaders of social Progressive groups became directors of the new Child Labor Committee, and their presence on both the new and the old organizations, plus the general agreement among all social reformers that the child labor laws had to be made effective, led to complete acceptance of the committee's leadership.[15] The uniting of the social Progressives and organized labor provided the most powerful force that could be established in support of social reform. Governor Odell's prompt endorsement of the Child Labor Committee's program, and the ease with which a conservative legislature passed most of the bills, indicate an ac-

[12] New York Child Labor Committee, *What the Newspapers Are Saying about Child Labor in New York State* (pamphlet), 1903.

[13] New York State Department of Labor, *Third Annual Report of the Department of Labor for the Twelve Months Ending September 30, 1903*, Vol. I, pp. 50–53.

[14] See pp. 79–80.

[15] Officers and major committee members found in New York Child Labor Committee, *Summary of Child Labor Laws in New York State* (pamphlet), 1903. Also see National Consumers' League, *Report for the Year Ending March 1903*, p. 24.

ceptance of the reformers' contention that they represented public opinion.

In the years after 1903 organized labor and the social Progressives continued to cooperate in promoting child labor legislation. The labor movement felt no threat to its prerogatives from the regulation or prohibition of child labor. Unions made no serious attempt to organize child workers, and there was little likelihood that the regulation of children's hours and working conditions would set a precedent for adult men. The need of the child for protection was recognized to be a special case. Thus the Workingmen's Federation supported all attempts to extend the laws concerning child labor, and it even claimed leadership in this area.[16] This claim represented organizational patriotism, for the social Progressives retained their leadership; organized labor's support of child labor legislation, however, illustrated its positive attitude toward social reform when the unions had no fear that their interests were threatened.

George Hall, a leader of the New York Child Labor Committee, remarked that "more difficult in some respects than obtaining this legislation was the Committee's struggle during its pioneer period to create a public opinion which would sustain the new laws." [17] In 1905 the supporters of the 1903 laws had to work hard to prevent the emasculation of the child labor laws.[18] The Child Labor Committee was able to resume the attack in the years 1907–1914 as the growth of Progressive opinion within New York stimulated an interest in all aspects of reform, and accelerated the campaign for new child labor regulations.

Against strong opposition, but with the support of Governor

[16] Workingmen's Federation of the State of New York, *Proceedings,* 1908: President Harris's Report. For continuing support of child labor reform see conventions of the Federation for 1906, 1907, 1908, 1909, and 1913.

[17] Frederick Smith Hall, *Forty Years, 1902–1942: The Work of the New York Child Labor Committee* (New York, 1942), p. 14.

[18] *Labor Advocate,* Aug. 26, 1905, p. 1.

Charles Evans Hughes and of the Commissioner of Labor, P. Tecumseh Sherman, the demands of the social Progressives and organized labor for an eight-hour day for children were partly met in 1907.[19] This measure applied only to factories and thus did not affect a majority of the employed children. The reform forces fought to include stores under the eight-hour provision, but the opposition of the Retail Dry Goods Merchants Association blocked action until 1914, when the work of the Factory Investigating Commission provided the push needed to pass the bill.

The New York legislature had set up the Factory Investigation Commission in response to the uproar raised by the Triangle Fire of 1911. Many social Progressives were employed by the Commission or contributed to its investigations of working conditions in the state. A host of recommendations for new labor laws ensued, and the legislature passed many of these in 1913 and 1914. What was equally important, the Commission's work publicized the whole issue of labor reform at a time when Progressivism in the nation had reached its zenith, and this gave important aid to the entire program of the social Progressives.

In 1909 the list of dangerous occupations prohibited for children was greatly enlarged, and in the same year the reformers opened an attack on the employment of children in canneries. Once again an investigation provided the basis for the social Progressives' attack. The study denied the owners' assertion that work in the canneries by the children of female employees really was a kind of play, which only incidentally aided in canning a perishable crop; instead, it concluded that cannery labor was regimented work, with long hours, which sapped the strength of children.[20] The owners successfully blocked any action until

[19] George A. Hall, "New York Child Labor Legislation," *Charities and The Commons*, XVIII (July 20, 1907), 434; New York State Department of Labor, *Sixth Annual Report of the Department of Labor for the Twelve Months Ending September 30, 1906*, Vol. 1, p. 58.

[20] National Child Labor Committee, "Child Employing Industries: The Proceedings of the Sixth Annual Conference on Child Labor, Boston,

1913, when the legislature approved the Factory Investigating Commission's recommendation to place canneries under the child labor laws.[21] Public support for Progressive reform was at its height, not only in New York but in the nation, and the canners could not contend against the political force of a reform-minded electorate. The social Progressives helped set this mood of reform, and in 1913 they reaped their greatest harvest. Although child labor continued illegally in the state after 1914, its use clearly was prohibited by law.[22]

The reform movement also was successful in its efforts to regulate tenement construction and manufacturing within those tenements. The regulation of tenement construction had the widest range of support, including charities and civic groups.[23] In this respect, the campaign that produced the tenement code of 1901 resembled the more conspicuous effort for child labor reform in 1903. Once again organized labor supported the reform movement, although it did not play so prominent a role as it had done in the child labor campaign.[24] The conservative reformers and civic associations held the leadership, and they received aid from the social Progressives and from organized labor. Humanitarian considerations again attracted support from the public. The reformers also stressed the evils which affected the entire population because of the proliferation of slums. As for the child labor amendment, no new function of state gov-

---

Massachusetts, January 13–16, 1910," *The Annals of the American Academy of Political and Social Science*, March 1910, Supplement, p. 153.

[21] New York State Department of Labor, *Bulletin*, Whole No. 55 (June 1913), contains summaries and texts of the thirty-five bills passed in this climactic year for the Progressive movement in New York.

[22] Evasion continued principally in the department stores of New York City and the upstate canneries.

[23] Lawrence Veiller Papers, manuscript letter or memo (undated, but presumably 1899). An excellent recent study of tenement house reform in New York is Lubove, *The Progressives and the Slums*.

[24] *New York Evening Journal*, March 18, 1901, p. 7; Workingmen's Federation of the State of New York, *Proceedings*, 1901: Sept. 18, afternoon session.

ernment was required for the reform of conditions in tenements; the only thing needed was the extension of the nineteenth-century principle that the government had responsibility for the regulation of some types of buildings.

The leaders of the tenement reform campaign chose to ask for a commission to study the problem, rather than to launch a frontal attack on the opposition.[25] With the support of Governor Theodore Roosevelt, the legislature sat up such a commission in 1900. Powerful real estate interests, backed clandestinely by Tammany Hall, had blocked legislation in the past, and the Commission would have to mobilize public sentiment if reform were to succeed.[26] The reformers gave organized labor a place on the new Commission to ensure continued support of the movement among all classes of the population. Public support developed because of the publicity from the reformers and the reform-dominated Commission, and in 1901 Governor Odell added his decisive influence to the campaign.[27] As in 1903 Odell recognized the political value of accepting reform at the correct moment. Much of the reformers' proposed building code became law in 1901. It required the lighting of hallways; the lighting of the 300,000 "dark" rooms in tenements which had no window; the erection of fire escapes that were themselves fireproof; doing away with privy sinks in yards; and leaving 30 per cent of any lot empty.

These were minimum standards, but after an attack upon the new code failed in the courts, the real estate interests offered a set of amendments designed to weaken the law. In 1903 their attack reached its height, and concessions had to be made; but the continued support of the tenement code by the civic organizations, the social Progressives, and organized labor, plus the reform spirit produced by the child labor campaign, prevented

[25] The Reminiscences of Lawrence Veiller (Oral History Project, Columbia University), 1949, p. 20.

[26] *Ibid.*, p. 6.

[27] *Ibid.*, p. 34.

the emasculation of the law.[28] The desire to maintain a united front against the amendments even led the Citizens Union to ask wealthy members for contributions to pay the fare of workers who were to take part in a demonstration in Albany.[29] During the period 1902–1906, a running battle continued between the forces who were attempting to extend and defend the 1901 law and the real estate interests who were demanding a relaxation of the code on the grounds that the necessary alterations were too expensive, and that the requirements would reduce building and thus raise the rents of the poorer classes.[30] As usual, the reformers had to fight attempts to weaken reforms once public attention had shifted to new interests.

A study in 1906 of the five-year-old tenement law and its amendments indicated that most of the bad conditions remained in old buildings, although the code prevented their repetition in newly constructed tenements.[31] The social Progressives were ready to suggest municipal housing as an answer to the slums, but this proposal was too radical for the basically conservative civic and charitable organizations that had fought for the regulation of tenement building. Louis Pink, a settlement worker who favored municipal housing, indicated that strong opposition to the proposal had immediately arisen since "vested property rights must not be interfered with whatever the cost to the community. Many of those who are most active in housing reform are bitterly opposed to city built tenements. A campaign for

[28] *Charities*, X (March 7, 1903), 209–215; *New York Evening Journal*, Feb. 16, 1903, p. 6.

[29] Richard W. G. Welling Papers (New York Public Library): Citizens Union to Welling, March 21, 1903.

[30] In 1905, for example, the New York County Republican Committee and the builders pressed Veiller to support amendments to the tenement house law. He acquiesced in one amendment on the promise that there would be no others in the future. See Veiller Papers: William Halpin to Veiller, Jan. 27, 1905; Adolph Block to Veiller, March 9, 1905, and March 29, 1905.

[31] Emily W. Dinwiddie, "The Work of New York's Tenement House Department," *Charities and The Commons*, XVII (Oct. 6, 1906), 11.

municipal construction of workingmen's homes would divide the friends of tenement house reform and would end in certain disaster." [32] Accordingly, no municipal construction took place during the Progressive period.

In the closely related area of regulating manufacturing within the tenement buildings, the social Progressive organizations clearly had the lead. In the first stage of the movement—before 1909—the aim was the regulation of working conditions within tenements. Prohibiting all home work would have been a more effective policy, but in the case of *In re Jacobs* (1885), the New York Court of Appeals had ruled that prohibition of home work invaded the constitutional rights of the individual. The more conservative Progressive forces would therefore not support anything more than regulation. Also, there was much less agreement among Progressives concerning the undesirability of home work than concerning the evils of New York City's degenerating tenement buildings. In general, the closer the reform approached to the regulation of the working conditions of adult laborers, the less the support from civic and charitable organizations, and from conservative opinion.

The basic code for the regulation of home work in the tenements passed the New York legislature in 1899. All tenement workshops, whether they were rooms set aside primarily for manufacture or merely living rooms in which some home work took place, had to be licensed by the state factory inspector. They could be so licensed only if the rooms met certain standards of ventilation and sanitation. The law applied only to the manufacture of clothing that was not laundered before sale.

Critics soon began to question the effectiveness of the new law. The licensing requirement meant that each individual work room in the tenements of New York City had to be inspected before being approved. In the first three months of the law's operation, when over 6,000 persons applied for licenses, only

[32] Louis H. Pink, "Old Tenements and the New Law," *University Settlement Studies*, III (June 1907), Supplement, 11.

fourteen inspectors were available. Thus at best they could only make a perfunctory inspection. After the license was obtained, there was nothing to prevent the tenement workers from operating in an unlawful manner since the danger of reinspection was very slight. The license thus became a certificate of cleanliness when in reality the old conditions prevailed.[33] Many tenement shops continued to operate without licenses, and they went undiscovered for years.

The evils of tenement work thus remained, and the social Progressives continued to point out the harmful effect of long hours of home work on family life and on individuals. The social Progressives also maintained that contagious diseases were common in the filthy tenements, and that the clothes worked on in these rooms were likely to transmit the contagion to the middle-class purchaser. The reformer emphasized that the public had more than a humanitarian interest in enforcing strict standards for this kind of work. C.A.I.L. took the lead in demanding more effective regulation, and it received solid support from organized labor and the other social Progressive groups.[34]

Organized labor supported the tenement reform program because home work usually meant low wages and unregulated working conditions, and the existence of thousands of tiny shops and individual home workers hampered the efforts to unionize the trades. The United Garment Workers strongly supported the social Progressives' demands for better regulation, and it also attempted to use a more direct method to further the campaign. The Union announced in 1901 that it would withdraw its label from any manufacturer who allowed even a part of his operation to be done by tenement labor.[35] This move was unsuccessful, however, because the great majority of New York City's garment concerns did not use the union label; and further legislation was required even to get accurate lists of manufacturers

[33] Henry White, *Gunton's Magazine*, XVIII (April 1900), 348–354.
[34] *Hammer and Pen*, Jan. 1900, p. 95.
[35] *New York Evening Journal*, May 13, 1901, p. 6.

who did employ tenement workers. If progress was to be made, legislation evidently would have to be the means.

In the years after 1899, the reform forces demanded a host of amendments to the law, all aimed at more effective enforcement. The amendments passed increased the number of inspectors, charged building owners with responsibility for conditions within the tenement—thus making it unnecessary for the inspectors to bring charges against each individual shop or worker —and placed new categories of goods under the law. But an insoluble problem still remained: inspectors simply could not reach all the tenement work rooms frequently enough to secure compliance with the law. Thus the social Progressives demanded, as a new approach to the problem, the complete prohibition of all manufacturing in tenement buildings.

As early as 1898 C.A.I.L. had called for the end of all tenement manufacturing,[36] but had failed to win wide support, and the 1899 law was regulatory. C.A.I.L. renewed its demand when the failure of regulation became apparent. The decision *In re Jacobs* still barred the prohibition of manufacturing in tenements, but nonetheless C.A.I.L. insisted that the law should be passed.

We do not, of course, know whether or not such a law, if passed, would be declared unconstitutional by the courts. But since the safety and well-being of the people is the highest law, all we can say is that no court in the world should be able to declare unconstitutional any legislation whose looked-for result can only be to banish from the city an evil, which in the face of stubborn facts, no one will dare to deny is a fruitful cause of disease, death and sin, a plague-spot in our midst whence issue ills and woes innumerable and unutterable.[37]

A bill to prohibit manufacturing activities in tenements was introduced into the legislature in 1904, but it did not receive serious consideration.[38]

[36] *New York Evening Journal*, May 12, 1898, p. 5.
[37] *Hammer and Pen*, Nov. 1903, p. 163.
[38] *Hammer and Pen*, May 1904, p. 34.

Florence Kelley and the National Consumers' League also believed that prohibition would be the only solution, but they realized that public opinion had not been aroused sufficiently to overcome the strong opposition from the clothing manufacturers and the deadening effect of the 1885 decision. Instead, the League demanded increased efforts for effective regulation.[39] When regulation continued to be unsuccessful, the social Progressives turned to their favorite weapon, the investigation. The national and New York consumers' leagues, the national and New York child labor committees, and the College Settlement jointly paid a professional social worker to undertake a full-time study. Her report, issued in 1907, asserted that the licensing requirements had done little to end the major evils of tenement manufacturing. The study blamed this on the weaknesses in inspection, and although the report did not call for prohibition, it pointed out the great expense that would be required in order to secure enough inspectors.[40] The investigation provided the impetus for several amendments in 1907, but it quickly became apparent that they were of little effect, and early in 1909 the National Consumers' League called for the end of manufacturing in the tenements.[41] In subsequent years this became the demand of all the social Progressives, but despite the increase in the reform spirit in New York, prohibition was not secured. The social Progressives faced the strong opposition of the clothing industry, lost much of the support from civic and charitable organizations on this issue, and were unable to stimulate public opinion sufficiently to overcome these two factors.

Another important problem which attracted the continuous attention of the social Progressives was the regulation of the

[39] National Consumers' League, *Fifth Annual Report, Year Ending March 1, 1904*, p. 25.

[40] Mary Van Kleeck, *Child Labor in New York City Tenements*, 1908, p. 13. This pamphlet is reprinted from *Charities and The Commons*, XIX (Jan. 18, 1908).

[41] National Consumers' League, *Report for Two Years Ending March 1909*, p. 18.

hours of women. In the nineteenth century the need for some protection for women had been recognized, and laws in 1886, 1896, and 1899 had set a standard of a ten-hour day and a sixty-hour week, without night work, for all women in factories, and for those under twenty-one who were employed in stores.[42] Women, like children, were regarded primarily as part-time workers, who were much weaker than men and who were much more prone to exploitation and quite unessential in most industries. Thus the public accepted the regulation of women's working time, although it would have opposed any widespread control over the hours worked by men.

The social Progressives, especially the consumers' leagues, considered the protection of female workers to be one of their main functions. The early laws potentially were able to provide basic protection for women, but the social Progressives sought to close loopholes and secure efficient enforcement. Thus until 1911 the reformers accepted the ten-hour day as the standard for female workers. Organized labor also cooperated in the defense of the ten-hour standard, although the consumers' leagues were most prominent in this effort.[43] The canners persistently attempted to win exemption from the ten-hour law. They argued that their work was seasonal and that it was necessary for their female employees to work longer than sixty hours per week if the perishable crops were to be canned before they spoiled. The reform forces nevertheless opposed these requests, fearing that any exemption would lead other industries to demand similar privileges.

The initial pressure for lower hours for women did not come from the social Progressives but from organized labor. Between 1901 and 1910 the Workingmen's Federation joined in defending the existing ten-hour standard against attack; but it also demanded a reduction of hours for women to nine per day and

[42] *History of Labor in the United States*, Vol. 3, pp. 466–469.
[43] *New York Times*, March 2, 1902, p. 24; *New York Evening Journal*, March 7, 1902, p. 5.

fifty-four per week.[44] This effort produced no results, since public opinion could not be rallied effectively. The social Progressives, whose access to middle-class opinion far exceeded that of organized labor, took little notice of the call for a reduction in the hours per day and per week. Instead, the reformers concentrated on the enforcement of the existing law.

Organized labor's interest in the fifty-four-hour week for women was influenced strongly by the effect this standard would have on the hours of certain groups of male employees. Large numbers of women worked in the textile factories of upstate New York, and the United Textile Workers Union had failed to organize them. The Union lacked the power to secure a reduction in hours by its own efforts and thus it turned to the Workingmen's Federation for support of a women's fifty-four-hour bill. Since men and women worked in interrelated processes in these textile plants, a cut in the hours of women would reduce the hours of male workers to the same figure. Thus the Federation sponsored a fifty-four-hour bill for women from 1901 to 1909—at times limiting the coverage only to the textile industry in an effort to cut business opposition, at times demanding inclusion of all women in an attempt to win support from the social Progressives. It was the growth of the Progressive spirit in the nation, and in New York, which led the Federation to hope for success in this campaign.

In 1910, the same year that the first workmen's compensation bill passed the New York State legislature, the annual call for a nine-hour day for women received its first serious consideration. Now, for the first time, the social Progressives began to support the Federation's fifty-four-hour bill. The reformers believed that the lower limits on hours could now be won because of the increasing public support for reform. But the bill failed to pass.

In 1911 the social Progressives backed the Federation's efforts

[44] See annual Workingmen's Federation Convention resolutions, also *Labor Legislative News*, March 13, 1903, p. 1, and Baker, *Women's Labor Legislation*, p. 73.

even more strongly.[45] The Democrats had won a majority in the state elections of 1910, and were in power for the first time since 1894. The Tammany-controlled Democratic Party had always pleaded its support for labor's interests, and the social Progressives thus concluded that the fifty-four-hour bill had a good chance in the new legislature.[46] The reformers did not attempt to take control of the campaign, especially since the 1911 bill covered all female workers in factories. The campaign for a fifty-four-hour week for women was led by organized labor and supported by the reform societies, just as the drive for stricter child labor laws in 1903 had had social Progressive leadership and support from labor.

The reformers were, however, to be disappointed in their estimate of organized labor's influence with the Democrats. The canners demanded an exemption from any fifty-four-hour maximum even more strongly than they had from the existing sixty-hour week. Their influence upon upstate members of the legislature was so strong that in February 1911 the leaders of the State Federation were warned to grant the canners an exemption or give up all hope for the fifty-four-hour bill.[47] The opposition from the textile industry also helped to stall the bill, and the Federation seemed ready to accept a compromise bill with a limit of fifty-six or fifty-eight hours per week.[48]

Then, in March, the Triangle Fire occurred, shocking the public and focusing its attention on the subject of labor legislation. The State Federation and the reformers now pushed the fifty-four-hour bill again, hoping to capitalize on this public indignation; but their refusal to concede the canners an exemption led to the defeat of the measure. An attempt to secure the

[45] *American Labor Legislation Review*, I (Jan. 1911), p. 93.

[46] Consumers' League of the City of New York, *Annual Report*, 1911, p. 33.

[47] *New York Call*, Feb. 25, 1911, p. 2; New York State Federation of Labor, *Proceedings*, 1911, p. 27.

[48] New York Women's Trade Union League, Papers: Legislative Committee Report, 1911.

support of the Tammany Hall boss, Charles Murphy, for the bill also failed.[49] Thus despite the public outcry after the Fire, the canners and textile interests managed to block the passage of the bill.

In 1912 the Federation, admitting the failure of the reform campaign to overcome the opposition in the legislature, decided to accept the compromise and exempt the canners. Even with this concession, which ended the most active source of opposition, the bill barely squeaked through the committee as the textile manufacturers continued to fight it.[50] Moreover, since the social Progressives did not like the exemption of the canneries,[51] they supported the bill with much less enthusiasm than in 1911. The end of the canners' opposition was the crucial factor, however, and on the last day of the session the bill slipped through the State Senate by the barest margin possible. To gain the victory, two supporters of the measure had to be shepherded back to the Senate chamber after having left the Capitol in the belief that the fifty-four-hour bill would never come to a vote.[52]

In the following year the canners' victory evaporated, as once again an investigation provided the basis for reform. The Factory Investigating Commission paid a team of social workers to study the canneries, and their report revealed that work in rural canning sheds was as tiring as in urban factories, which meant that unlimited hours, even for a short period, could be harmful for women. The Commission recommended a compromise figure of from sixty to sixty-six hours per week, with any work over sixty hours to be permitted only in emergencies and with the approval of the Department of Labor. The State Federation and the social Progressives actively supported this bill, and it

[49] *New York Call,* July 1, 1911, p. 2; New York Women's Trade Union League, Papers: Legislative Committee Report, 1911.

[50] New York State Federation of Labor, *Proceedings,* 1912, pp. 62–64.

[51] National Consumers' League, *Report for the Year Ending January 19, 1912,* p. 28.

[52] New York State Federation of Labor, *Proceedings,* 1912, p. 64.

passed without difficulty. The election of 1912, in New York and the nation, had shown the attractiveness of the Progressive program to the voters, and the New York legislature of 1913 responded with a burst of reform legislation including the new compromise hours law for canneries. A year later, the combined campaign of the reform societies and organized labor, and the continued importance of the Progressive political mood in the State, produced a fifty-four-hour law covering female workers in department stores.[53]

Even before the passage of the fifty-four-hour law, the Women's Trade Union League began to demand a forty-eight-hour week and an eight-hour day for all women workers,[54] and by 1916 it had gained the support of the consumers' leagues and the State Federation for these new maximums.[55] A minimum-wage bill for women, and the forty-eight-hour week, were the two most important demands of the reform forces in the years following World War I, but neither became law before the period of the New Deal.

The campaign for legislation on women's working hours illustrates how organized labor could take the initiative, even concerning unorganized workers, when the reform in question had an effect upon a significant group in the state labor movement. Organized labor often accepted the leadership of the social Progressives when the issue did not affect the trade unions directly. On the other hand, the labor movement indicated that it would demand control of reform campaigns when its interests were significantly involved. Thus the effect of a fifty-four-hour bill on the United Textile Workers Union led the State Federation

[53] The opposition of the New York City department stores had prevented the extension of the sixty-hour week to adult women workers in the mercantile area until 1913.

[54] New York Women's Trade Union League, *Annual Report*, 1911–1912, p. 23.

[55] New York State Federation of Labor, *Proceedings*, 1914, p. 138; New York Women's Trade Union League, *Annual Report*, 1916–1917, p. 24.

of Labor to assume a major role in directing the campaign to reduce women's working hours through legislation.

Without doubt, organized labor's most important legislative effort was its attempt to win remuneration for workers injured in industrial accidents. Before 1902 New York State required only that employers not contract with their workers to exempt the employer from the requirements of the common law on accidents.[56] Under common law, an injured worker might sue his employer for damages before a judge and jury. In order to collect, the worker had to prove not only the negligence of the employer, but also that he had not been guilty of contributory neglect. In addition, any negligence by a fellow employee was not the responsibility of the employer and might be grounds for dismissing the suit. Finally, the worker had no claim if he had known of the risks involved in a certain job, but still worked at it; and it was the employee's responsibility to disprove any claim the employer might make about this assumed risk. Thus a costly lawsuit resulted from a worker's attempt to win damages, and employees collected in only a small fraction of suits following industrial accidents. If a worker did win damages, approximately 40 per cent usually went to the attorney, further reducing the chance that a seriously injured worker would receive adequate recompense.[57]

The failure of the common law to provide payment automatically for industrial injuries, together with the large number of such accidents and the chaos caused in a family with only small savings when the major wage earner became disabled, led organized labor and certain social Progressive organizations to demand a more equitable system. As early as 1898 the Social Reform Club demanded a revision of the principles of the common law. Miles Dawson, a well-known actuary, insurance

[56] *History of Labor in the United States*, Vol. 3, p. 568.

[57] Crystal Eastman, "Employers' Liability: A Criticism on Facts," *Publications of the New York Branch of the American Association for Labor Legislation*, No. 1, 1909, p. 17.

lawyer, and writer on insurance—and a leading member of the Club—expressed the prevailing sentiment when he argued that the common law had been designed to meet the needs of an agricultural society. In an industrial age, Dawson pointed out, accidents were frequent and often the employee could not prevent them even by exercising due caution. Since workers often had to perform tasks with an intrinsic danger of injury, it was only just that they not suffer alone if an accident should strike.[58] The Club then introduced a bill into the legislature of 1898 calling for automatic workmen's compensation of up to 50 per cent of a worker's wages for a period up to three years, with payments to vary according to the seriousness of the injury. The bill did not completely repeal the common-law idea of a suit against the employer for negligence, for it made compensation applicable only in cases where no one was clearly at fault.[59]

Despite the support of this bill by the A.F.L., the Workingmen's Federation refused to support it, demanding instead a bill that would limit the employer's appeal to the common-law defenses as a basis for defeating damage claims. Workers won many damage suits before the jury, but courts of appeal often voided the judgment because of assumed risk or contributory negligence by the worker or a fellow employee.[60] The Federation argued that a weakening of the employer's defenses would produce a greater number of court victories, and for sums much higher than compensation would provide. The opposition of the Workingmen's Federation led the Social Reform Club to give up the compensation bill, and it supported labor's efforts to pass an employers' liability law weakening the common-law defenses of the employer.

Up until 1909, organized labor in New York continued to support employers' liability legislation. In 1902, after several disappointments, the Workingmen's Federation, with the support

[58] Social Reform Club, Leaflet, Nov. 23, 1897.
[59] *New York Times*, March 1, 1898, p. 4; March 10, 1898, p. 9.
[60] *New York Times*, Dec. 13, 1897, p. 5.

of the Social Reform Club, won a weak Employers' Liability Act. The law left the defense of contributory negligence virtually intact, contained ambiguous language that led the railroad brotherhoods to charge that railroads would be excluded from the law by court interpretation, and exempted injuries to domestic servants and farm laborers from coverage. An amendment in 1906 specifically included railroads and made it easier for a worker to prove negligence by the employer.[61] These statutes did not produce a rash of damage suit victories, for the defense of contributory negligence was still possible, and was used as before. Organized labor did not win any further amendments to the employers' liability law, and thus the problem of industrial accidents remained unsolved as well as oppressive.

The 1909 session of the legislature was marked by a renewal of interest in workmen's compensation, when a commission was set up to study the problems of workmen's compensation and unemployment. The impetus for this step came from the New York branch of the American Association for Labor Legislation, rather than from organized labor. The 1908 convention of the Workingmen's Federation did not consider workmen's compensation, but the idea had been discussed extensively by the middle-class reformers within the A.A.L.L.[62] The demand for a commission had the support of Governor Hughes, who recognized the role of the Association by appointing two of its members to the commission.[63]

Organized labor in New York now reacted much more positively to the new campaign for workmen's compensation than it had in 1898. The failure of the employers' liability laws

[61] Workingmen's Federation of the State of New York, *Proceedings*, 1906, pp. 28–29.

[62] For example, see Henry Seager's program of labor reform presented in 1907. American Association for Labor Legislation, *Proceedings of First Annual Meeting*, 1907, pp. 86–94.

[63] American Association for Labor Legislation, *Third Annual Meeting: Proceedings, Reports, Addresses*, 1909, p. 30.

to produce payments in more than 25 per cent of all industrial accidents made the Workingmen's Federation more amenable to the workmen's compensation approach.[64] Organized labor nevertheless sought to continue and strengthen employers' liability as well, giving the employee a choice of remedy. It also demanded that compensation payments for temporary disability equal 65 per cent of the wage rate, with a four-year maximum; that death benefits be a third more than the highest possible total of disability payments; and that the State of New York guarantee that the compensation payments would be made.[65]

The Commission's proposal to the 1910 legislature, however, was much weaker. In an effort to avoid constitutional difficulties, coverage was limited to a few hazardous trades, and the choice of compensation was made voluntary for the employer. The scale of benefits was lowered, without a guarantee of payment by the State. Finally, although the employers' liability laws were to be strengthened, the use of this remedy by the worker meant the forfeiture of compensation payments, whereas an employer who accepted the workmen's compensation program became exempt from all lawsuits.[66] The social Progressives believed that the system of employers' liability had been ineffective, and thus demanded the regularity of compensation. Conservatives also supported workmen's compensation with the aim of minimizing the effect of the employers' liability laws. Because of the possibility of a huge award in an accident suit, employers often paid more for insurance than they lost to their employees in damages. Compensation would regularize accident payments, and thus reduce insurance costs significantly.[67] Organized labor at first opposed the compensation bill; but since the measure was a

[64] *New York Call*, Nov. 27, 1909, p. 1; American Association for Labor Legislation, *Proceedings, First Annual Meeting*, 1907, p. 94.

[65] *New York Call*, Feb. 21, 1910, p. 1.

[66] *New York Call*, April 1, 1910, pp. 1–2.

[67] Seth Low Papers (Columbia University): Box 72, Low to J. Mayhew Wainwright, Feb. 11, 1910.

great advance over past practice, the opposition was intended to force additional concessions, not to kill it.[68] Once the bill had reached the crucial stage in the legislature, organized labor gave it strong support.

In the matter of workmen's compensation legislation, unlike the less immediate issues of child labor and tenement reform, the labor movement refused to allow the social reformers to dictate their policy. Once the social Progressives had raised the issue of compensation, organized labor acted swiftly to seize control of the campaign from the middle-class reformers in order to legislate its own program. In 1910 and the succeeding years, cooperation between the reformers and labor was tenuous. The trade unions saw that they might eventually have to accept the social Progressives' proposals since these had won the support of the public and the necessary conservative votes in the legislature; but they did so only when organized labor could not dominate the reform forces.

In 1910 organized labor and the A.A.L.L. had split temporarily over the commission's compensation bill. The reformers agreed that the bill was far from perfect, but contended that nothing more could be gained at the time.[69] Labor continually demanded the maximum that might be achieved, and in this it often differed from the social Progressives' more cautious program. The trade unions and reformers contended for leadership in this area of reform, and each was forced to compromise to secure the support of the other. The adjustment of interests between labor and the social Progressives thus became in important feature of the campaign for a compensation law.

The compensation law of 1910 had a short life, for on March 24, 1911, the New York Court of Appeals unanimously ruled it unconstitutional.[70] The court declared that the law made the

[68] New York State Federation of Labor, *Proceedings*, 1910, p. 20.
[69] *New York Call*, May 26, 1910, p. 1.
[70] *Ives v. South Buffalo Railway Company*, 201 N.Y. 271, 1911.

question of negligence superfluous, but the judges believed that no man could be required to make payment for injuries unless he were directly at fault. Thus the law violated the due process clauses in the constitutions both of New York and of the United States. The police power was not found to be a proper justification for the law since compensation did nothing to conserve the health, safety, or morals of the employees.

The decision raised a storm of criticism from the social Progressives and from the conservative supporters of the 1910 law.[71] It also led to the immediate introduction of an amendment in the legislature of 1911 designed to make workmen's compensation and other forms of labor legislation constitutional. The State Federation sponsored this amendment, and took the lead in working for its passage. Although the A.A.L.L. at first cooperated with the State Federation, a split quietly developed between the Association and organized labor.[72] In addition, the social Progressives disagreed among themselves concerning the scope of the proposed amendment. It failed to pass.

The split that occurred among the social Progressives concerned a part of the amendment that would have sanctioned additional forms of labor legislation in the future. A majority of the reformers argued that the Federation's amendment was too broad and that it would therefore hinder the campaign for effective workmen's compensation.

We here make the point that industrial accidents have become pretty much a live issue in this State, and that with vigorous united action, we can get the people behind us on the right sort of constitutional amendment. But that old age pensions, invalidity and possibly sickness insurance are matters so remote from practical

[71] John Bauer, "New York Workmen's Compensation Act Unconstitutional," *American Economic Review*, I (Sept. 1911), 634–637 and James Parker Hall, "The New York Workmen's Compensation Act Decision," *The Journal of Political Economy*, XIX (Oct. 1911), 694–700, exemplify the criticism outside the usual social Progressive sources.

[72] New York Association for Labor Legislation, *Third Annual Report*, 1911, pp. 35–36.

accomplishment that to include these matters in a constitutional amendment, at the present time, would only provoke needless opposition.[73]

The social Progressives realized that a division among the reform forces would seriously imperil all efforts for compensation legislation,[74] yet the disagreement over the form of the amendment was not resolved.

Mary Dreier, president of the New York Women's Trade Union League, supported the Federation's position, asserting that the vague wording of the A.A.L.L.'s substitute amendment might not cover future reforms. She contended, "It would be a pity not to try to get the whole thing as we have to make a struggle anyway." [75]

But the most significant reason for the failure of the State Federation and the social Progressives to cooperate on a compensation amendment revolved about the role that the private casualty insurance companies were to play under any compensation law. Organized labor called on employers to insure themselves by means of a state insurance fund for workmen's compensation payments they might have to make. The casualty insurance companies, which had insured employers against damage suits under the common law and the employers' liability statutes, thus were eliminated completely. Organized labor and the social Progressives had attacked these casualty companies for their interest in profits rather than persons. Workers' damage claims had been contested interminably in the courts, and often the worker would settle out of court for a pittance, rather than live on charity, as he was often obliged to do, until the case finally was decided. The companies contended in reply that many of the workers' suits were fraudulent. The State Federation's president, Daniel Harris, denied this, and charged that the

[73] Paul Kennaday to Mary Dreier, Andrews Papers, Dec. 7, 1911.
[74] Paul Kennaday to Samuel Gompers, Andrews Papers, Nov. 11, 1911.
[75] Mary Dreier to Paul Kennaday, Andrews Papers, Dec. 6, 1911.

casualty companies contested the workers' accident claims in order to increase their already substantial profits.[76] Harris argued that if the casualty companies were permitted to insure employers under a workmen's compensation law, they would continue to try to keep their payments low by opposing compensation claims in the courts, or by seeking to sabotage the effectiveness of the law.

The social Progressives agreed that the casualty companies were penurious in paying claims. Miles Dawson pointed out that intense competition made soliciting costs so high that the companies had to be economical in meeting claims.

Take the case of an employer of many workmen who, as he could be sure of a fair, average experience, might safely carry his own risk. He insures in a stock company only if convinced that it will be profitable to do so; that is, if its premiums are actually below the net cost to him or are so little above it that he is not justified in taking the risk of fluctuations rather than pay the excess. If the management expense is, as in Great Britain, more than 35 per cent, or as in the United States, about 50 per cent, the stock companies must merely, in order to recoup their expenses, be able to adjust the claims of this employer's employees for under 65 per cent in one case, and under 50 per cent in the other, of what it would cost the employer to pay them.[77]

Dawson declared that a state insurance fund would have lower administrative costs and would be more liberal in accepting claims. Even so, the agreement between organized labor and the social Progressives concerning the policies of the casualty companies did not lead to solid cooperation against them.

The A.A.L.L.'s opposition to the State Federation's compensation amendment became public in 1912. The Association insisted that it did not support the casualty companies, which were frantically resisting the attempt to remove them from one of their main fields of business, but it argued that the Federa-

[76] New York Call, May 15, 1913, p. 1.
[77] American Labor Legislation Review, III (June 1913), 261.

tion's attempt wholly to exclude the companies would bring about the defeat of the entire compensation amendment.[78] Instead, the A.A.L.L. supported the compromise Bayne-Phillips amendment, which established a state insurance fund while permitting the existing firms to continue their business.[79] The Federation refused to support this amendment, which nevertheless passed the legislature without serious objection. The Association's compromise was most congenial to politicians who had to contend with the influence of the insurance companies, and with the growth of reform sentiment in the state.

In 1912 the election as governor of William Sulzer, who had supported organized labor consistently during his seventeen years as a Democratic congressman, together with the Progressive mood displayed by the electorate in the presidential and state races, encouraged the State Federation to renew the attempts to secure the kind of compensation legislation called for by its interests. A new, compulsory compensation bill was introduced by the Federation in 1913 under the assumption that the Bayne-Phillips amendment would be passed by the legislature for a second time—as required by the New York State constitution—and be approved by the electorate at the November election. Ignoring the provision in the amendment permitting private insurance firms to continue their operations under a workmen's compensation law, the State Federation's bill completely eliminated the casualty companies, and would have placed all insurance under a state insurance fund. The measure also provided a liberal system of payments, contained no contribution of any kind by workers, and set up a Workmen's Compensation Commission to handle claims and administer the state fund. The bill represented the interests of labor fully, and bore little resemblance to the act which had been declared unconstitutional in 1911. Obviously, organized labor believed that the

[78] New York State Federation of Labor, *Proceedings*, 1912, pp. 29–32.
[79] New York State Department of Labor, *Bulletin*, Whole No. 51 (June 1912), p. 151.

Progressive spirit in the state, plus the election of Governor Sulzer, offered hope that the casualty companies' victory in the battle over the amendment might now be reversed. State Federation officials also insisted that Tammany Hall's leaders, who controlled the Democratic majority in the legislature, had promised to pass organized labor's bill.[80] The A.A.L.L. supported the Federation's bill, thus reversing its stand in 1912 concerning the casualty companies. The reformers agreed the moment had arrived when public opinion might force political leaders to support the position of labor.

The casualty companies then offered their own bill, which did not provide for a state insurance fund. Despite a concerted campaign by the State Federation, including threats of reprisal against the Democrats in the election of 1913, and despite support from reform organizations such as the A.A.L.L.,[81] the State Federation's bill did not pass, even after it had been amended to allow mutual insurance by groups of employers, or self-insurance by firms certified as financially stable by the Workmen's Compensation Commission. The refusal of the reform forces to permit the casualty companies any place in the field of compensation blocked the Federation's measure. The Democratic leadership hoped to avoid the complete alienation of labor and reform opinion on this issue, and thus it supported a compromise bill, based on the Bayne-Phillips amendment, which permitted both casualty companies and a state fund to operate. The State Federation denounced the compromise; but the casualty companies, armed with their large political contributions, could not be beaten, and the measure passed. The State Senate approved the bill only after a "remarkable exhibition of lobbying" by insurance company agents, along with sustained

[80] *New York Call*, May 15, 1913, p. 2; New York State Federation of Labor, *Proceedings*, 1913: Reports by President Harris and Legislative Chairman Fitzgerald.

[81] *New York Call*, March 4, 1914, p. 3; Paul Kennaday to the members of the New York State Senate Committee on Insurance, March 10, 1913. Andrews Papers.

pressure by the Democratic leaders.[82] The compromise did not become law, however, for Governor Sulzer vetoed it.

Sulzer, by a sudden reversal of his long record of party regularity, had in fact confounded the Tammany boss, Charles Murphy. The Governor sponsored investigations of scandals in the previous Democratic administration, and refused to meet Murphy's demands for patronage. The Tammany boss accordingly planned to break Sulzer and destroy his attempt to gain control of the Democratic Party in New York. Sulzer's veto message cited the opposition by the State Federation and important social Progressive groups as proof that the compensation bill did not represent the interests of those it was supposed to protect.[83] Of even greater importance was the Governor's hope that a veto would win the support of organized labor and the social reformers for his battle with Tammany.

Despite wide support from organized labor, the social Progressives, and the general public, late in 1913 Sulzer was impeached and removed from office by the Tammany-dominated legislature. After the impeachment and trial, a special session of the legislature met to reconsider workmen's compensation. The former lieutenant-governor, Martin H. Glynn, who had become governor, had been friendly to organized labor during his term as a congressman and his tenure as state comptroller in 1906–1908. But he was also a party regular, and it seemed clear that the Democratic leadership had not changed its attitude toward the casualty companies. Glynn conferred almost daily with the State Federation during late November 1913 concerning a new bill,[84] but his final proposal did not bar the casualty companies, although it met almost every demand from labor except this crucial one.[85] Despite the Progressive mood in

[82] *New York Times*, May 1, 1913, p. 2. The *New York Call*, May 2, 1913, p. 1, also agreed on the overt nature of the lobbying.
[83] New York State Federation of Labor, *Proceedings*, 1913, p. 41.
[84] New York State Federation of Labor, *Proceedings*, 1914, p. 42.
[85] *New York Times*, Dec. 9, 1913, p. 2.

the state, and the united efforts of the State Federation and the A.A.L.L., the insurance companies' influence was not to be overcome. The Glynn bill became law in December 1913, and it was hailed as the most advanced compensation law in the nation.[86] Thus the growth of Progressivism as a political movement from 1910 through 1914 once again led to a notable advance in labor law.

The Progressive spirit had grown steadily in New York State since 1906, but in the short period between the elections of 1914 and the entrance of the nation into World War I it diminished sharply, and the reform forces now had to battle to preserve their gains, with little hope of extending them. A sharp recession in 1914 interrupted the course of prosperity, and business became hostile to reforms it had accepted in previous years. The recession came on the heels of the most successful year the Progressives in New York had ever had—namely 1913—and many spokesmen for business charged that the new legislation had produced the downturn in economic activity.[87] Elbert Gary of the United States Steel Corporation pointed out that the recent reforms had made management timid because "there has been a decided sentiment, important and quite extensive, against successful business." He admitted that some business leaders had ignored the interests of the public and of their own employees, but argued that this situation had been largely corrected. Only demagogues, he said, continued to attack business instead of working for class cooperation and a renewed prosperity.[88]

Moreover, the deterioration of the Progressive Party in New

[86] *New York Times*, Dec. 12, 1913, p. 2. Also see the comments by Henry Seager in Andrews Papers, Box 71, Dec. 9, 1913.

[87] New York State Department of Labor, *Fourteenth Annual Report of the Commissioner of Labor for the Twelve Months Ending September 30, 1914*, p. 17; *Legislative Labor News*, Feb. 22, 1915, p. 1.

[88] *Addresses Delivered at Members' Council Luncheon of the Merchants Association of New York on the Subject of "Unemployment in New York" by William C. Breed, Esq., Hon. John Purroy Mitchel, Hon. Elbert H. Gary, Hon. Henry Bruere* [1915], pp. 10–11.

York led many independent Republicans to return to the G.O.P., and to vote for candidates chosen by the conservative forces that now controlled the party. The Progressives had no answer to the recession, except to insist that their reforms had not produced it. The Democrats had suffered a severe setback with independent voters because of the removal of Governor Sulzer. The legislature of 1915 thus was dominated by conservative upstate Republican leaders, and they soon unleashed a concerted attack on the reforms of the previous decade. State Senator Elon Brown, who dominated this group, declared that the Republicans had been elected in 1914 to retrench and end the "dictation of organized labor without consulting the business interests of this state." [89] Florence Kelley summed up the reaction of the social Progressives when she remarked, "This is such a dreadful Legislature that it is no use asking anything of them, but that they stop sinning a little." [90] The conservative attack covered the whole range of labor reforms. Organized labor generally cooperated with the social Progressives in an attempt to defend the hard-won gains.

The most controversial bill of the session proposed the merger of the recently formed Workmen's Compensation Commission and the Department of Labor into a new Industrial Commission. This plan produced stiff opposition from organized labor and from most of the reformers. The consumers' leagues, the New York Child Labor Committee, and several settlements led the defense of the system of labor law enforcement which had been developed slowly during the past two decades. The State Federation had secured from the Democrats the appointment of the former A.F.L. vice president, John Mitchell, as chairman of the Compensation Commission, and of John Lynch, the former president of the International Typographical Union, as commissioner of labor. The Federation opposed the merger because it would mean the loss of these two pro-labor adminis-

[89] *New York Times*, March 14, 1915, Section II, p. 7.
[90] *Legislative Labor News*, April 9, 1915, p. 1.

trators if they were not appointed to the new five-man Industrial Commission.[91] The reformers had no special preference for administrators drawn from organized labor, but they believed that fifteen years of practice in slowly developing more effective enforcement procedures within the existing structure of the Department of Labor might be endangered.[92]

The American Association for Labor Legislation came under fire from both organized labor and other social Progressives for supporting this particular legislation. The Association opposed the bill originally because of specific defects in the structure of the new Industrial Commission, but it strongly favored the principle of a single administrative body with some degree of quasi-legislative authority. The Wisconsin Industrial Commission of 1911 provided a model for the A.A.L.L.'s leaders. Other reformers agreed that the administration of the labor law could be made more efficient, but they warned that "those now in charge of the Department are in sympathy with the spirit and aim of the law, whereas any changes that would be made would be by those who have openly expressed antagonism to many of the most vital provisions of the law." [93] The Republican leaders took advantage of this division in the reformers' ranks by asking the A.A.L.L. to revise the Industrial Commission bill. The revamped measure then was pushed through the legislature without a hearing, over the objections of other social Progressive groups. Samuel Gompers resigned his membership in the A.A.L.L. because of its support of this bill.[94]

The Association answered this criticism by reiterating the independent character of social Progressive societies. The A.A.L.L. argued that it had an obligation to support legislation on the basis of its own study of the problems. Cooperation with other reform organizations, or with organized labor, was determined

91 *Legislative Labor News*, March 15, 1915, p. 1.
92 *Legislative Labor News*, March 22, 1915, p. 2.
93 Bernard Sheintag to Andrews, Andrews Papers, March 11, 1915.
94 *Legislative Labor News*, June 1915, p. 5.

by the nature of each issue, and was not to be expected as general policy. The A.A.L.L. contended that its bill would gain the advantages of an efficient single administrative body without weakening enforcement in practice, and despite the objections of other reform forces, the Association continued to support the bill it had revised.

Organized labor and the social Progressives also cooperated in fighting proposals to shift the enforcement of the building requirements for factories within New York City—many of which had been added only during 1912 and 1913—from the Department of Labor to the five borough governments.[95] Experience had shown that local enforcement was less effective than coordinated action by the state, and the reformers had battled for ten years to have mercantile inspection placed in the Department of Labor before they won their point in 1908.

A host of other bills attacking the recent reforms appeared in the legislature, and the canners took advantage of the reaction to repeat their demand for an extension of the hours permitted their female employees. Three bills introduced in 1915 sought to extend the permissible limit from sixty-six to seventy-two hours per week, to stretch the limit for night work from 10 P.M. to midnight, and to permit Sunday work. The consumers' leagues, the New York Women's Trade Union League, and the child labor committees, joined by the State Federation, attacked the bills, but they were passed by the legislature.[96] The new Republican governor, Charles Whitman, objected, however, and the bills were then recalled by the legislature and killed.[97]

A joint labor-reformer meeting in March 1915 singled out ten "ripper" bills for condemnation,[98] and only one of these—the merger of the Labor Department and the Workmen's Compen-

---

[95] *New York Call*, March 24, 1915, p. 1; March 27, 1915, p. 1; Consumers' League of the City of New York, *Annual Report*, 1915, p. 16.

[96] *Legislative Labor News*, March 1, 1915, p. 3.

[97] *New York Call*, April 18, 1915, p. 1; April 22, 1915, p. 1.

[98] *New York Call*, March 27, 1915, p. 1.

sation Commission—passed in that year. Much of this success in defending the labor law was the result of Governor Whitman's vetoes of several important bills. The Governor and State Senator Elon Brown were engaged in a struggle over patronage and leadership within the State Republican Party.[99] Brown, as head of the group of conservative upstate Republican leaders who controlled the legislature in 1915 and 1916, attempted to weaken the influence of the Governor, whose strength lay in the moderate Republican forces of New York City; and as one step in this program, Brown courted the important business interests in the state with an attack on the labor laws. Whitman in his turn vetoed bills that did not have overwhelming support from conservative forces in order to block Brown's attempt to compile a substantial legislative record. Whitman also sought to maintain his popularity in New York City as a basis for control of the party. It was in the city that the social Progressives and organized labor had their greatest influence, and Whitman thus opposed the most unpopular of the "ripper" legislation. Had Brown and Whitman not been in conflict during these years, the labor laws might have been seriously emasculated.

The resistance to reform legislation continued during 1916 in New York and in other states.[100] Despite the passage by Congress of the first Child Labor Act and the Adamson Act, for the most part the social Progressives' successes had ended at the state level. Little more was accomplished in the area of social reform before the New Deal.[101] The State Federation sought to blunt the continuing reaction in New York by developing a compromise labor program with the State Association of Manu-

[99] *New York Times*, March 12, 1915, p. 6.

[100] See Henry Seager's remarks in the *American Labor Legislation Review*, VI (March 1916), 87.

[101] Social workers became less interested in social reform in the 1920's as the emphasis switched from the environmentalism of the Progressive period to a casework approach based on psychological factors. See Kathleen Woodroofe, *From Charity to Social Work in England and the United States* (London, 1962), pp. 92–99, 133–135.

facturers and the new Industrial Commission.[102] Commissioners
Mitchell and Lynch played a vital role in the preparation of the
compromise which finally went before the legislature in an omnibus labor bill. This course of action, however, divided the reform forces as effectively as the conservative attack in 1915 had
led them to cooperate.

Among the provisions of the omnibus bill was a proposal to
permit women to work more than sixty-six hours per week in
canneries during rush seasons, under the supervision of the Industrial Commission. In 1915 the State Federation had opposed
this measure, and it found the cannery proposal "a source of
regret" in 1916.[103] Yet the Federation supported Lynch and
Mitchell when they defended the omnibus bill as a whole—with
the cannery provision included.[104]

Considerations unrelated to canneries had motivated the complete about-face by the State Federation. A disastrous factory
fire in Brooklyn in late November 1915 had caused many deaths,
and the social Progressives charged that Lynch, the commissioner most directly responsible for the enforcement of the labor
law, had been lax in his duties.[105] They accordingly demanded
that he not be reappointed to a new term on the Industrial
Commission. Mitchell, who had charge of workmen's compensation, was under heavy attack from conservative forces because
his successful operation of the state insurance fund had made it a
significant competitor of the casualty companies. The State Federation had been largely responsible for the appointment of
Mitchell and Lynch, and found itself obliged to support these
two men—especially Lynch, whose appointment expired in
1916—or face a loss of prestige and influence should they be dis-
credited and ultimately replaced by conservatives. Thus the pol-

[102] *Legislative Labor News*, March 6, 1916, p. 4.
[103] *New York Call*, April 29, 1916, p. 2.
[104] *Legislative Labor News*, May 1916, p. 4.
[105] Nellie Swartz to Low, Low Papers, Box 89, Feb. 10, 1916; *Labor Herald* (Rochester), Dec. 10, 1915, p. 1.

icies of the State Federation diverged from those of the social Progressives at a time when unity was essential.

The Consumers' League of New York City declared that the support of the Federation for the cannery feature of the omnibus bill was "entirely unaccountable," [106] as indeed it was in relation to the past policies of organized labor in the state. The New York Women's Trade Union League openly attacked the Federation for its support of the cannery provision, and it circulated a letter throughout the state castigating the Federation's leadership. This letter had the support of the Brooklyn Central Labor Union. [107] The Central Federated Union of New York City did not criticize the Federation leadership directly, for the president of the State organization, James Holland, was a C.F.U. man; but it did attack the Federation's support of the cannery provision. [108]

Lynch defended his support of the omnibus bill by pointing out that the sixty-six-hour limit in canneries was widely evaded in rural sections. The new provision was intended to set up reasonable standards which would be obeyed. [109] This argument had been used by state officials in the past to justify lax enforcement or special exemptions for specific industries, and the reformers and labor had always opposed it as an admission that reform would have to await the approval of the most conservative minorities in the state—an impossible and undemocratic situation. In 1916 the Consumers' League of New York City repeated its opposition to any special exemptions. A concession inevitably led to further demands for special privileges, and to the ultimate deterioration of the law. [110] The Federation thus

[106] Consumers' League of the City of New York, *Annual Report,* 1916, p. 17.

[107] *New York Call,* April 29, 1916, p. 2. Also see the long debate on this opposition to the State Federation in its *Proceedings,* 1916, pp. 197ff.

[108] See pp. 32–33.

[109] New York State Federation of Labor, *Proceedings,* 1916, p. 77.

[110] Consumers' League of the City of New York, *Annual Report,* 1916, p. 18.

allied itself with the State Manufacturers Association and the conservative Republicans in the legislature against a united social Progressive movement buttressed by important support from within organized labor. The omnibus bill passed the legislature, but Governor Whitman vetoed it after a tense and crowded hearing.

These events indicate the tenuousness of the cooperation between the social Progressives and organized labor, and the devotion of the State Federation to what it believed to be its own best interests, even though this put it in alliance with the apparently incompatible elements of business and political conservatism. The Federation was determined to protect its newfound influence in the administration of the labor law, through the defense of commissioners Mitchell and Lynch, even though this policy produced a split in the labor movement, and aroused the active opposition of the social Progressives.

Despite their cooperation, the reformers and the union movement never really shared an identity of interest. Cooperation was always temporary, fragile, and limited.[111] Major areas of reform were not equally important to organized labor and the reform societies. The social Progressives exhibited little interest in labor's efforts to obtain special legislation for the benefit of

[111] For works that stress the contribution of the social Progressives to reform, especially in the area of legislation for women and children, see Leo Wolman, *History of the State of New York*, Vol. 10, p. 73; Josephine Goldmark, *Impatient Crusader*, p. 206; Mollie R. Carroll, *Labor and Politics: The Attitude of the American Federation of Labor toward Legislation and Politics* (Boston and New York, 1923), pp. 83, 87; Aaron Abell, "Labor Legislation in the United States: The Background and Growth of Newer Trends," *The Review of Politics*, X (Jan. 1948), 36–37; Robert Hunter, *Labor in Politics* (New York, 1915), pp. 104–107; and Baker, *Women's Labor Legislation*, p. 150. George G. Groat, *An Introduction to the Study of Organized Labor in America* (New York, 1916), p. 358, stresses the importance of organized labor in the campaigns for reform. Beyer, *Labor Legislation in Three States*, pp. 1–3, also comments on the importance of organized labor's legislative activities. The first chapter of this study is a perceptive analysis of the various forces working for labor legislation.

particular trades. Proposals to limit the use of injunctions in labor disputes, to prohibit the use of alien labor on public contracts, and to prevent the counterfeiting and misuse of union labels had vigorous support from labor, but received only scattered help from the reform societies. The social reformers were interested mainly in direct legislative reform to relieve industrial evils, not in the encouragement of unionism, which they never fully trusted. Even in the vital area of workmen's compensation, only the A.A.L.L. gave consistent support. The influence of the social Progressives was most important in securing reduced hours and improved working conditions for women and children, reforms in tenement construction and in the regulation of labor in these buildings, and improved procedures for enforcing the labor laws.

In the years before 1910, the social reformers achieved only spotty success in their legislative campaigns. The record of the social Progressives was not significantly better than the efforts of organized labor when it worked for legislation without much support from the middle-class reformer. Both groups won several important victories but most reform bills disappeared without ceremony in the legislature's committees.[112] Conservative political leaders favored reform only when they were convinced that the mass of organized workers in the state, or a significant portion of the middle class, actively supported the bill. This happened only rarely before 1910, for the mood of the state was generally conservative, and most citizens were poorly informed concerning the activities of organized labor and the social Progressives in Albany.

---

[112] The reformers led the successful campaigns for the tenement manufacturing law of 1899, the tenement construction law of 1901, the child labor amendments of 1903, and the eight-hour day for children in 1907. Organized labor secured the prevailing-wage and eight-hour-day law amendments in 1899 (and a constitutional amendment on the same subjects after laws were declared unconstitutional in 1902 and 1903), the employers' liability laws of 1902 and 1906, and a semimonthly pay bill for railroad workers. That outstanding legislation can be enumerated so easily for the period before 1910 indicates the paucity of reform.

It was only after the election of Charles Evans Hughes as governor in 1906 that the interest of the public in all areas of reform activity began to increase sharply. This development came about as a result of the Governor's active campaigns for more effective regulation of insurance and public service corporations, his leadership in an antigambling campaign, his support of direct primary legislation, and his general appeal to the public as a force for moderate reform. The growth after 1910 of political Progressivism in the nation and in New York —especially with Theodore Roosevelt as its leader—added immeasurably to Hughes's reform impulse. The Triangle Fire, the continuing publicity for reform by the Factory Investigating Commission, and the expanded activities of the social Progressives and of organized labor, further increased the attractiveness of labor reform. It was in this atmosphere—so different from the years before Hughes's first election—that the great bulk of reform legislation was enacted.

After 1910 the Republican and Democratic leaders steered a course between the need to appeal to the reform sentiment apparent in the electorate, and the influence of conservative interests opposed to reform. The awakening of public opinion to the need for moderate social and political reform, and the importance to the politician of this new mood in the electorate, were basically responsible for the legislative victories gained by organized labor and the social Progressives. It was not the inherent strength of either the social Progressive societies or organized labor that produced the reforms, but rather the acceptance of their reform programs as expressive of the public's attitude. In 1915 and 1916 the decline of the public's interest in reform produced a complete about-face by the legislature. The trade unions and social Progressives still demanded reform, but public opinion no longer sustained them. In the campaign for specific laws, different reform societies, combinations of social Progressive and labor groups or organized labor alone, had taken the lead; but after 1910 both were beneficiaries of a reform spirit in the electorate they had only in part helped to produce.

VI

Organized Labor and the Social Progressives: Areas of Disagreement

DISAGREEMENTS between organized labor and the social Progressives occurred frequently over specific pieces of legislation. Often the principle would have been accepted by both, and the difference was merely one of form and tactics. On several important issues, though, organized labor and the social Progressives disagreed basically on the action to be taken. Under the pressure of a growing spirit of Progressive reform, organized labor was often split on the same issues, and it was not uncommon to find important elements in the labor movement allied with the social Progressives. Reform was usually impossible until the disagreements were resolved. These disputes not only reveal what the basic differences were between organized labor and the social Progressives but also indicate certain changes in the trade unions' attitudes which foreshadow their policies during the 1930's.

The campaign for minimum wage legislation in New York produced considerable friction between organized labor and the social Progressives, and also split the labor movement. Social Progressives initiated the demand for minimum wage rates, and as early as 1907 Henry Seager proposed a minimum wage law to cover men and women.[1] The National Consumers' League soon considered the idea as a solution for the abysmally low wages

[1] Henry R. Seager, *Labor Essays*, p. 85.

paid to unorganized women workers in many trades. After a year-long study, the National League concluded that government minimum wage legislation was the only answer to excessively low wages for women.[2] In the 1912 investigation by the New York City Consumers' League of department stores in the city, 60 per cent of the 225 saleswomen over sixteen years of age who were interviewed were found to receive wages below $6.50 per week. Many of these women were self-supporting, and $9.00 per week was estimated to be the minimum necessary for proper maintenance.[3] The New York City League thus concluded that minimum wage rates were necessary for women in New York State.

In 1913 the Consumers' League asked the Factory Investigating Commission to study the wages of women, but the Commission answered that it did not have the funds to undertake such a task at the time. The New York City League then conducted its own investigation throughout the state. It discovered, once again, that large numbers of working women earned less than the weekly minimum of $9.00. Of the 877 department store workers questioned, 54.5 per cent had incomes below the minimum figure, while 89.5 per cent of employees at five-and-ten-cent stores earned less than $9.00 per week. These figures did not include overtime work, bonuses, or commissions, but they also ignored deductions for fines or illness.[4] This study further convinced the Consumers' League that a minimum wage law for the state was necessary.

The National Women's Trade Union League also became interested in minimum wage laws. It took less than a decade for the league to conclude that the thorough organization of women into trade unions was almost a utopian concept. After 1909 the

[2] National Consumers' League, *Report for the Year Ending March 1910*, p. 22.

[3] Consumers' League of the City of New York, *Annual Report*, 1912, p. 10.

[4] Consumers' League of the City of New York, *Annual Report*, 1913, pp. 17–18.

National League demanded minimum wage rates for women. The argument that women worked to earn extra money, not to support families, and that lower wages were thus not a social evil, met with a strong rebuttal from the reformers. Margaret Dreier Robins, president of the National W.T.U.L., retorted that over 80 per cent of working women had been found to be contributing their full wages to the family fund, and that many were relied upon as a primary source of income.[5] Studies in New York City that had set minimum income requirements for working-class families had revealed that in the cross section selected for the studies, a significant number of families fell short of the minimum figures, even with more than one wage earner.[6]

The argument that minimum wage regulations would infringe upon the businessman's right to privacy in his relations with workers, and reduce his right to control the wages of his employees, also brought a sharp reply. Owen Lovejoy, the secretary of the National Child Labor Committee, pointed out:

If it is contended that minimum wage boards would unveil the private concerns of any industry, the reply is that there are not private concerns of industry. The industry that seeks to shield from properly constituted authorities information as to its wage questions and other data related to the earnings of employees is in the category with the man who maintains his right to guard his private cesspool from the public health authorities who have discovered in that cesspool the genesis of the city's epidemic.[7]

The climax of the social Progressives' campaign for minimum wage legislation in New York came as a result of the final report of the Factory Investigating Commission to the legislature in

[5] National Women's Trade Union League of America, *Proceedings, Fourth Biennial Convention*, 1913, p. 3.

[6] Louise B. More, *Wage-Earners' Budgets: A Study of Standards and Cost of Living in New York City* (New York, 1907), pp. 264–269; Robert C. Chapin, *The Standard of Living among Workingmen's Families in New York City* (New York, 1909), pp. 245–249.

[7] As quoted by President Robins of the National Women's Trade Union League in *Proceedings, Fourth Biennial Convention*, 1913, p. 5.

1915. The Commission had devoted the year 1914 to an investigation of wages within the state, and after examining the incomes of 109,481 workers, it reported that the conclusions reached by the New York City Consumers' League after its limited investigation in 1913 had been essentially accurate. Fifty-four per cent of the women employed in mercantile establishments earned less than $7.50 per week, and 25 per cent made less than $5.50. The Commission agreed with the reformers' assertion that women were not simply earning extra "pin money," since it found that from two-thirds to three-quarters of the working women were unmarried and were employed either because the family income was insufficient or because they were entirely self-supporting. Finally, in calculating what the minimum wage in New York State should be, the Commission concurred with the Consumers' League figure of $9.00 per week for a single woman in New York City, adding that a slightly lower figure would be acceptable in other parts of the state.[8]

The Commission then proposed a voluntary minimum wage plan, in which boards composed of employers, employees, and public representatives would set minimum figures in industries where wages were below the necessary minimum. The plan would cover women and minors only. The social Progressives' persistent demands for minimum wage legislation had influenced the Commission to make its cautious recommendations. However, the reform spirit in the state had cooled, and the legislatures of 1915 and 1916 gave the proposal little attention.

Since the Commission's plan did not include adult men or make the law compulsory, it ignored two basic tenets of the social Progressives' thinking on minimum wage legislation. Possible constitutional objections, and the desire to avoid too radical a bill, played a part in this decision. But perhaps the most important reason for these qualifications was the opposition of organized labor.

[8] *Fourth Report of the New York State Factory Investigating Commission* (Feb. 15, 1915), Vol. 1, pp. 33ff.

The proposal for a minimum wage split the labor movement deeply. The A.F.L. always had argued that there was no necessary connection between social legislation and a high standard of living for the worker. Industrial conditions were poor in paternalistic nations such as imperial Germany, and the A.F.L. insisted that history showed the soundness of achieving gains for labor through strong trade unions.[9] Yet important exceptions had been made, including limits on the hours worked by women and children, the control of working conditions that might be unsafe, compulsory workmen's compensation, and the regulation of hours, wages, and working conditions on government projects or for government workers. However, these laws had been clearly labeled as exceptions, and the A.F.L.'s leadership continued to oppose legislation that would apply to other areas which the trade unions regarded as their preserve.

The supporters of this traditional A.F.L. policy opposed minimum wage legislation as a threat to established unions. Helen Marot warned that even the regulation of women's wages would weaken the union movement. Once minimum wage rates were established for unorganized workers, they would become the center of gravity for the wages of all, even the unionized workers who might have a higher wage scale.[10] This group of labor leaders also questioned whether the enforcement of the minimum wage law could be trusted to the middle class. Emphasizing the strong feeling among labor leaders that different social classes had sharply different interests, John Manning, editor of the United Garment Workers' journal, declared that righteousness and honesty could not be legislated into human beings, and that enforcement of the law would thus be crucial. Only strong

[9] For an example of this view see W. Macarthur, "Political Action and Trade Unionism," *Publications of the American Academy of Political and Social Science*, No. 434, 1904.

[10] *Fourth Report of the New York State Factory Investigating Commission* (1915), Vol. 1, pp. 774–777.

trade unions could enforce minimum wage laws so as to protect the workers' interests, yet the form of the proposed minimum wage boards, with labor selecting only one-third of the representatives, placed control in the hands of nonlabor authorities.[11]

Samuel Gompers's views usually were copied by much of the labor press, and he had a larger audience than any other trade union leader in America. In 1915 Gompers attacked the Factory Commission's proposal for minimum wage boards. Experience throughout the nation had shown, he declared, that laws might be of minor value because of lax enforcement. Public interest passed on to other subjects, and the laws meant little when politicians controlled their enforcement. Many labor leaders agreed with Gompers's statement that "free workers must never delegate to outside authority ultimate control over the determining conditions and terms of personal relations between employers and employees, but the workers themselves must assume responsibility for their own welfare." [12] Gompers also feared that the minimum wage for women would eventually lead to regulation of men. Women and men had to win their gains by the same means—organization—and not by overnight reform.[13] Such important New York State labor leaders as Edward Bates, long time secretary-treasurer of the State Federation of Labor, agreed. Bates said that regulation of women's wages ultimately would mean similar laws for men, and that state regulation of wages was "a condition akin to slavery." [14]

This view generally represented the interests of the stronger unions, which were able to secure higher wages than unorganized workers could hope for. Most social Progressives already believed that minimum wage legislation for men in unorganized

[11] *Hammer and Pen*, June 1912, p. 7.
[12] *Official Record*, March 1915, p. 1.
[13] *American Federationist*, May 1915, pp. 364–365.
[14] *Fourth Report of the New York State Factory Investigating Commission* (1915), Vol. 1, p. 769.

trades was essential. The reformers' assurance that the regulation of men's wages would be confined to nonunion trades [15] was flimsy; and one opponent of government regulation pointed out that the promoters of minimum wage boards in California used the likelihood that state action would weaken unions and reduce strikes as an argument for their plan.[16] Organized labor frequently disagreed with the social Progressives, yet the reformers' attitude toward the trade unions was more favorable than the views of other possible representatives of the public on the minimum wage boards. With organized labor a minority on these boards, the fortunes of union workers would be placed in potentially unfriendly hands.

Some supporters of minimum wage legislation recognized that it would eventually cover all workers, and attempted to prove that the establishment of minimum wage levels in organized trades would aid unionization. Henry Seager attacked the idea that union wage rates would be forced to the minimum and that the labor movement would be weakened. He asserted that the minimum wage would become a base for further action by the unions. The British coal miners had minimum wage rates set by law, yet their union had grown more powerful.[17]

Even though there were influential unionists among the opponents of a minimum wage law for women, organized labor moved toward the acceptance of legislative reform for both women and men. The New York State Federation of Labor had been a major force in the campaign for shorter hours of work for women, and in 1913 the A.F.L. formally approved legislative reform in this area by calling for the eight-hour day for women through state legislation. When the Factory Investigating Commission queried important labor leaders in New York

[15] Florence Kelley in *New York Call*, March 8, 1915, p. 3.

[16] "The Minimum Wage Board and the Union" (by a Trade Unionist), *The Unpopular Review*, IV (Oct. 1915), 398.

[17] Seager, *Labor Essays*, p. 284.

concerning minimum wage boards for women, the respondents overwhelmingly supported the plan. Homer Call and Emanuel Kovaleski, vice presidents of the State Federation; James Lynch, commissioner of labor at the time; and John Mitchell, the chairman of the Workmen's Compensation Commission, all supported minimum wage boards for women. Other labor leaders went even further. James Holland, a future president of the State Federation, and Tim Healy, a labor leader with long-standing connections in the social Progressive movement, argued that the minimum wage was necessary for "all classes of wage earners," but most particularly for women—a "helpless class of labor." [18]

In 1915 the Brooklyn Central Labor Union distributed a pamphlet throughout the state supporting minimum wage boards for women. It paid homage to the traditional A.F.L. view that the organization of workers and economic action by trade unions were the keys to progress, but agreed with the social Progressives' argument that women were practically impossible to organize under the existing conditions, and that therefore the state must aid them. They might, it was believed, be more easily organized once their broken spirit had been reinforced by a minimum wage. The Brooklyn Central Labor Union thus attacked the contention that the minimum wage would weaken the chances for the future organization of women. The pamphlet also recognized no difference between support for the regulation of women's hours, which had become general throughout the labor movement, and for minimum wages for women.[19]

The State Federation, however, awaited the lead of the A.F.L.,

[18] For the opinions of these labor leaders see *Fourth Report of the New York State Factory Investigating Commission* (1915), Vol. 1, pp. 769–780.

[19] Brooklyn Central Labor Union, *Why New York Should Enact a Legal Minimum Wage for Women and Minors* (pamphlet), 1915.

and thus it dodged a decision on the issue of minimum wage regulation for women in both 1914 and 1915.[20] Although Gompers personally opposed the minimum wage for women, the 1914 convention of the A.F.L. excepted women in defeating a resolution to legislate hours and wages for men. Gompers was a member of the New York Factory Investigating Commission, and he recognized the A.F.L.'s resolution when he failed to dissent from the Commission's recommendation of minimum wage boards for women. Gompers seemed to be clearly in the minority in 1915, when once again the A.F.L. convention excepted women from a resolution attacking wage and hour legislation for men. The vote on this resolution indicated that legislation covering men might soon receive approval. Only 8,500 votes were tallied in favor of the resolution, with 6,396 against and 4,061 abstaining. Thus the resolution did not receive approval from the majority.[21] At this point the New York State Federation of Labor began its campaign for legislation that would provide an eight-hour day and a minimum wage for women.[22] The inability of the State Federation and the social Progressives to win either of these reforms made further discussion of legislation for men academic until the climactic events of the 1930's.

The increasing sentiment among unionists in favor of legislation reflected the limited power of many trade unions. The union that had little success in increasing its membership or in securing better wages, hours, and working conditions would be attracted by the possibility of legislative reform, even though the organs of legislation and enforcement were under the control of the middle class. There was a limited precedent in New York State for the regulation of wages. The Prevailing Wage Act of 1899 obliged government bodies within New York to

[20] New York State Federation of Labor, *Proceedings*, 1914, p. 74; 1916, p. 115.
[21] Philip Taft, *The A.F. of L. in the Time of Gompers*, pp. 147–148.
[22] Baker, *Women's Labor Legislation*, p. 172.

pay the "prevailing wage" to all workers on public works projects, and the law often had been interpreted to mean the union scale. This law particularly aided unions that did not have significant job control, and which thus could not force union wages and a closed shop upon the employer. The interests of the weaker union were in reality closer to those of the unorganized worker. Thus a basic difference in effectiveness and power among the unions produced the split within the labor movement on the issue of legislative reform.

The legislature in 1916 considered another new reform: compulsory health insurance. Once again, the social Progressives suggested this important reform. The bill proposed to cover workers earning less than $100 per month, which meant almost all. The employer and employee were each to bear 40 per cent of the cost, and the State of New York was to add the other 20 per cent. The bill provided medical expenses for a maximum of twenty-six weeks, plus an additional payment to help workers contend with the loss of wages due to illness.[23]

Organized labor's reaction to this proposal followed the pattern of the minimum wage issue. Gompers and other opponents of government regulation criticized the bill as another step toward control of the worker by government commissions. They preferred to have wages raised so that the worker might have the money to look after his own health, and called also for improved working conditions so that dangers to health would be lessened.[24] If the reformers wished to assist the workers, the argument continued, they should strengthen the ability of the trade union to improve conditions through collective bargaining. Gompers did not, however, suggest open opposition to health insurance, but proposed caution and further study.[25] Undoubtedly, the appeal of health insurance to the labor movement accounted for this cautious approach.

[23] *New York Times*, Jan. 8, 1916, p. 8; Jan. 24, 1916, p. 20.

[24] *Legislative Labor News*, March 13, 1916, p. 4.

[25] Form letter signed by Andrews, Andrews Papers, Box 79, Dec. 29, 1916.

Labor leaders who had supported minimum wage legislation also adopted a positive attitude toward the measure. John Mitchell saw in the success of the workmen's compensation program in New York an indication that health insurance would benefit the workers without weakening the unions.[26] President Holland, speaking for the State Federation, appeared to represent majority opinion within the New York labor movement when he attacked the specific bill before the legislature, but not the principle of health insurance. Organized labor particularly opposed any contributions by workers to a health insurance fund.[27] Holland preferred trade union health plans, but instead of condemning the social Progressives' bill he called for a commission to study the problem.[28] The history of commissions in New York during the previous two decades had indicated that reforms did not die upon being consigned to their study. Instead, the publicity engendered by the commission's activities often strengthened the movement for the reform. The reaction of organized labor in New York to the health insurance bill clearly revealed the increasing appeal of legislation to trade unionists.

In the vital area of labor law enforcement, organized labor and the social Progressives also found cooperation difficult, despite their agreement that the law must be strictly enforced. The labor movement consistently demanded that the enforcement of the labor law be placed as much as possible in the hands of unionists. Organized labor therefore sought the appointment of its leaders to the top positions in the Department of Labor, and the appointment of qualified unionists to posts as inspectors, especially where special requirements made experience in the trade desirable. Despite these demands, no nominee of organized labor was appointed commissioner of labor until James Lynch was

[26] *New York Times*, Jan. 24, 1916, p. 20.
[27] Andrews to John Commons, Andrews Papers, March 16, 1916.
[28] *Legislative Labor News*, March 20, 1916, p. 4; New York State Federation of Labor, *Proceedings*, 1916, pp. 63, 91.

named to the position in 1913, although former unionists, with political connections, often did get key posts.[29]

The New York State Federation of Labor and city central labor councils continually charged that the labor law was not properly enforced. Their remedy was the appointment of unionists who would have a definite interest in the successful operation of the laws. The social Progressives did not agree with this prescription. Admitting that the enforcement of the law was often remarkably ineffective, the reformers agreed with labor that the blame lay with the politically appointed personnel, who often had little experience with the problems of labor, and even less desire to learn in the face of quiet opposition from influential politicians and businessmen. However, the social Progressives did not believe the solution was the replacement of one interest group, the politicians, by another, the union leaders.[30] Instead, they believed that the law should be enforced by "impartial" personnel chosen by civil service examination. In effect this meant middle-class personnel, since the tests usually were designed so that only a man with a good education could pass. Labor leaders often lacked the theoretical information demanded by the examinations, and fared poorly as a result.[31] Thus the trade unions did not support civil service for the Labor Department; instead they demanded a continuation of appointments—but with unionists as the appointees.

The labor movement admitted the special interests of different groups in the community, and asked that laws framed to benefit workers be enforced by men who would execute these stat-

[29] John McMackin, labor commissioner 1901–1905, and John Williams, labor commissioner 1907–1913, were former unionists turned successful politicians. Neither had been suggested by the Workingmen's Federation.

[30] See the detailed attack on the link between politics and the appointment of labor unionists to the Department of Labor and the Workmen's Compensation Commission in Mary Chamberlain, "The Tammany Tiger's Paw on Labor Laws in New York State," *The Survey*, XXXII (Aug. 15, 1914), 499–504, 514.

[31] New York State Federation of Labor, *Proceedings*, 1912, p. 22.

utes.[32] The social Progressive, however, refused to admit that self-interest influenced the views of such impartial judges as the "public" or the "expert," who were unbiased sources of truth amid the propaganda of special interests. The experts selected by civil service examinations would administer the law without prejudice, and in the interests of the community.

Although the social Progressive and organized labor sought the same general end—efficient enforcement—they did not cooperate very effectively. Each time a new commissioner of labor was to be appointed, the reformers and unionists suggested different men. The social Progressives' attacks on former unionists who held office in the Labor Department received little support from organized labor even though the trade unions also may have been dissatisfied with the enforcement of the law. In 1904 the reformers severely criticized the labor commissioner, John McMackin, a former unionist turned Republican politician. Organized labor either took no side in the dispute or supported McMackin, although he had received numerous rebukes from these same labor sources.[33] The support of the State Federation for James Lynch in 1916, when he was attacked by the reformers, has already been noted. Organized labor generally regarded criticism of former unionists who held public office as an attack on the labor movement, and even if the reformers' charges were accurate, they usually aroused the hostility of labor leaders.

The simmering dispute over civil service erupted into an open battle during the years after 1911. The social Progressives were

[32] See John Fitzpatrick (president of the Chicago Federation of Labor) to Andrews, Andrews Papers, Feb. 17, 1911, for a fine example of this attitude.

[33] The Central Federated Union of New York City took no action on the reformers' calls for cooperation against McMackin. See *New York Tribune*, Dec. 26, 1904, p. 12. The Albany Central Federation of Labor supported him. See *Official Record*, Feb. 1905, p. 2. For other labor support of McMackin, see *Labor Advocate*, Feb. 3, 1904, p. 5, and Feb. 10, 1904, p. 1.

campaigning for a larger force of inspectors in the Department of Labor, including eight new supervisory posts. They demanded that these places be filled by civil service procedures. The Governor and the labor commissioner, John Williams, notified the American Association for Labor Legislation that the new positions would not be approved by the legislature if they were placed under civil service.[34] After the passage of the bill in 1912, Williams exempted the eight supervisory posts from civil service. The entire galaxy of social Progressive societies opposed this ruling, leading Daniel Harris, president of the State Federation of Labor, to attack the reformers for meddling in "matters that are of great importance to the labor unions of this state." [35] The social Progressives were at the height of their influence in New York, and Williams ultimately compromised by placing four of the positions under civil service.

With the appointment of James Lynch as commissioner of labor in 1913, the struggle over the staffing of the department reached a climax. The social Progressives met with Lynch on March 2, 1914, and in angry tones demanded the answers to certain questions: Was it not true that two incompetent Democratic politicians had been given top posts in the Labor Department, while John Shillady, a competent official, had been dismissed? Was it not true that Lynch gave positions to unionists regardless of their fitness for the job? And was it not true that the Commissioner had sabotaged civil service procedures in the department by transferring twenty-one positions to an appointment basis?

Lynch conceded nothing to the reformers. He insisted that his two appointees were fit, and denied any political pressures. The Commissioner retorted that Shillady was "unfit for work," but balked at explaining his reasons for any specific action to the social Progressives. Lynch emphasized that he had been a union official, and that thus he could be trusted to manage the depart-

[34] Henry Seager to Andrews, Andrews Papers, Aug. 4, 1911.
[35] New York State Federation of Labor, *Proceedings*, 1912, p. 23.

ment in the best interests of the working people. John M. Glenn of the Russell Sage Foundation immediately responded that the reformers represented the public, and thus had a vital interest in the organization of the Labor Department. The conference ended on this contentious note, without any agreement.[36]

The social Progressives continued their attempt to collect evidence of shortcomings in the Labor Department, although plans for a public investigation collapsed.[37] The hostility between Lynch and the reformers never really ended, and it broke out with new intensity after the Brooklyn factory fire of 1915.

Organized labor and the social Progressives also disagreed on the desirability of arbitration as a means for solving industrial disputes. In those between the special interests of organized labor and organized capital, the social Progressives demanded arbitration by representatives of the impartial public. In 1886 New York had set up a Board of Mediation and Arbitration, which had the power to investigate on its own initiative though not to take any further action without the consent of all parties. The board had considered only 157 of the 2,156 strikes that occurred in New York between 1894 and 1900. Eleven were arbitrated successfully, and seventy-six were settled by conciliation.[38] Opposition from organized labor, and from businessmen who did not want an investigation of their labor policies, combined to make voluntary arbitration ineffective.

During the period 1901–1904 attempts were made to set up an arbitration board with compulsory powers. Organized labor strongly opposed this proposal, and the bills, lacking united business support, made little progress. In response to a social reformer's query about compulsory arbitration, the Central Fed-

---

[36] Summary of Conference with Commissioner of Labor James Lynch, Andrews Papers, March 2, 1914.

[37] See Andrews Papers for Mary Van Kleeck to Andrews, March 18, 1914; G. M. Price to Andrews, March 13, 1914; and George Hall to Andrews, April 13, 1914 and May 26, 1914.

[38] Thomas S. Adams and Helen L. Sumner, *Labor Problems* (New York, 1913), p. 299.

erated Union of New York City concisely summed up organized labor's attitude: "Since the working men have no part and small influence in the government, we do not favor compulsory arbitration." [39]

The conservative Henry White, secretary of the United Garment Workers, discussed organized labor's opposition to compulsory arbitration more fully. Although not a Marxist by any stretch of the imagination, White viewed the issue in class terms. He recognized a class conflict between labor and capital, and he also believed that every individual was bound by his class position, which determined his attitudes. White believed that the middle-class arbitrators thus would tend to favor the position of capital if organized labor were to press demands that were in any way extreme. Yet labor's demands often were extreme—that is, by society's standards—for labor represented a class that had little and sought to achieve much. White believed that labor would frequently find that its demands conflicted with the standards of the time and with the predispositions of an arbitrator from outside the working class.[40]

On occasion organized labor did favor arbitration. When a union was weak and unable to gain its demands through economic action, and especially when the workers were laboring under substandard conditions which would appeal to an arbitrator's sense of injustice, arbitration and public investigation might be valuable processes. The protocols in the garment industry used the impartial public representative on the final appeals board. In exchange, the International Ladies' Garment Workers' Union won equal footing with the employers' representatives and thus, in practice, the union recognition the employers had refused to admit in theory. Organized labor in New York, and in the nation, did not oppose conciliation and arbitration outright, but it did object to the compulsory variety which made unions extraneous.

[39] *New York Evening Journal*, Nov. 27, 1899, p. 9.
[40] *The Garment Worker*, V (May 1901), 3–6.

Labor recognized that it did not share in many of the principles of American society, and this feeling of alienation was a basic reason for the disagreements between the social Progressives and organized labor in New York. Trade unions refused to trust nonlabor forces because they believed that even the social Progressives had interests which might conflict with the workers' demands. However, organized labor's growing acceptance of legislative reform during the progressive period was a sign of the allure of immediate gains and of the failure of weaker trade unions to make significant advances. Like socialist critics of the Progressives' piecemeal reform, who held out hopes to the laborer of a total transformation of society—in the future—the opponents of legislative reform within the A.F.L. discovered that the appeal of immediate gains was irresistible, regardless of the source.

VII

The Problem of

Labor Law Enforcement

ORGANIZED labor and the social Progressives applauded Governor Theodore Roosevelt's first labor program in 1899 even though he did not suggest a new series of reforms. Roosevelt simply proposed to enforce the labor laws already on the statute books. However, like so many other men before and after him, T.R. failed to make the law the law in fact. From 1897 to 1916, the lag between enforcement and legislation constituted a major problem for the reform forces in New York. By the end of this period, it had been only partially solved.

The difficulties in enforcement began with the wording of the laws. Many key statutes became entangled in court tests and were inconsistently administered because they lacked definition or had loopholes which employers used to evade the purpose of the measures. The important law providing for the eight-hour day on public works permitted exceptions in the event of an emergency—but it offered no criteria for determining what was an emergency.[1] The decisions by inspectors, or by the commissioner of labor, inevitably drew fire from labor or employer. "Clean and healthful" conditions were required for a license under the law of 1899 which regulated tenement manufacturing;

[1] New York State Department of Labor, *Sixth Annual Report of the Commissioner of Labor for the Twelve Months Ending September 30, 1906*, p. 70.

however, each inspector interpreted these terms differently,[2] and often the social Progressives thought the definitions much too broad. The law requiring the "prevailing wage" for workers on public works contained no procedures for determining that wage, and although unions might manage to have their rate schedules accepted, the issue remained in almost constant dispute. Before the work of the Factory Investigating Commission, the laws on factory ventilation, sanitation, and lighting were unenforceable because they lacked definite requirements.[3]

On the other hand, difficulties also arose because statutes did not provide for the exceptional industry or situation. The canners, for example, insisted that the perishable nature of the crop, and the limited labor supply in rural areas, necessitated special rules for their industry. A succession of commissioners unsuccessfully sought a solution that would recognize the canners' complaints without offending the reform forces.[4] Commissioner of Labor P. Tecumseh Sherman recognized that the fault lay in the undue simplicity of the legislation, and in 1906 he suggested a labor code for each industry.[5] Several European countries already had adopted multiple codes. These nations also had set up administrative bodies with the power to recognize exceptions to the laws, and to make rules with the force of law where specific situations required.

[2] National Consumers' League, *Annual Report for the Year Ending March 4, 1902*, p. 12.

[3] New York Women's Trade Union League, Papers: Monthly Meeting Minutes, Jan. 8, 1912.

[4] The list of labor commissioners from the consolidation of the Bureau of Labor Statistics and Bureau of Factory Inspection into the Department of Labor in 1901 is as follows: John McMackin, 1901–1905; P. Tecumseh Sherman, 1905–1907; John Williams, 1907–1913; James Lynch, 1913–1915. An Industrial Commission of five members was responsible for labor law enforcement after 1915, but Lynch, one of the five commissioners, had immediate control.

[5] New York State Department of Labor, *Sixth Annual Report of the Commissioner of Labor for the Twelve Months Ending September 30, 1906*, p. 62.

Many social Progressives, especially within the American Association for Labor Legislation, proposed a similar system of regulation on this side of the Atlantic, and they strongly endorsed the Wisconsin Industrial Commission of 1911—the first American agency to be based on the European practice in labor law regulation.[6] After the social Progressives' recommendations had been adopted by the Factory Investigating Commission, New York established an Industrial Board, which also followed European practice in the enforcement of laws governing construction standards and safety procedures for factories.[7] The Board was originally a part of the Department of Labor, and its quasi-legislative functions passed to the Industrial Commission after the merger of the Labor Department and the Workmen's Compensation Commission in 1915. Thus New York took the first cautious steps toward meeting the problem of an inflexible labor law.

Both Republican and Democratic administrations, in the state and in the cities, refused to enforce the labor law strictly. Such administrative inaction blunted the effect of hard-won reforms. Only rarely did officials have the candor of the New York State commissioner of public works, Colonel J. N. Partridge. In 1899 he answered a complaint concerning a violation of the eight-hour day and prevailing-wage laws on a public works project by commenting that "it was the policy of the State to economize and employ the cheapest labor procurable, and that in his opinion the eight hour day law and prevailing rate of wages laws were not good legislation."[8] Of course Partridge had no authority to substitute his judgment for that of the legislature, but countless administrators did the same thing through the years.

The Tammany administration in New York City between

[6] Andrews to George M. Price, Andrews Papers, Jan. 2, 1911.

[7] New York State Department of Labor, *Bulletin*, Whole No. 56 (Sept. 1913), pp. 189, 389–390.

[8] *New York Evening Journal*, March 20, 1899, p. 7. The quotation represents the *Journal's* paraphrase of Partridge's statement.

1897 and 1901 promised organized labor everything, but failed to deliver anything. Tammany largely ignored the labor laws, and the Central Federated Union constantly battled with various municipal agencies in an attempt to secure proper compliance.[9] Labor used cajolery and threats alternately, but Tammany grew increasingly less responsive, and by 1900 the Hall no longer even bothered to make specious promises or claims of action.[10] The same problem recurred in subsequent Tammany governments.

The social Progressives also attacked Tammany's enforcement of the law. The statutes of 1896 concerning working conditions for women in department stores called for enforcement by local boards of health. In 1897 the reform mayor of New York City, William L. Strong, provided for special investigators to enforce the law. After its victory in the election of 1897, Tammany abolished this special force, and placed the enforcement duties on the already overworked sanitary inspectors of the Board of Health. A department store manager noted that "it was an open secret that under the new regime the law was not to be enforced."[11] Although the Low administration, elected in another anti-Tammany victory in 1901, did not restore the special mercantile inspectors, it attempted to enforce the law, and the social Progressives applauded these efforts.[12] The social Progressives had supplied money and leadership for Low's campaign, and thus he could be expected to have a more positive attitude toward the enforcement of many portions of the labor law.

Organized labor discovered that the general improvement in the caliber of city government and labor law enforcement under

[9] For details of the activities of the Central Federated Union of New York City during the years 1897 to 1901, see the Monday issues of the *New York Times*, and the labor column that appeared daily in the *New York Evening Journal*.

[10] See *New York Evening Journal*, July 23, 1900, p. 5, for an example.

[11] Consumers' League of the City of New York, *Annual Report*, 1898, p. 19.

[12] Consumers' League of the City of New York, *Annual Report*, 1901, p. 11.

reform administrations did not necessarily mean strict attention to all labor laws, especially not to those offering protection for union activities or regulating working conditions for public projects. In 1902 a series of scandals in the building trades involved several important labor leaders. William Jerome, who had been district attorney in New York City since Tammany's defeat in 1901 and was the symbol of good government and civic reform, condemned labor leaders as a group because of these scandals. This naturally led the Central Federated Union to attack Jerome,[13] and relations between organized labor and the District Attorney remained cool despite efforts to patch up the quarrel. Since officials such as Jerome had important responsibilities concerning the labor law, the quality of enforcement often depended on the existing relations between organized labor and the politician. In many areas of the state, local officials were almost always unfriendly to trade unionism, and the labor law suffered accordingly.[14] Violations of the eight-hour day and prevailing-wage laws for public works had to be prosecuted by local district attorneys after the Department of Labor had cited the offender. Many of these cases never reached court, and the evasion continued.[15] In rural areas, local opinion favored the canners' demands for unlimited hours of work since the canneries would buy from the farmers only what they could process without spoilage. Thus rural grand juries often refused to indict offenders, and the hours laws remained hardly more than a dead letter in these areas throughout the period.[16]

In the years after 1906, the growing spirit of reform in New

[13] *New York Evening Journal*, Oct. 1, 1902, p. 9.

[14] New York State Department of Labor, *Third Annual Report of the Commissioner of Labor for the Twelve Months Ending September 30, 1903*, pp. 18–20.

[15] New York State Department of Labor, *Bulletin*, Whole No. 11 (Dec. 1901), p. 311.

[16] New York State Department of Labor, *Eighth Annual Report of the Commissioner of Labor for the Twelve Months Ending September 30, 1908*, p. 31; *The Child Labor Bulletin*, III (May 1914), 132.

York led to an increase in the personnel of the Department of Labor, and to a greater persistence by that personnel in enforcing the laws. Inspection became more thorough, though by no means completely so, and commissioners Sherman, Williams, and Lynch increased the number of cases brought into court for prosecution. Despite this effort, much evasion continued.[17] The Department's search for violators of the child labor laws indicated the extent of this evasion. The Department's yearly investigations of mercantile establishments during the period 1909–1915 revealed that from 35 to 50 per cent of the total number of children employed were working illegally.[18] Much of this evasion continued because of the attitude of the courts toward labor law violations.

Although the Department of Labor prosecuted many more violators after 1909, Commissioner Williams considered court action to be a hindrance to enforcement since it revealed the lack of sanctions behind the law.[19] During 1914 the Department of Labor brought 1,107 cases into court in New York City, of which 240 were still pending. Of the remaining 867, six had been withdrawn, and 180 defendants had won acquittal or had their cases dismissed. The reformers blamed the high percentage of cases lost on the conservatism of the judges, rather than on the innocence of the defendants or poor presentation by the Department. In the cases that produced a conviction, almost half of the offenders had their sentence suspended by the court, and those actually fined paid an average penalty of only $27.00. Up-

[17] Katharine Anthony, *Labor Laws of New York: A Handbook* (The Brooklyn Auxiliary of the Consumers' League of the City of New York, March 1917), p. iii. See also John Fitch to Andrews, Andrews Papers, March 18, 1914.

[18] *Annual Report of the Industrial Commission for the Twelve Months Ending September 30, 1915* (Albany, 1916), Vol. I, p. 81.

[19] New York State Department of Labor, *Tenth Annual Report of the Commissioner of Labor for the Twelve Months Ending September 30, 1910*, p. 24.

state, 198 cases came to trial in 1914, and 116 resulted in dismissal or acquittal. Forty offenders received suspended sentences, and the average fine was only $23.00.[20] Similar patterns appeared in other years as well.[21]

The reformers attacked the attitude of the courts as a major barrier to effective labor law enforcement. The social Progressives had always maintained that the great majority of businessmen in the state would comply with labor law regulations. The minority who violated the laws, they believed, should not be regarded as misguided or misinformed; rather, the reformers' investigations indicated that those who ignored the law in the first instance would do so again and again. Thus it was argued that only prosecution and stiff fines could prevent this evasion.[22] The low fines imposed by the courts, even where multiple convictions had been secured, did not reward the effort expended by the Department of Labor, and certainly did not inhibit further violations. Thus the reformers sadly agreed with Commissioner Williams that court action weakened the labor laws, and they demanded that their program of strict prosecution and stiff penalty be adopted. However, even during the height of the Progressive period in New York, prosecutions continued to be wasted motion in many cases. Thus the increased efficiency in inspection after 1906 did not end evasion of the labor laws.

Despite these difficulties in the courts, the social Progressives

[20] New York State Department of Labor, *Fourteenth Annual Report of the Commissioner of Labor for the Twelve Months Ending September 30, 1914*, pp. 55–56, 64.

[21] In the annual reports of the Department of Labor, 1909 to 1914, see the reports by the Commissioner of Labor, Chief Factory Inspector, and Chief Mercantile Inspector. The Consumers' League of Buffalo, *Annual Report*, 1911, 1912, also provides some interesting figures on the courts' disposition of child labor violations.

[22] New York Child Labor Committee, *A Report to Governor Frank W. Higgins upon the Failure of Commissioner John McMackin to Enforce the Labor Laws* (pamphlet), Jan. 16, 1905, pp. 15–18.

and organized labor worked continuously to secure a larger staff of inspectors for the Department of Labor. In the years before 1906, the conservative Republican administrations in Albany refused to increase enforcement costs. As Governor Odell noted, the Republican state government regarded the maintenance of a low tax rate as most important.[23] Although the law provided for fifty field inspectors, the Labor Department never had this number because its appropriations became a favorite spot for budget-cutting. Unable to secure more inspectors, the reformers and Workingmen's Federation called for the appointment of fifty voluntary, unpaid inspectors. Social Progressives and labor leaders were ready to assume these positions, but the legislature failed to accede to the demand, since the zeal of such voluntary inspectors would not be considered a virtue in the enforcement of labor laws. The reform forces did not win an appropriation that allowed for the full staffing of the Labor Department until 1906.[24]

Complaints about the Labor Department's failure to discover violations of the labor code almost inevitably brought the defense that the Department was understaffed and thus unable to do its job properly. Considering that a force of between thirty-seven and fifty persons had to inspect at least 12,000 tenements in New York City, and all the factories and stores in the state, plus bakeries, mines, and public works—and since reinspection was considered necessary if violations were not to be conveniently hidden while the inspector was present—it is evident that the Department's defense was not fanciful. Clearly the limited force could not provide thorough enforcement. The reformers realized this, but they insisted that the lack of comprehensive regulation could be partially offset by a zeal for prosecution, and by reinspection when violations were discovered. The failure of the courts to support the Department did not change

[23] *New York Evening Journal*, Dec. 10, 1900, p. 9.
[24] National Consumers' League, *Annual Report for the Year Ending March 1906*, p. 15.

the social Progressives' policy. The reformers insisted that only continued prosecution, plus sustained public pressure for realistic penalties, could make the courts realize their responsibilities.

In 1904 the social Progressives bitterly criticized the work of the labor commissioner, John McMackin. They charged that he failed to prosecute offenders, and that the Department often issued orders to correct violations without checking further to see whether these directives had been carried out. In every case where compliance could not be achieved by persuasion, the reformers argued, prosecution should have been used.[25]

McMackin answered the charges against him by stressing the enormity of the job to be done and the lack of personnel. He justified his failure to prosecute in all cases by asserting that each court action required four days of preparation, which had to come from inspection time in the field, and that extensive prosecution and full investigation thus were not possible at the same time.[26]

The validity of McMackin's defense became apparent when his successor, P. Tecumseh Sherman, discussed the changes he hoped to make in the operation of the Department. Sherman was a favorite of the social Progressives, and he agreed with the reformers that McMackin's zeal for enforcement had not been remarkable. However, he believed that the basic problem had been the shortage of inspectors. Sherman sustained McMackin's assertion that a basic dichotomy existed in the Department's activities: if it inspected and reinspected thoroughly, there was no time for prosecution; if it prosecuted extensively, inspection had to suffer. McMackin had chosen the first course; Sherman would follow the social Progressives' thinking and take the second. With fewer man-hours available for field work, Sherman had to change the pattern of inspection. Full-time inspectors

[25] New York Child Labor Committee, *Attack on McMackin*, p. 23.
[26] New York State Department of Labor, *Fourth Annual Report of the Commissioner of Labor for the Twelve Months Ending September 30, 1904*, pp. 265–287.

were placed in certain key areas while other sections of the state were ignored completely.[27]

Before the Progressive upsurge of 1906 to 1914 strengthened the determination to enforce the labor laws, the problem of political influence upon the Department of Labor also weakened enforcement. Florence Kelley pointed out that employers and politicians constantly put pressure on inspectors to be lax in their enforcement duties, while much less pressure came from the reformers, labor, and the public to act as a counterbalance. Her study of the situation indicated that zealous inspectors soon were charged with blackmail, bribery, or undue persecution of employers, and that the more conscientious and effective an inspector, the shorter his term of office.[28] McMackin declared that his enforcement of the law had been as good as the realities of political conduct in the state permitted. He asserted that "if the Department was handed over to the people you want to select, whether it is Mrs. Florence Kelley or not, the Department would not be in existence for a year." [29] McMackin, however, did not foresee the effects of Progressivism after 1906, and the Department's attempt to enforce more effectively led not to its dissolution in the face of political opposition but rather to its expansion.

The first step toward the enlargement of the Department took place in 1908, when the social Progressives finally won their twelve-year battle to transfer the inspection of mercantile establishments from the local boards of health to the Department of Labor. Despite the weaknesses in state enforcement, it was more effective than the work of a Tammany-controlled Board of Health. Additional inspectors were added to cover the new area of jurisdiction. However, the great increase in the strength

[27] New York State Department of Labor, *Fifth Annual Report of the Commissioner of Labor for the Twelve Months Ending September 30, 1905*, pp. 18–19. Commissioner Williams continued the same general policy.

[28] Florence Kelley, "An Effective Child Labor Law," *The Annals, American Academy of Political and Social Science*, May 1903, p. 163.

[29] *New York Tribune*, Dec. 26, 1904, p. 12.

of the Department occurred, as did the great rush in legislation itself, following the Triangle Fire and the formation of the Factory Investigating Commission in 1911. In that year the legislature increased the number of factory inspectors from fifty-eight to eighty-four, and six more positions were added in 1912. In response to the Factory Commission's call in 1913 for a larger Department, the legislature increased the number of factory inspectors to 158, and enlarged the mercantile inspection force from ten to twenty-one.[30] Thus the total strength of the Labor Department nearly doubled, and its appropriation also rose almost 100 per cent to an all-time high of $691,220.[31]

This greater interest in enforcement significantly changed the Department of Labor's expenditures per worker. In 1899 the State had spent 13.7 cents per wage earner to enforce the labor laws in manufacturing and mining establishments. By 1909 this figure had fallen to 12.1 cents, as expenditures rose more slowly than the number of workers. However, in 1919, despite a continued increase in the labor force in manufacturing and mining, the Labor Department spent 19.0 cents per worker. Illinois and Massachusetts had substantially higher expenditures per worker in 1909, but New York led all states in 1919.[32]

The more vigorous inspection methods of the enlarged Labor Department brought renewed political opposition when the social Progressives' influence faded after 1914. In 1915 the legislature cut the Department's appropriation[33] and weakened important statutes designed to ensure effective enforcement. A 1915 law permitted employers to arrange workmen's compensation settlements directly with their employees. Previously all

[30] New York State Department of Labor, *Thirteenth Annual Report of the Commissioner of Labor for the Twelve Months Ending September 30, 1913*, p. 10, summarizes the growth of the Department since 1910.

[31] New York State Department of Labor, *Bulletin*, Whole No. 55 (June 1913), p. 142.

[32] Leo Wolman, *History of New York State*, Vol. X, p. 89.

[33] *Annual Report of The Industrial Commission for the Nine Months Ending June 30, 1916*, pp. 10-11.

claims had had to be adjusted through the State Workmen's Compensation Commission, directed by John Mitchell. The Commission had attempted to protect the rights of workers, and thus the State Federation strongly opposed the amendment. Organized labor feared that coercion might be used against workers if employers—or rather their insurance companies— could settle compensation claims without recourse to the Workmen's Compensation Commission. Many workers would accept a pittance immediately rather than contest the case before the Commission.[34] In 1915 the legislature also repealed the twenty-year-old law barring alien labor from public works. This law had been ignored until the expansion of the Labor Department, but once enforced, it had threatened to choke off the supply of cheap foreign labor.[35]

The legislature also attempted to shift the enforcement of building requirements for factories in New York City from the Department of Labor to the five borough governments. Only a veto by the mayor, acting under the Home Rule provisions of the state constitution, defeated the bill. The new, comprehensive code on this subject had been enacted in 1913, and the Labor Department had attempted to enforce it. The reformers protested that a fracturing of responsibiliy would mean overlapping and a lack of clear responsibility for different areas of enforcement. In New York City, the enforcement of different sections of the tenement law by different city and state departments usually had produced confusion and inefficiency.[36] Mercantile inspection had been placed under the jurisdiction of the State Department of Labor in 1908 to end divided enforcement. In 1911 the Factory Investigating Commission discovered that the state factory inspector and the local health officer in Troy had never met, although they worked in the same area, enforcing related laws, and

[34] *Legislative Labor News*, Feb. 15, 1915, p. 4; April 9, 1915, pp. 5–6.
[35] *Legislative Labor News*, March 8, 1915, p. 1; March 15, 1915, p. 1.
[36] Paul Cravath to Francis V. Greene, Francis V. Greene Papers (New York Public Library), Dec. 18, 1900.

no doubt each had information that could assist the other.[37] The reformers thus regarded the shift of responsibility for the factory building laws from the state to the five borough governments in New York City as a deliberate attempt to weaken the labor law. The actions of the 1915 and 1916 legislatures indicate that Commissioner McMackin had not offered a mere rationale for his personal conduct when he warned the reformers in 1904 that a conservative state government would seek to prevent strict enforcement.

The problem of enforcing the labor law provided ammunition for the group in organized labor that attacked widespread reform through legislation. The social Progressives admitted the weaknesses in enforcement, but they insisted that just as legislation had been won by continuous campaigning, so enforcement must be secured by expanding the Department of Labor, by centralizing responsibility in one agency, by forming an expert force of inspectors and administrators chosen by civil service procedures, and by developing a continuous reform attitude among the people which would inevitably force the courts and politicians to a more realistic approach. This last requirement was all-important but most difficult to achieve. An increasing acceptance of legislative reform by organized labor and middle-class opinion meant that the problem of enforcement had to be solved. The key lay in forming a public attitude that would value enforcement of the laws for the protection of those without property just as fully as it did the laws for those with property. The reform spirit of 1906 to 1914 had to become a permanent part of public thinking; yet the collapse of Progressivism in New York after 1914 indicates how thoroughly the reformers had failed in this basic matter.

[37] New York Women's Trade Union League, Papers: Monthly Meeting Minutes, Jan. 8, 1912.

VIII

Organized Labor
and Political Action, 1897-1904

THE campaigns for reform in New York indicated clearly that conservative politicians would give their support only if they feared a revolt by important groups of voters, or if they hoped that specific reforms would win new voters for the party. Thus the social Progressives and organized labor continuously stressed their ability to speak for large numbers of the electorate.

Although the social Progressive societies depended upon the power of an aroused electorate, they did not enter politics. Prominent members of these organizations aided the Citizens Union and other independent political groups in New York City. Many social Progressives continued to support the Republicans nationally while attacking the G.O.P. on the state level for its opposition to their demands. Other reformers entered the Socialist Party's right wing, where they continued the social Progressives' emphasis on specific reform within the capitalist structure even if they had hopes of an ultimate social reconstruction. Many reformers became supporters of the Progressive Party after Theodore Roosevelt split the New York Republican organization in 1910.[1] Some social Progressives could be found

[1] The fullest discussion of the Progressive Party in New York is in Herbert H. Rosenthal, "The Progressive Movement in New York State, 1906–1914" (unpublished doctoral dissertation, Harvard University, 1955). Rosenthal confines his study to the political aspects of Progressivism, including the relation of the Progressive Party in New York to the

in the national Democratic Party, especially in 1912; but within New York, the influence of Tammany Hall made the Party uncongenial to reformers, who regarded city machines as the incarnation of all they detested in politics. These political differences among the social Progressives prevented any reform society from attempting political action.

Moreover, the social Progressives did not organize their reform campaigns on a class or party basis; instead, the appeal was to the "public," regardless of its political affiliation. The few major reforms passed before 1910 had bipartisan support in the legislature because of their popularity with the voters. Between 1910 and 1914 a majority of the electorate seemed to approve of a program of social reform, and the Democrats and Progressive Republicans responded. The social Progressives depended on nonpartisan public support which did not have to be marshaled behind any candidate or party, but whose influence was politically potent.

Organized labor's legislative program did not enjoy widespread support at any time. Many of labor's bills concerned small groups of workers or individual unions. Some proposals received the social Progressives' support, but there were often serious differences over the exact provisions of these bills. A Progressive mood in the electorate did not necessarily aid organized labor's own measures, and therefore the labor forces attempted to apply independent pressure on the legislature.

The opposition of most A.F.L. unions complicated any attempt at political action. The A.F.L. disapproved of most political action because of failures in the past and because of its divisive effect upon labor unity. The great majority of national and local unions, state federations, and city central bodies had constitutional provisions prohibiting politics, yet some sort of political action seemed necessary in the face of hostile conserva-

national movement. Also see Allen F. Davis, *op. cit.*, for the attitude of one important group of social Progressives toward the Progressive Party and the national campaign of 1912.

tive opinion. Accordingly state and city bodies often ignored these prohibitions in their constitutions, although local unions usually did not engage directly in politics.

The A.F.L. had sanctioned efforts by unionists to elect labor men to office, and to reward and punish legislators according to their attitude toward organized labor's demands. In the 1880's the Workingmen's Assembly of New York ran candidates for various offices on a labor ticket. The failure of this policy led the Assembly to switch to one of reward and punishment through an annual honor roll and blacklist.[2] Despite the reward-and-punish policy, the Assembly and its successor, the Workingmen's Federation, formally forbade politics in their constitutions. This prohibition was a useful device: it could be ignored when necessary, yet it could be used to choke off attempts at political action beyond the established policy of evaluating the legislature. Thus a resolution attacking militarism, presented to the Federation's convention in 1900, clearly implied an attack on the colonial policy of the McKinley administration. The chairman ruled the motion out of order because it savored of politics, and the convention upheld him.[3]

City labor councils often intervened in elections for assemblyman or for local office, yet their constitutions also forbade political action. The Utica Trades Assembly, for example, supported labor candidates for local offices in 1896. None were elected, but the Republicans nominated and elected a labor candidate the following year.[4] In 1899, however, the Trades Assembly did not wish to interfere openly, and it denied charges of partisanship during the election campaign by pointing out that the organization's constitution forbade political action.[5]

[2] George G. Groat, *Trade Unions and the Law in New York* (New York, 1905), pp. 26–28.
[3] *Official Record*, Oct. 1900, p. 3.
[4] *Utica Advocate*, Oct. 15, 1898, p. 1.
[5] *Utica Advocate*, Dec. 30, 1899, p. 5.

The Central Federated Union of New York City also resorted to political action, even though the C.F.U. constitution had the usual no-politics clause. Political bickering marred many C.F.U. meetings, and one delegate noted wistfully that a meaningful no-politics clause had been a wise device for avoiding conflict within the labor movement.[6] In 1899 the C.F.U. organized an Independent Labor Party to elect labor candidates to office in New York City. In 1900 a motion to oppose Jacob Ruppert's candidacy for the State Assembly, because of the antiunion record of his brewery, produced a no-politics ruling from the presiding officer. After some vitriolic charges against the brewer, the C.F.U. overrode its chairman and denounced Ruppert. As one delegate pointed out, the no-politics clause had been ignored before.[7]

Politics played an important part in the C.F.U.'s discussions at other times as well, but the organization did not always take formal action. The C.F.U. adopted no official position in the mayoralty races of 1897 and 1901 because of the deep political differences within the body. Action would have weakened the central organization's effectiveness in meeting industrial problems. In both elections, labor leaders formed workingmen's political leagues in which they were represented as individuals, not as spokesmen for their unions. Political action was clearly a part of organized labor's activities, as tempered by the needs of each instance.

New York's labor organizations rarely cooperated effectively on political matters. The Workingmen's Federation used an annual honor roll and blacklist as the basis for its policy of reward-and-punish; but city labor councils and local unions failed to support the Federation by publicizing its list or by setting up political leagues to carry out punitive action. The poor response at the local level greatly weakened the effective-

[6] *New York Evening Journal*, Oct. 30, 1899, p. 6.
[7] *New York Times*, Nov. 5, 1900, p. 3.

ness of the state organization's policy.[8] Accordingly, the suggestion was made that local legislative committees be formed to support the Federation's political activities.[9] The Federation had found that visits by a local labor committee influenced a legislator more than the state organization's lobbying, since it more directly represented the electorate within his district.[10] However, nothing came of this proposal.

The Federation's legislative chairman, James Hooley, believed that local support was the key to the success of the Federation's political activities. He even demanded that local unions hold their members "under penalty to cast their votes for legislators on election day exactly as those legislators cast their votes at Albany on the legislation asked for by the labor unions." Union funds also were to be used in this new political effort.[11] Hooley's conduct as legislative chairman was under attack at the time, and his call for united political action had no chance of acceptance. However, the frequent demands for some form of intensified local support of the Federation indicate the ineffectiveness of political recommendations by labor bodies which could not implement them at the vital point—among the voters.

The Workingmen's Federation relied almost entirely on the reward-and-punish method of political action, and it was also used extensively by city labor councils. In 1902 the C.F.U. attempted to block New York City's approval of a contract allowing the Pennsylvania Railroad to build a tunnel under the Hudson River. Organized labor opposed the contract because it did not provide specifically for the eight-hour day and prevailing rate of wages for construction workers. Aldermen were

[8] Workingmen's Federation of the State of New York, *Proceedings*, 1899, p. 22.

[9] *Utica Advocate*, Sept. 15, 1900, p. 5; *New York Evening Journal*, Sept. 12, 1900, p. 7.

[10] Workingmen's Federation of the State of New York, *Proceedings*, 1904: Legislative Chairman Hooley's Report.

[11] Workingmen's Federation of the State of New York, *Proceedings*, 1905: Legislative Chairman Hooley's Report.

threatened with political retaliation should they support the contract, but it passed anyway. The C.F.U. immediately prepared a blacklist, hung it for the next ten months in the labor organization's meeting hall, and distributed 250,000 copies of it before the 1903 election.[12]

The Workingmen's Federation insisted that its honor roll and blacklist were nonpartisan since they rated individuals, not parties. However, an examination of the period 1897–1904 indicates that the blacklist and honor roll did become a means of labeling parties as well.

The legislative report of the Federation in 1898 cited twelve Republican assemblymen and only one Democrat on the blacklist. Every one of the Republicans was from an upstate district. The report reviewed the State Senate for the sessions of 1897 and 1898, and placed six Republicans on the blacklist. Not one Democratic senator was considered unfriendly to organized labor.[13] The following year the same pattern appeared. Fifty-six of the sixty-three Democratic assemblymen made the honor roll because of their support of three key measures, while only seventeen of the eighty-three Republican assemblymen appeared on the same list.[14] In 1900 the Federation's major proposal was defeated on a roll-call vote in the Assembly. Of the sixty-three legislators who voted for the Federation's bill, only nine were Republicans.[15] The legislative reports for 1903 and 1904 indicated that the Republican majority overwhelmingly opposed most important labor bills, whereas the Democrats provided most of the affirmative votes.[16] The Federation also criticized Republican governors, especially Theodore Roosevelt in 1900 and Benjamin Odell in 1904, for their failure to sponsor impor-

[12] *New York Evening Journal*, Dec. 22, 1902, p. 10; Oct. 5, 1903, p. 6.
[13] *New York Evening Journal*, Sept. 17, 1898, p. 5.
[14] *New York Evening Journal*, Oct. 12, 1899, p. 8.
[15] *New York Evening Journal*, April 10, 1900, p. 7.
[16] For the 1903 record see *Labor Legislative News*, Oct. 1, 1903, pp. 3–9. For 1904 see Workingmen's Federation of the State of New York, *Proceedings, 1904: Legislative Chairman Hooley's Report.*

tant labor legislation.[17] Thus the Federation's reports were clearly anti-Republican even though it was individual legislators, not political parties, who were rated.

Any other result would have been most surprising. Members of the legislature usually voted according to party policy,[18] and the Republican leadership opposed most of organized labor's program. Until 1900 "Boss" Thomas C. Platt, and the small group of Republican leaders in his "Amen Corner," controlled the majority in the legislature.[19] After 1901 Governor Odell challenged the party leadership, and by degrees he replaced Platt as the main source of political power. However, Odell also relied on conservative Republican leaders for support, and his attitude toward labor legislation was hardly more positive. The party leaders determined the membership of the committees in both Senate and Assembly, and without fail prominent opponents of the Workingmen's Federation became the Republican members of the Labor and Industries committees. Senator Thomas Costello, who characterized labor's lobbyists as "fakirs," "liars," and "disturbers of the peace" [20] during one of his frequent outbursts, headed the Senate Labor Committee, and his influence blocked labor legislation year after year. In 1904 the Assembly's Labor and Industries Committee did not even meet for seven weeks of the session. This prevented action on all labor bills until the date the Rules Committee—controlled by the Republican leadership—took command of the order of bills.[21] Not one labor measure survived these tactics.

There was little reason for Republican leaders to favor labor

[17] *New York Evening Journal*, Sept. 15, 1900, p. 5; Workingmen's Federation of the State of New York, *Proceedings*, 1904: Legislative Chairman Hooley's Report.

[18] H. F. Gosnell, *Boss Platt and His New York Machine: A Study of the Political Leadership of Thomas C. Platt, Theodore Roosevelt and Others* (Chicago, 1924), pp. 151, 166.

[19] Gosnell, *Boss Platt*, pp. 155–158. For the membership of Platt's "Amen Corner," see *ibid.*, pp. 59–68.

[20] *New York Evening Journal*, April 10, 1900, p. 7.

[21] *The Labor Advocate*, Feb. 26, 1904, p. 1; April 1, 1904, p. 1.

legislation, especially when business was almost invariably opposed. Employers' liability, anti-injunction measures, bills to provide semimonthly pay and full crews of workers on railroads, and a host of special proposals concerning individual trades, had little support in upstate rural districts and among the middle class in the cities. Yet these groups supplied most of the Republican votes in New York, and the G.O.P. leaders saw no reason to favor legislation that did not excite its traditional supporters.[22] The great accomplishment of the Progressive spirit in New York, after 1906, was its conversion of many middle-class Republicans to support of social and political reform. The appearance of the Progressive Party in New York indicated the reluctance of upstate Republican leaders to accept reform, even under these circumstances. In the years before 1904, organized labor certainly could have expected little from a Republican-dominated legislature.

By comparison the Democratic minority in the legislature had a more positive record on labor legislation. However, this support of organized labor rarely had to meet any real tests. On most roll-call votes the Democratic minority realized that the bill could not pass because of Republican opposition, and that therefore they could safely build a favorable record for the labor voters in their districts by support of these measures. The test of the Democratic Party's attitude came in cities which had strong Democratic organizations. The policies of Tammany Hall in New York City provide clear evidence that organized labor could not really rely upon the Democratic Party.

In 1901 a Fusion Party composed of the Republicans, independent reform groups such as the Citizens Union, and renegade Democrats, defeated Tammany Hall and elected Seth Low mayor. Mayor Low's administration favored immediate approval of the Pennsylvania Railroad's tunnel to Manhattan, but a temporary alliance of dissident fusion aldermen with the Tam-

---

[22] Gosnell, *Boss Platt*, pp. 124–125.

many minority threatened to block favorable action. Despite organized labor's frantic opposition to the tunnel contract, three Tammany men switched to support of the bill, and thus it passed by one vote. The Hall did nothing to block the shift by the three aldermen.[23] Tammany denied that it had ordered the change in votes, but a sudden reversal in attitude by three organization stalwarts could not have occurred without the approval of the leaders. It was revealed later that Charles Murphy, the Tammany boss, had important holdings in construction firms which had received large contracts for work on the tunnel. Furthermore, while the Democratic minority in the legislature compiled a favorable voting record during the years 1898–1901 by support of organized labor's doomed bills, a Tammany administration in New York City weakened the existing laws by poor enforcement and created such animosity that important anti-Tammany political action developed within organized labor in 1899 and 1901.

The Democrats also placed many more unionists on their tickets than the Republicans. In 1900 twelve unionists were elected to the legislature as Democrats, whereas only one Republican was a union man.[24] In 1903 two Democratic state senators and nine Democratic assemblymen were unionists; only two Republican assemblymen came from organized labor's ranks.[25] Considered together with the voting record of the Democrats, this indicates the sources of the Democratic vote in New York. Most of the Democrats' support came from Tammany-dominated New York City, and from Buffalo and other industrial centers upstate. The Republicans could count on most of their votes even if they ignored labor reform; the Democrats had to appear more responsive to organized labor's interests. Open and consistent opposition to labor bills eventually might have reduced Democratic strength in working-class districts. Thus

[23] *New York Times,* Dec. 16, 1902, pp. 1–2.
[24] *New York Evening Journal,* April 10, 1900, p. 7.
[25] *Labor Legislative News,* Jan. 16, 1903, p. 2; Jan. 23, 1903, p. 1.

the glowing promises in platforms, the favorable voting record in the legislature, and the sprinkling of unionists sent to Albany were methods of continuing the impression that the Democrats had an interest in the welfare of the worker.

There is no doubt that Tammany Hall had close connections with big business interests, such as the Belmont, Ryan, and Whitney combinations; there is no doubt that Tammany Hall devoted itself more to private gain than the political well-being of the biggest city in America; but there is also no doubt that Tammany had strong popular support from working-class districts, and that despite its primary concern with the interests of the organization, it could more truly represent the workers of the city and state than the Republicans. The composition of the Republican Party vote meant that labor bills could not pass without conservative business and middle-class support, or without political conditions which dictated an appeal for labor votes. Tammany, however, could support labor legislation much more fully because of the Hall's working-class vote. Thus the potential for labor legislation was greater in a Democratic administration; but in practice the requirements of the Tammany organization itself, and the special interests of important business supporters of the Hall, often meant disappointment for organized labor.

In the opinion of many union leaders, the reward-and-punish policy of the Workingmen's Federation could not be effective because of the political conditions within the state. Assemblyman Henry Streifler, a unionist from Buffalo who sat in the legislature from 1897 to 1900 as a Democrat, was one of the strongest supporters of additional action by labor through "a political alliance independent of the labor organizations but maintained on the same principles plus political action." [26] He favored workingmen's political leagues in which unionists did not represent their organizations. These leagues would attempt

[26] *Utica Advocate*, Aug. 27, 1898, p. 3.

to elect union men to public office.[27] Party labels supposedly would be scrapped, and Streifler looked forward to a statewide workingmen's political league which would control a large block of votes. If swung to Republicans or Democrats, this vote could determine which party would have a majority in the legislature, and he foresaw the two major parties bidding for the support of the proposed state league by placing labor leaders on their tickets.[28] Streifler opposed a labor party because he believed it would make few inroads into the middle-class vote. Labor candidates on major party tickets, he thought, had a much better chance of election.

In 1900 the Workingmen's Federation supported the idea of a state workingmen's political league, but although several disconnected organizations were established in such cities as Binghamton, a state league never developed.[29] The Federation returned to this idea after the demoralizing legislative session of 1904, but again nothing materialized.[30]

The workingmen's political leagues in several upstate cities were very active, and they secured nominations on major party tickets for a number of Workingmen's Federation leaders.[31] In New York City, a Workingmen's Political League was organized in 1897, and it operated fitfully during the following years.

Although the leagues did help place some important unionists on the ballot, their overall influence was small. In upstate areas many workers voted Republican. In an effort to offset this tendency, the Democrats often nominated labor men in working-class districts. The leagues encouraged these nominations, which occurred even where they did not function. Less formal pressure

[27] *New York Evening Journal,* June 8, 1897, p. 9.
[28] *Utica Advocate,* April 21, 1900, p. 5.
[29] *Farm and Factory,* May 5, 1900, p. 3; May 12, 1900, p. 8.
[30] Workingmen's Federation of the State of New York, *Proceedings,* 1904: Resolutions.
[31] *New York Evening Journal,* Oct. 26, 1899–Nov. 9, 1899, provides information in its labor column on the extent of this movement in upstate areas.

by organized labor could produce the same result. Nomination of a unionist by the Democrats often meant that the Republicans would do the same. Thus the leagues were not essential to having union men nominated.

The workingmen's political leagues were not supposed to be partisan: this was to be a cornerstone of their strength since they could play off one party against the other. However, in practice the leagues often became adjuncts of specific political parties, and they would then work for all the candidates of that party, not simply the labor nominees. The Workingmen's Political League of New York City was attacked as a tool of Tammany from the time of its formation in 1897.[32] Although several of the League's leaders were connected with Tammany, they contended that this fact did not prevent them from being nonpartisan.[33] During the following years, this league did not once oppose a Democratic candidate, and the charge that it was Tammany's method of influencing organized labor, and not vice versa, seems justified.

In 1901 the Workingmen's Political League of New York City discovered it had competition from a new organization, known as the Trade Union Political League. Organized in April 1901, the new organization proposed to operate "in a nonpartisan way to bring about the nominations of men who have the confidence of organized labor." [34] It soon became obvious that men with the "confidence" of organized labor did not have to be unionists, and thus a basic premise of the political league idea had been scrapped. During the heated mayoralty race of 1901 in New York City, the Workingmen's Political League supported the Tammany ticket from top to bottom. The Trade Union Political League, however, endorsed the entire fusion slate. This was hardly unexpected, since the new league had been organized by anti-Tammany members of the building

[32] *New York Times,* June 7, 1897, p. 7.
[33] *New York Times,* July 5, 1897, p. 8.
[34] *New York Evening Journal,* April 23, 1901, p. 5.

trades unions.[35] Thus there were two competing workingmen's political organizations, neither of which achieved the aim of electing unionists to office through nonpartisan action.

The labor leaders who directed these political leagues often found that the most desirable labor candidates were themselves. This produced charges that the organizations were merely vehicles for advancing the interests of the few who controlled them.[36] In New York City this personal factor, plus the inability of any of the leagues to establish a truly nonpartisan character, made them useless as spokesmen for organized labor. In addition, they produced discord which weakened labor's unity in the more important economic functions. The permanent, statewide organization envisaged by Streifler never made any headway. The leagues were usually dormant during the periods between elections, and their sudden appearance at election time made it possible for ephemeral organizations, with little more than a few union leaders and a name, to claim that they represented organized labor's interests.[37] The failure of the workingmen's political leagues to produce any real results led other labor leaders to continue the demands for a true labor party.

During the years from 1897 to 1904 there were several weak efforts to set up a statewide labor party. In 1898 one plan proposed the formation of a state political convention which would organize a labor party. This party would attempt to elect enough legislators to be the balance of power between the Republicans and Democrats.[38] Opponents contended that a labor

[35] *New York Times,* Oct. 17, 1901, p. 5. The board of delegates of the United Building Trades fathered the Trade Union Political League, and on Oct. 19 the board of delegates endorsed the fusion ticket under its own name as well. See *New York Times,* Oct. 19, 1901, p. 2.

[36] *New York Times,* Sept. 19, 1898, p. 10.

[37] During 1899 a United Workingmen's League meeting this description appeared in New York City. It supported the Independent Labor Party and promptly disappeared after the election. See *New York Evening Journal,* June 6, 1899, p. 6; Sept. 20, 1899, p. 9.

[38] *Utica Advocate,* July 2, 1898, p. 2.

party could not elect enough candidates, and the proposed convention never met. The Workingmen's Federation convention of 1899 passed a resolution in favor of independent political action, but it did not spell out what sort of action.[39] This resolution never was implemented, and the convention of 1900 refused to pass a similar proposal.[40] A resolution specifically demanding a "State Labor Party" came before the disgruntled delegates to the convention of 1904. They had witnessed the complete failure of organized labor's program during the past legislative session, yet the resolution could not get significant support. The delegates insisted that their union constitutions prevented such political action.[41] Thus the Workingmen's Federation would not accept any form of independent political action in these years—but New York City labor did.

The building trades unions of New York City were the driving force behind the independent political movement of 1899. These unions complained bitterly that the Tammany administration refused to enforce the labor laws, especially those concerning wages and hours on public works.[42] Pleas and threats had failed. In July 1899 a trolley strike erupted on the Brooklyn lines, sparked by the company's evasion of the ten-hour law for surface motormen. The strike indicated the neglect of both city and state, neither of which attempted to enforce the law. City police protected strikebreakers, and thus helped keep the cars moving. The strike provided an emotional climax to the less sensational but equally substantial grievances of organized labor against the Tammany administration.

The Central Federated Union of New York City initiated the independent political movement by calling a conference for

[39] *New York Evening Journal*, June 22, 1900, p. 6.
[40] *New York Evening Journal*, Sept. 13, 1900, p. 7.
[41] *The Labor Advocate*, Sept. 23, 1904, p. 1.
[42] See the "Labor Notes" column in the *New York Evening Journal*, April–July 1899, for protests over Tammany's failure to enforce labor laws.

August 7, 1899, to set up a labor party. Over five hundred unions in the city received invitations, and the optimistic leaders predicted that three hundred would attend the meeting. However, only one hundred and five unions sent representatives, and about half of these were weak Knights of Labor locals.[43] Thus the movement lacked united suport from its inception. The C.F.U. continued, however, to support the labor party to the very end because of the influence of the strong building trades unions. The adherents of independent politics also hoped the Workingmen's Federation would sponsor a statewide labor party,[44] but there was no chance that upstate unions would accept this kind of action. As later events proved, the failure to coordinate the political program of New York City labor with the Federation's policies could lead to serious conflict.

The August 7 conference first stated the independent nature of the proposed labor party.

Whereas the delegates to this convention have been sent by their respective organizations with the understanding that an independent labor party is to be formed, and that no alliance will be made with either of the two dominant parties, therefore be it Resolved that this conference declare itself against any attempt to commit the convention, or political organizations to be formed by it, to any candidate for political office not nominated by this party.[45]

After a vaguely socialistic preamble to the platform, reminiscent of other statements of aims by nonsocialist American unions, the conference drew up a platform composed of political and economic demands. These included municipal ownership of public utilities, initiative, referendum and recall, enforcement of the eight-hour day and prevailing-wage laws, an employers' liability law, the end of sweatshops in tenements, prohibition of labor by all children under sixteen, adequate schools, and day labor in

[43] *New York Evening Journal*, Aug. 5, 1899, p. 8; Aug. 8, 1899, p. 6.
[44] *New York Evening Journal*, Aug. 14, 1899, p. 5.
[45] *New York Evening Journal*, Aug. 8, 1899, p. 6.

place of contract labor on public projects.[46] This platform merely repeated previous legislative aims of the A.F.L. or the Workingmen's Federation. What is of significance is the attempt to enforce these demands through a labor party.

The newly formed Independent Labor Party (I.L.P.) made plans to enter New York City races for judgeships, seats in the State Assembly, and for sheriff of New York County. As these plans unfolded, however, the Independent Labor Party's course changed sharply. The I.L.P. soon diluted its original character by opening the membership to middle-class supporters of organized labor.[47] The two socialist parties also were invited to join the campaign,[48] and on September 12 the new party appealed to the general public for funds,[49] continuing its movement away from a pure labor organization.

The change in policy indicated the basic weakness of this attempt at independent political action. Even though many powerful building trades unions supported the I.L.P., the failure of many other labor organizations to give any aid suggested that the new party would not be able to draw on a united labor vote. Furthermore, in New York City a labor party could not be the balance of power because of the Republicans' weakness. Tammany's power in the city could be challenged only through a fusion of all the opposing forces, and this often did not occur because of the conflicting aims of the various reform groups and the demand of the Republican Party that it be the main beneficiary of any fusion victory. The most sanguine observers credited the Independent Labor Party with only 30,000 votes out of a total of about 250,000. Alone, the I.L.P. could not

[46] *New York Evening Journal*, Aug. 18, 1899, p. 7.

[47] *New York Evening Journal*, Aug. 23, 1899, p. 4; Aug. 28, 1899, p. 7; *New York Times*, Sept. 1, 1899, p. 2.

[48] *New York Evening Journal*, Sept. 1, 1899, p. 5.

[49] *New York Times*, Sept. 12, 1899, p. 4. One of the leaders of the I.L.P., John Parsons, had promised $100,000 from wealthy contributors if the party were launched. However, the treasury of the I.L.P. contained exactly $10 on August 18.

expect to win even one office because its votes would come from the strongest Tammany districts, and would be merely a fraction of the Democratic total. Thus the idea of independent political action was impractical from its very inception, and the movement of the I.L.P. toward cooperation with middle-class opponents of Tammany was not a perversion of its purpose but the true motive for the party's formation.

The independence demanded by the resolution of August 7 was continued overtly by a set of Labor Party nominations during the first week of October.[50] However, at the same time negotiations had begun with the Republicans, the Citizens Union, and other nonlabor groups interested in a fusion campaign against Tammany.[51] Labor leaders who favored Tammany, and those who wanted a truly independent labor party, objected to these consultations as a violation of the August 7 resolution. At a meeting of the C.F.U. on October 8, opponents charged that the Independent Labor Party had been promised representation on a fusion ticket in exchange for its support. Delegate Samuel Prince, a supporter of Tammany who subsequently was elected to the legislature on the Democratic ticket, commented that the Labor Party could get more from bargaining with Tammany than through negotiations with the fusionists. He thought fourteen nominations of unionists for assemblyman would be the price Tammany might pay to end the I.L.P.[52] Apparently Tammany's offer never was made, for the Labor Party announced on October 13 that it would drop its original slate for judges and assemblymen and join in a fusion effort. As its share of the fusion ticket, the I.L.P. received two judgeship nominations and that of sheriff of New York County.[53]

It would seem that fusion was the initial intention of the building trades leaders who guided the Labor Party. During its brief

[50] See the *New York Evening Journal*, Oct. 1–3, 1899.

[51] *New York Times*, Oct. 6, 1899, p. 2.

[52] *New York Times*, Oct. 9, 1899, p. 3.

[53] *New York Times*, Oct. 10, 1899, p. 2; *New York Evening Journal*, Oct. 13, 1899, p. 8.

life the Independent Labor Party grew less independent, and slowly moved toward cooperation with other anti-Tammany reform forces. The Socialist Democratic Party cited this inherent admission that an independent labor party could not succeed as the reason for its refusal to support the I.L.P.[54] As the Labor Party moved toward fusion, the original platform had to be ignored, and the campaign concentrated on the one issue of beating a Tammany administration which had been unfair to organized labor. This, however, was the true issue: the I.L.P. had been formed to admonish Tammany for not enforcing the existing labor laws, not to promulgate a broad reform program. Furthermore, the new party never had been an independent organization intent on running a campaign; rather, it was basically a workingmen's political league hoping to earn several nominations in a fusion campaign against Tammany. A majority in the C.F.U. recognized this, for they approved of the initial overtures to nonlabor elements, the scrapping of the Independent Labor Party ticket in violation of the August 7 statement, and even the endorsement of assemblymen blacklisted by the Workingmen's Federation, as part of the effort to gain key nominations for labor leaders or labor's friends.

Fusion linked the Labor Party with some of the most conservative elements in the city, and it forced the I.L.P. to support several Republican assemblymen—as part of the fusion ticket—who were on the blacklist of the Workingmen's Federation, or who were opposing honor roll incumbents. Republican Assemblyman Slater had drawn particular criticism from the Workingmen's Federation, but he had the endorsement of the I.L.P. The Labor Party's reply to criticism on this point illustrates its impossible position. William O'Brien, a prominent figure in the C.F.U. and the building trades councils, received the fusion nomination for sheriff. He defended the support of Slater by insisting that he did not want to see him elected, but that the Labor Party had endorsed him because to have run an

[54] New York Evening Journal, Oct. 10, 1899, p. 8.

opponent would have drawn votes from the Democratic opponent and led to Slater's re-election.[55] Thus the Labor Party
was supporting a man it hoped would lose. Independent political
action had to be sacrificed for the necessities of fusion unity.

In addition to the endorsement of Slater, fusion forced the
I.L.P. to oppose two Democratic state assemblymen who were
unionists. The two men had been placed on the honor roll of the
Workingmen's Federation, and the incongruity of a labor party
opposing union men who had worked faithfully for organized
labor's interests in the legislature led the state organization to
enter the New York City campaign. The Federation sponsored a
mass rally in Manhattan to discuss its honor roll, and to "con-
demn the attempt to deliver the labor vote to any political
party." The legislative chairman, James Hooley, attacked the
Independent Labor Party for opposing men on the honor roll,
be they unionists or not, and he disclosed the basic reason for the
Federation's intervention when he asserted that the state organization would lose all influence in Albany if important labor
bodies freely ignored its recommendations on voting.[56] The
I.L.P. had been interested primarily in New York City affairs,
but the necessity for fusion had brought it into conflict with the
Federation. As usual, the state organization lost the support of
important groups within organized labor when their interests did
not agree. The Independent Labor Party continued to pursue its
own course with the approval of the C.F.U.

By the time of the election, the I.L.P. had alienated important
sections of labor opinion, and instead of representing a united
labor movement, it comprised just one contending faction. The
voting results reflect this clearly: the Labor Party vote was frac-
tional and nowhere near the promised 30,000. William O'Brien
led the fusion ticket in his unsuccessful race for sheriff, yet he
lost by over 55,000 votes in a total vote of 240,000.[57] O'Brien's

[55] *New York Times*, Oct. 23, 1899, p. 3.
[56] *New York Evening Journal*, Nov. 4, 1899, p. 6.
[57] *New York Times*, Nov. 8, 1899, pp. 1–2.

great personal popularity among organized workers in New York City undoubtedly accounted for his high vote. The fusion forces did not contest some Democratic districts, and here the Labor Party ran candidates independently. The voting figures in these working-class districts show no reduction of the Democratic vote.[58] The two unionist assemblymen easily overcame their fusion opponents who had been endorsed by the I.L.P. In all, the Labor Party had no significant influence on any phase of the election.

The problems facing the Independent Labor Party indicate the difficulty of any attempt at political action by organized labor. The opposition by many unions to all political action, the difficulty of coordinating the policies of state and local organizations, and the personal antagonism that developed among labor leaders all contributed to the failure of political action. Yet even more basic to the failure of these political efforts was the reaction of working-class voters to labor's candidates, programs, and voting recommendations. Reward and punishment, working-men's political leagues, and independent labor parties rested on the assumption that the recommendations of a labor body, or the presence of a labor candidate on a ticket, could influence a block of working-class votes. This "labor vote" would be composed of both unionists and unorganized workers, the key factor being the responsiveness of these voters to labor's political efforts. With few exceptions, such a labor vote failed to materialize in New York during this period.

The Central Federated Union attempted to defeat the three Tammany aldermen who had changed their votes and thereby permitted the Pennsylvania Railroad's tunnel contract to pass. Although two of the three represented working-class districts, all were re-elected. Comptroller Edward Grout and the president of the Board of Aldermen, Charles Fornes, also had been blacklisted for their role in pushing through the contract. Using an old Tammany tactic, Charles Murphy convinced these re-

[58] *New York Evening Journal*, Nov. 8, 1899, p. 9.

spected, independent Democratic members of the Low administration that Low and the fusion candidates could not be re-elected, and that they could save their political careers only by joining the Hall's ticket. Running as Democrats, Grout and Fornes had to face their blacklisting by the C.F.U., yet their total vote was larger than that of Mayor-elect George B. McClellan, who had extensive labor support.[59]

Trade union candidates occasionally had better success in producing a labor vote. Two of the most vocal unionists in the State Assembly had similar experiences in two very different districts. Henry Streifler ran as a Democrat in a Republican district of Buffalo which had a large working-class population. After two unsuccessful tries he was elected to the Assembly in 1897. Streifler won re-election in 1898 and 1899, when the races were not obscured by a presidential contest, but in 1900 his trade union origins and strong pro-labor record were not enough to overcome the propensity for voting a straight ticket in a national election. McKinley carried the district, and the rest of his Republican ticket also won. Samuel Prince, on the other hand, ran as a Democrat in a strongly Democratic district of New York City, and he was elected in every contest from 1899 to 1903. However, in the presidential election of 1904 Theodore Roosevelt carried the district, and despite the large working-class population in the area, the straight-ticket vote led to Prince's defeat.

On the whole, trade union candidates in New York City made no significant impact on the vote. When unionists ran as Tammany men in Democratic districts, they usually were elected; when labor candidates ran in opposition to the traditional voting patterns within the city, workers generally ignored them. As has been indicated, William O'Brien led the fusion ticket in 1899. It would appear that those extra votes came from workers who respected him despite the unfortunate situation of the Independ-

[59] See *New York Times*, Nov. 4, 1903, pp. 1–2, for the election figures.

178

ent Labor Party. Yet his margin over other members of the ticket was not substantial, and if there were laborers who did vote specifically for him, their number was small. In 1901 O'Brien ran once again for sheriff, this time on Seth Low's fusion ticket. O'Brien was nominated to attract Democratic working-class voters, yet when his percentage of the vote is compared with the anti-Tammany ballots in the 1897 race for sheriff, no significant difference appears even though the candidates in 1897 were not unionists.[60]

Unlike O'Brien, William Jerome was able to win many of Tammany's working-class votes in his campaign for district attorney on the fusion ticket of 1901. His compelling personality and lively campaign attracted the attention of the press, and by election day Jerome had become an almost apolitical incarnation of reform after a scandal-filled Tammany administration. The voters responded by giving Jerome a greater vote than Low. In the Democratic, working-class districts of Manhattan, he ran well ahead of O'Brien, Low, and the fusion candidates for the Assembly.[61] Jerome's appeal to these voters was not through his identification with their social position; rather, it was the result of an exciting campaign conducted by a fiery candidate who had struck the right issue at the right time.

Despite the tendency among workers to follow traditional voting patterns, they were not completely unresponsive to labor candidates or to recommendations of state and city central bodies. The nomination of a pro-labor candidate by the minority party in a working-class district might occasionally produce victory for that party. Streifler's victories in 1897–1899

[60] Figures from *The City Record* (Supplement, Dec. 1897), p. 15, and *The City Record* (Supplement, Jan. 4, 1902), p. 9. At some time during the months following an election, the official figures, down to the election district level, appear in this official publication of New York City. For voting figures on statewide races, or elections to the legislature, a most helpful source is the *Manual for the Use of the Legislature of the State of New York* for the year following the election.

[61] *New York Times*, Nov. 6, 1901, pp. 1–2.

illustrate this well. Republicans from New York City districts with significant working-class populations tended to be more responsive to the wishes of organized labor. Since many elections for the Assembly could be decided by even a small change in the vote, these Republican assemblymen often did not join the Party majority in its opposition to labor bills. In Albany, Thomas Fitzgerald, president of the Allied Printing Trades Council of New York, won an election in 1897 on an independent labor ticket. Fitzgerald had been promised the nomination for alderman by the Democrats; when they reneged, he ran as an independent, with united labor support, and carried the district.[62]

Thus it cannot be maintained that there was no labor vote. Instead, it would appear that the number of labor votes was relatively small, and that they were tapped most effectively in local elections where organized labor could campaign intensively without the need for a large expenditure. As will be seen in the subsequent discussion of the political efforts of William Randolph Hearst and Henry George, the general failure of the worker to respond to the political policies of organized labor did not mean he was a mere automaton who voted without discrimination in every election.

Organized labor's propaganda was only one of the political influences upon the worker. Religion and nationality, family voting traditions, and the partisan popular press had an important effect upon the laborer. Usually these forces had a greater influence than the comparatively feeble efforts of the labor movement. Organized labor failed to produce a permanent political organization which could command the allegiance of union leaders and workers. The appearance of an independent labor party a few months before an election; the ephemeral workingmen's political leagues, which lasted only a few years and were almost entirely inactive between elections; and the refusal of many local unions to publicize the Workingmen's Federation honor roll and black-

[62] *New York Evening Journal*, May 27, 1898, p. 4.

list among the rank and file, should be contrasted with the propaganda sources available to the major parties, and the force of traditional voting habits upon workers. There is no doubt that organized labor, dabbling in politics as a subsidiary function, could not contend with the effective methods of the professional political machines; and nowhere is this clearer than in Tammany Hall's command of the working-class vote in New York City.

Tammany Hall's strength among the workers of New York City was an essential fact of politics; and attempts to weaken it made little real progress during the period 1897–1904, despite such occasional intrusions as William Jerome's campaign of 1901. The workers who lived in the tenement districts of Tammany's fief generally supported the Hall in both winning and losing efforts. This support continued despite the undoubted corruption within Tammany administrations, and the opposition of almost all the organs of middle-class opinion in the state and nation.

Lincoln Steffens recognized the distinctive character of Tammany when he wrote that "Tammany corruption is democratic corruption." [63] It was the sort of corruption that upset the rich but not the poor; for as George Gunton noted,

Tammany, whatever else it does, all the year around, fifty-two weeks in the year, constantly pays attention in one way or another to the laboring people of this city. It is always doing something for them. Never on a high plane; it never advocates any great reform for them, never was known to do it. It never introduced any public policy that was of permanent service to them. It never cleaned their streets. It neglected them until the filth forced itself in at their doors. But in the small way of employments and attentions, it always kept itself in their consciousness, in some kind of personal touch.[64]

[63] Lincoln Steffens, *The Shame of the Cities* (New York, 1904; Sagamore Press ed., 1957, used here), p. 204.

[64] *Gunton's Institute Bulletin* (The Institute of Social Economics), III (Feb. 3, 1900), 403.

The critics of Tammany agreed that the Hall had the votes of the populace because it served them every day of the year with the tangibles of gifts, jobs, and aid in legal difficulties, rather than with promises of civic reform which meant little to the tenement masses. Tammany was the greatest charity in the city, and in exchange for its aid it asked not the long forms and self-abasement required by the philanthropic societies, but only the vote of the citizen.[65] Since so many voters supported Tammany for reasons other than its political principles or program, the Hall could steal planks from opponents, make amazing about-faces in policy, and lure opposing candidates to its ticket. Of course the Hall did not hesitate to use illegal methods of voting when necessary, but in most elections the great majority of Tammany's votes were honestly cast.

Irish voters supplied a significant part of Tammany's voting strength. Their support for the organization could be traced back to the Hall's interest in the Irish immigrants during the Know-Nothing agitation of the 1850's. The Irish subsequently had gained control of Tammany, and the adherence of Irish voters to an Irish-dominated Tammany organization became traditional.[66] For many poor men in the tenement areas, Democratic politics became a means for social and economic advancement. Other immigrant groups also received favors from Tammany, and with few exceptions they gave the Hall significant support, which also became traditional and hard to crack.[67]

[65] Sydney Brooks, "Tammany," *The English Review*, III (Nov. 1909), 721.

[66] Gustavus Myers, "The Secrets of Tammany's Success," *The Forum*, XXXI (June 1901), 495, and Burton J. Hendrick, "The Twilight of Tammany Hall," *The World's Work*, XXVII (Feb. 1914), 436–438, present contemporary comments on this voting pattern.

[67] Germans and Jews from Eastern Europe who brought socialist ideas with them to the United States tended to resist Tammany's domination. However, the great majority of voters in both these groups, as well as the Italian voters, supported Tammany in most of the elections during the Progressive period.

Many labor leaders opposed Tammany, knowing full well how piddling the Hall's gifts were in comparison with the effect of its insistence that its own interests came before the demands of organized labor. The inability of trade union leaders to oppose Tammany successfully only made the Hall's neglect of organized labor more oppressive. Yet where could the worker who sought to escape Tammany turn?

Even some Republicans admitted that their party had no place for the laborers' interests.[68] The fusion movements promised organized labor more than the Republicans did, partly because of the necessity of securing as many votes as possible among the workers, and partly because of the important social Progressive element in the fusion movement. James Reynolds, a leader in the Social Reform Club, the University Settlement, and the fusion political combinations, spoke for many social Progressives when he suggested that the encouragement of trade unions would be a means of destroying Tammany's hold over much of the working-class vote.

The impending threat of beggary or the poorhouse which hangs over the independent laborer is the power which drives so many into the arms of the political boss, who undertakes to provide an assurance of steady employment with out-of-work and death benefits for the laborer's family in return for the surrender of the laborer's political independence. In relieving the laborer of this temptation to political serfdom, the trade union renders an incidental civic benefit, in addition to the direct benefits to the laborer himself.[69]

In 1897 civic reformers in the Citizens Union ran Seth Low for mayor on an independent ticket, and during the campaign they set up a special Committee on Labor and Social Reform. The Committee sought to win part of the working-class vote

[68] *Gunton's Institute Bulletin*, III (Feb. 3, 1900), 403. In the 1897 mayoralty campaign only the Republicans refused to promise enforcement and extension of the eight-hour day and prevailing-wage law. See *New York Evening Journal*, Oct. 2, 1897, p. 3.

[69] James B. Reynolds, "Eight Years at the University Settlement," *University Settlement Studies*, II (July 1906), 36–37.

from Tammany Hall. Reynolds headed this committee, which was composed of unionists and social Progressives. It vigorously attacked Tammany's labor record, especially during the depression of 1892–1894, and pointed to Low's record as a respected arbitrator in labor disputes.[70] The Committee also stressed Low's support of reforms such as an effective eight-hour day law.[71] Fusion movements in 1899 and 1901 gave unionists places on the ticket, and although this won important support from trade union leaders, it converted few of the traditional Tammany votes in the working class districts of Manhattan.[72]

Despite these concessions on program and candidates, there could be no lasting alliance between the civic reformers and organized labor. Conservative business interests, which sought to end Tammany's extravagances and exactions, joined the wealthy civic reformers in supplying the money for fusion campaigns.[73] Although the Citizens Union and other civic reform groups worked zealously for a more efficient and honest city govern-

[70] The Citizens Union, *Tammany's Million Dollar Fraud on the Workingmen* (pamphlet), 1897.

[71] The Citizens Union, *Workingmen as Citizens* (pamphlet), 1897; Knights of Labor, District Assembly 49, New York, *Annual Official Handbook*, No. 15, 1897, back cover advertisement; Samuel Donnelly (president of Local 6, International Typographical Union) to Low, Low Papers, Sept. 6, 1897.

[72] Milo T. Bogard, a fusion leader, asserted that the 1901 campaign was the first time that union labor was "properly recognized in a campaign for pure government, and the portion of labor in the redemption of the City cannot be underestimated." The figures, however, indicate that Tammany held its working-class districts solidly. The fusion victory came through a united middle-class, anti-Tammany vote, centering mainly in Brooklyn and the Bronx.

[73] See Charles L. Bernheimer Papers (New-York Historical Society): Box 8B, Bernheimer to Isaac Seligman, Aug. 18, 1913, Finance Committee Meeting Minutes, Aug. 19, 1913, and Memorandum, Aug. 22, 1913, for interesting details on fusion's reliance on a few rich contributors. A full list of contributors to the 1913 fusion campaign, with the amounts given, also is included. This list of contributors has been printed as Citizens Municipal Committee of the City of New York, *Treasurer's Report for the Campaign of 1913* (New York, 1913).

ment, they held definitely conservative views on most social reform issues. Mayor Low turned down the suggestion that he appoint Lawrence Veiller—the leader in the campaign for the Tenement Building Code of 1901—as tenement commissioner in the new fusion administration, because Veiller was considered too radical.[74] During the following years, the social Progressives criticized Veiller for being too conservative.[75] During the two years he held office, Low battled almost continuously with the Central Federated Union over the failure of certain commissioners to enforce the labor law fully, and over their refusal to give preference to union labor even where the law did not require it. The Low administration also pushed through the Pennsylvania Railroad's tunnel contract, in 1902, over the vehement objections of the C.F.U.

Following the defeat of Low in 1903, an observer commented on the reasons why the fusion ticket had gone down to defeat: "Only a few months ago, New York 'Reform' had an overwhelming defeat. Why? Because it was neither radical nor democratic. Its watchwords were the hackneyed ones of a 'business administration, honesty, efficiency and economy.' "[76] Low had placed honest and efficient men in administrative posts, and he had provided sound government—but it had been government that "did not reach the people." The Fusion administration ignored demands for new parks, more schools, or municipally built tenements in an effort to provide efficient government at the least possible cost to the 10 per cent of the city's population who paid the real estate taxes.[77] Low did not raise taxes despite rising prices. Although some labor leaders supported fusion campaigns, neither organized labor as a whole nor the individual

[74] Veiller, *Reminiscences*, p. 39.   [75] *Ibid.*

[76] "Why Municipal Reform Succeeds in Chicago and Fails in New York," *The Independent*, LVI (April 14, 1904), 830.

[77] *Ibid.*, pp. 830–831. Also see Steven C. Swett, "The Test of a Reformer: A Study of Seth Low, New York City Mayor, 1902–1903," *New-York Historical Society Quarterly*, XLIV (Jan. 1960), pp. 5–41.

working-class voter gave the civic reformers much assistance. The Citizens Union continued the Mugwump reform movement of the late nineteenth century, and the gap between its aims and the demands of organized labor was sizable.

The workers' support of Tammany Hall indicated not only the force of traditional voting patterns, the effectiveness of the machine, and the personal touch of the Hall's activities, but also the absence of a positive alternative. When such an alternative appeared—as it did in the person of Henry George in 1897, and still more clearly in the fantastic political career of William Randolph Hearst—the working-class voter responded dramatically.

Henry George had run for mayor of New York City in 1886 on an independent labor ticket, and although he lost, a sizable number of voters deserted Tammany to support him. After that campaign George had little contact with New York City politics, or with organized labor within the city. In 1897, however, several labor leaders, dissatisfied with the reform administration of Mayor William L. Strong, which was coming to a close, and ill disposed to see Tammany return to power, persuaded George to make another independent race. Tom L. Johnson, who soon afterward achieved national prominence as the reform mayor of Cleveland, supplied the all-important financial support.

From the very start of his campaign, labor leaders announced their support, and many prominent men in the Central Labor Union [78] openly worked for George.[79] Attempts to have the central body endorse George met opposition from the Tammany group in the organization, and a deep split developed. Although George did not receive the endorsement,[80] there was no doubt that a large number of delegates favored him. However, these labor leaders were unwilling to split the Central

[78] The Central Federated Union of New York City was known as the Central Labor Union until 1899.

[79] *New York Evening Journal*, Oct. 2, 1897, p. 2; Oct. 7, 1899, p. 3.

[80] *New York Times*, Oct. 18, 1897, p. 2; *New York Evening Journal*, Oct. 7, 1899, p. 3.

Labor Union over the issue. Only seven small unions formally endorsed George, but even his opponents admitted his appeal to labor voters. The *New York Press* said editorially that Low had had some labor support in the days before George's late entrance into the campaign, but that now Low would not get enough working-class votes to win a single district.[81]

The reporter for *The Spectator* noted the difference between George and Low. Low depended for support on rich and educated gentlemen, "quite alienated from the masses." The populace disliked the moral sternness and the emphasis on efficient government that characterized the activities of these Mugwumps. The civic reformers ignored the basic reforms that would have touched the masses personally. George, however, represented this ideal of social reform in his person—a reform "looking to vast economic changes." [82] His single-tax ideas were not the reason for his popularity; instead, he represented some dim ideal of thoroughgoing social change.

Although George was credited with drawing many voters from their traditional allegiance to Tammany, the issue did not come to the test.[83] An apoplectic stroke led to George's death just before the election, and on election day Tammany held its working-class vote and won handily. It would seem that George had made significant inroads into the Hall's vote, but his death makes generalization difficult. It remained for William Randolph Hearst to indicate clearly the appeal of the vital, well-publicized social reform candidate who presented a definite alternative to Tammany Hall and its conservative opponents.

[81] Low Papers: 1897 Election Materials, undated clipping from the *New York Press* (some time in Oct. 1897).

[82] "The Tammany Victory," *The Spectator*, LXXIX (Nov. 6, 1897), 637.

[83] Lothrop Stoddard, *Master of Manhattan: The Life of Richard Croker* (New York, 1931), p. 179; *New York Evening Journal*, Oct. 29, 1897, p. 1. Also see the informal polls conducted by the *Evening Journal* and reported in its issues of Oct. 1897. Charles Barker, *Henry George* (New York, 1955), pp. 616–618, believes George's vote would have been below the figure needed to produce a plurality for Low.

IX

Hearst and Labor

IN the years before 1905, William Randolph Hearst prepared himself for the exciting climax of his political career. His main organ of expression, and greatest political weapon, was the Hearst press.[1] These papers were among the leaders in circulation, and Hearst clearly aimed to keep them attractive to the less educated members of the population. The workers and the lower middle class of New York City bought Hearst's morning and evening dailies, and year after year these papers provided the means for building up Hearst's own political personality.

The Hearst papers continuously attacked the trusts, political corruption, and the ties between business and politicians. In every manner conceivable, Hearst attempted to produce the impression that his newspapers protected the small businessman, the workers and shopkeepers of the lower middle class, and the mass of the laborers. News and editorial blended imperceptibly, and in successive crusades for the smashing of a trust, the unseating of a corrupt politician, or the passage of laws favored by social Progressive and labor organizations, Hearst presented the picture of a man struggling against the weight of conservative opinion in order to express the wishes of the lower classes in

[1] Before 1903 Hearst published a New York morning paper under various titles using the words "Journal" and "American." In 1903 the *New York American* became the fixed name of the morning paper. The evening paper remained the *New York Evening Journal* throughout the Progressive period.

society. He constantly demanded that all levels of government respond to the demands of the public—by which he meant the public who bought his dailies. The abuse heaped on Hearst because of his unorthodox ideas and methods came primarily from newspapers long associated with political and journalistic conservatism, and it only reinforced the image of Hearst the reformer.

The support of the Hearst press for strikes and labor legislation contrasted sharply with the antiunion attitude of the other major newspapers. Not only did many strikes receive sympathetic treatment, but a regular labor column appeared daily in the *New York Evening Journal*. Only the pro-Tammany *New York Daily News* attempted to match the *Journal*'s coverage of labor news. Hearst's support of organized labor's major bills in the legislature naturally won the approval of the Workingmen's Federation. For example, the *Labor Legislative News* congratulated Hearst for supporting the New York City street cleaners' demands before the legislature in 1903: "As usual the *New York Journal*, with its persistent efforts in favor of uplifting and bettering conditions of the working man, deserves the thanks of the men in the street cleaning department of New York for its support of their measures." [2]

Despite attacks on Tammany Hall for its supposed corruption and deceptions, Hearst was essentially a Democrat, and during 1903–1907 he represented a Tammany working-class district in the House of Representatives. As part of his campaign for labor support in the congressional race of 1902, Hearst called for the Democrats to become the party of the people through a close association with organized labor. Labeling the Republicans as the comrades of trusts, he asserted that a labor-Democratic alliance meant the Party's support of demands by the trade unions for shorter hours and higher pay as a prerequisite for labor's support of the Democrats.[3] During this campaign Hearst re-

[2] *Labor Legislative News*, March 20, 1903, p. 4.
[3] *New York Evening Journal*, Nov. 6, 1902, p. 16.

ceived the active support of several labor leaders,[4] and he easily carried the strong Democratic district.

Hearst's record in Congress was mediocre, as newspaper activities continued to take most of his time. The campaign for Congress had been comparatively quiet, and his margin of victory reflected the Democratic character of the district more than it did the appeal of Hearst himself. It was through his newspapers that Hearst hoped to establish his political appeal, and as events in 1905 were to prove, he did this with great skill.

As early as 1904 Hearst began to suggest that he might make a good presidential candidate for the Democratic Party. Alton Parker's weak race against Theodore Roosevelt only reinforced this idea. Hearst needed some political office as a stepping stone to his ultimate ambition, and after accepting another term in Congress in 1904, he made overtures to Tammany chief Charles Murphy, concerning the Democratic nomination for mayor of New York City in 1905. Murphy enjoyed cordial relations with Mayor George B. McClellan at this time, and thus he refused. If Tammany had accepted Hearst in 1905, he in turn would have accepted Tammany and run under its banner.[5] Instead, Hearst had to look for other sources of political strength.

Hearst now climaxed his years of muckraking journalism by setting up the Municipal Ownership League—a new political organization pledged to the public ownership of major utilities. As usual, he had picked an issue that appealed to the lower middle class and the workers. The legislature in 1905 had failed to support an attempted cut in the gas rate in New York City, despite substantial evidence that the rates were higher than in other areas, and that they were kept so by a lack of competition and the compliance of important New York City politicians. Despite solid Progressive support, the legislature also defeated a

[4] *New York Evening Journal*, Oct. 28, 1902, p. 8.
[5] Ferdinand Lundberg, *Imperial Hearst: A Social Biography* (New York, 1936), p. 102.

bill to provide for the automatic reversion of new privately built subway lines to New York City after an initial operating period of either twenty-five or fifty years. Hearst's new demand thus continued his image as a representative of the interests of the poorer elements in society, and it also drew to him a collection of social Progressives, single-taxers, and right-wing socialists.[6]

During the campaign of 1905, Hearst was the only candidate to support municipal ownership unequivocally;[7] but the significance of this issue far exceeded the particular appeal of public ownership. Even Hearst's opponents recognized that his popularity was the result of a popular resentment against the "money power," which the attacks of the muckrakers had done much to develop.[8] The Hearst press had been a continuing source of such attacks, and many persons interpreted Hearst's own campaign as an assault on entrenched wealth, particularly when it was crystallized by the issue of municipal ownership. It was this image of Hearst as a social reformer, who represented the interests of the populace against the machinations of financiers and politicians, that underlay his tremendous appeal. The widespread acceptance of Hearst as such a reformer was the culmination of years of clever and careful newspaper work.

In the initial stage of the 1905 campaign, Hearst's Municipal Ownership League took part in negotiations for a fusion ticket to oppose Tammany. As usual, the discussions primarily concerned the assignment of nominations among the cooperating groups, and the disputes on this point so divided the prospective fusion forces that no candidates could be chosen.[9] Hearst later charged that the Republicans had been paid by the financier Thomas F. Ryan to kill attempts at fusion and thus to ensure

[6] See *New York Evening Journal* for the month of October 1905 for the names of Hearst's supporters.

[7] "New York's Municipal Campaign," *The Independent*, LIX (Oct. 19, 1905), 937.

[8] *New York Times*, Nov. 1, 1905, p. 8.

[9] For the course of the futile fusion discussions, see *New York Times* for the month of September 1905.

the re-election of Tammany's slate headed by Mayor McClellan.[10] The state Republican leader, Benjamin Odell, denied this
charge, of course, and it would not seem that Hearst really was
upset over the collapse of fusion. During the negotiations his
name had not been suggested by the Municipal Ownership
League; for Hearst wanted the mayoralty nomination, and it
seemed clear that the Citizens Union and the Republicans would
not give a new, untried political organization the top spot, especially considering its Democratic antecedents and reform program. After the collapse of fusion, Hearst rushed into the race
for mayor as the candidate of his Municipal Ownership League,
even though all concerned believed the collapse of fusion, whatever the reason, ensured the re-election of Mayor McClellan.[11]

Nevertheless, Hearst's appeal to the voters quickly became evident, as even his bitterest opponents had to admit.[12] The Republicans and Hearst each soon realized that a partial alliance
might be to their mutual advantage, and it was arranged to have
Hearst's ticket include twenty of the thirty-five Republican
Assembly candidates in Manhattan, plus nine of the twenty-one
candidates in Brooklyn. Hearst also endorsed Republican candidates for alderman. In general, Hearst supported Republicans in
Democratic districts where a straight-ticket vote on the Municipal Ownership line would be of great assistance to the G.O.P.[13]
In return, Hearst was supposed to receive Republican votes for
mayor.[14] This meant that organization Republicans would have
to knife their own candidate. Since his chances of election were
nil, the advantage of Hearst's support in the other races was of
greater value.

Hearst intended to capture the votes of the independents who

[10] *New York Evening Journal*, Oct. 5, 1905, p. 10.
[11] *New York Times*, Sept. 28, 1905, p. 1.
[12] *New York Herald*, Oct. 17, 1905, p. 1.
[13] *New York Times*, Oct. 28, 1905, p. 4.
[14] *New York Times*, Nov. 8, 1905, p. 1.

were usually attracted by reform, and the working-class vote which was the backbone of Tammany's power in New York City. Without a substantial shift away from Tammany by the workers, Hearst's independent ticket would be buried. The failure of the Independent Labor Party to win many votes from Tammany in 1899 indicated that his would be no easy task; but unlike organized labor, Hearst could reach all the workers, not only the union leaders, and he could appeal to them as a reformer who had proved he could stand up to the moneyed forces in business and politics.

Hearst's newspapers became daily campaign sheets which supported his candidacy while viciously attacking the Tammany slate. McClellan was linked to the gas interests in New York City and labeled "The Gas Man," and Murphy was depicted in the striped garb of a prisoner, no further caption being necessary. With his customary flair for the sensational, Hearst leveled attacks, "exposed" plots against the public interest, supported key reforms of the social Progressives and organized labor, and in general ran the race of the social reformer—but in his own individual style. His campaign in the Hearst press was keyed to its usual readers among the lower middle and working classes, for theirs were the votes he needed to challenge Tammany effectively. Hearst also addressed numerous meetings throughout the city, molding his speeches to fit the nature of his audience. Thus he could be conservative before business audiences in Republican districts and a reformer before labor meetings in Tammany strongholds. The reform posture predominated, however, and the appeal to the working class was basic.

Hearst did not leave the task of winning the workers' votes to his papers and to meetings alone. In addition he organized a Workingmen's Municipal Ownership Association, which technically was to act for the general cause of public ownership. Naturally the Association discovered that the cause could be served best by the immediate election of Hearst. The organization contained many prominent figures from the New York City labor movement.[15] The strong support of Hearst's candidacy by these labor leaders was the first hint of his appeal to the workers. Hearst's past support for strikes and labor legislation, and his generally friendly attitude toward organized labor, paid off in this substantial support among the labor leaders of the city. Unlike the political organizations set up by labor unions, the Workingmen's Municipal Ownership Association did not operate on a shoestring. Instead, emulating Tammany Hall's clubhouses before the election, the offices were open until 10 P.M. so that workers might come in during the evening hours.[16] The Association organized a gigantic labor parade for the week preceding the election—copying a parade during Henry George's strong race for mayor of New York in 1886. The individual members of the Association came from many different unions within the city, and they planned to work at the local union level.[17] The organization used the structure of earlier workingmen's political leagues even though it was organized and guided by a nonlabor figure.

In his newspapers and meetings, Hearst emphasized the antilabor policies of the Tammany administration and his own support of organized labor. He attacked the transit interests in the city for their opposition to unionization, and said again and again that he believed these transit companies were allied with the Tammany organization.[18] Hearst repeated all the Central Federated Union's charges that the McClellan administration had not enforced the labor law.[19] In contrast, Hearst fully supported organized labor's major demands in the legislature,

[15] *New York Evening Journal*, Sept. 19, 1905, p. 13.

[16] *Daily Trade Record*, Sept. 20, 1905, p. 1.

[17] *New York Evening Journal*, Oct. 14, 1905, p. 2; Oct. 23, 1905, p. 4.

[18] *New York Evening Journal*, Oct. 12, 1905, p. 17.

[19] *New York Evening Journal*, Oct. 13, 1905, p. 13. Hearst also attacked Charles Murphy for paying only $1.33 per day to workmen employed by his construction companies. This exposé was to be a late campaign bombshell. See *New York Evening Journal*, Nov. 2, 1905, p. 3.

and he promised unequaled enforcement of the labor laws within the city.[20]

When the female starch workers in Troy, New York, struck in late September 1905, the editor of the *New York Journal* quickly appeared before a strikers' meeting to offer a special edition of his newspaper in their behalf. Twenty-five thousand copies would be sold at ten cents per copy, with all the proceeds to go to the strikers. In addition, an appeal for funds would be made in the regular issues of the Hearst press. When this special edition reached the newsstands, the New York Women's Trade Union League, which was aiding the strikers, thanked Hearst for the funds and for the publicity produced by his support of the strikers.[21] Hearst had no doubt of the political value of this action in Troy nor did it mark a departure from his previous record: he had supported other strikes in the past, though often with moral encouragement only. Even token support was so unlike the antilabor tone of other newspapers and magazines that it had gained for Hearst the reputation of being pro-labor. To capitalize on this reputation became the main objective of his campaign.

Hearst was so successful in building the image of social reform about his campaign that even the Socialist Party feared his effect upon its own election total. The municipal ownership plank had an attraction for right-wing socialists who voted the Party's ticket on account of a vague feeling that some social reorganization was necessary rather than because of a commitment either to Marxian theory or to extensive socialization. Some workers voted Socialist as a protest, but now Hearst not only embodied the protest motif in himself, but was making a serious run for office. The Socialist Party admitted that Hearst had appeal as a reformer, and that he was a more satisfactory alternative than the old parties or fusion forces for middle-class individuals who

[20] *New York Evening Journal*, Oct. 14, 1905, p. 9; Oct. 18, 1905, p. 15.
[21] New York Women's Trade Union League, Papers: Executive Board Minutes, Sept. 29, 1905; Oct. 26, 1905.

wanted social reform. However, the Socialists attacked Hearst as a danger to the working class, arguing that he could not accomplish his reforms since the Municipal Ownership League did not have a full ticket of aldermen. Hearst's attacks on Tammany were questioned since he generally had supported the Hall until 1905. His program for public ownership of utilities ended, according to the Socialists, where their reforms would have begun.[22] Hearst thus threatened to lead the more radical vote among the workers to an unproductive dead end.

These fears among Socialists about Hearst's effect on their vote indicate the tremendous impact he had had upon all segments of working-class opinion. As a proponent of immediate social reform, as a representative of the poorer and weaker classes against the moneyed, influential few, Hearst gained the workers' support; and the details of his program, or the fact that as mayor he would lack the machinery to implement it, mattered little in comparison with the strange sight of a man running for an important office in New York City who seemed to represent the lower middle and working classes.

Hearst's campaign forced Tammany to place more of an emphasis on its own labor record, and the Hall had to work hard to hold its supporters. A Public Ownership League which had been formed in 1899 suddenly entered the campaign during its late stages to support Mayor McClellan. This League supposedly represented "the sentiments of organized labor in a large degree."[23] Its appearance during the campaign was reminiscent of the activities of the Workingmen's Political League of New York during the years 1897–1901: the latter organization also had revived at election time with just enough energy to support Tammany before expiring. Tammany tried to counter Hearst's attacks on its labor record by charging that the printers in his employ were treated more poorly than on other dailies.

[22] The Socialist Party, *Should Wage-Earners Vote for Hearst?* (pamphlet), 1905.

[23] *New York Times*, Nov. 3, 1905, p. 2.

Despite considerable support for Hearst among labor leaders, the Central Federated Union did not endorse him formally. The universal opinion that Hearst could not win made the C.F.U. hesitant about antagonizing the Tammany administration by open support of its bitter opponent in the election. Following open opposition to Tammany in the election of 1899, the relations between the C.F.U. and the Democratic government of Mayor Van Wyck had hit an all-time low. Thus despite the extremely strong support Hearst gained among labor leaders, he did not have the formal endorsement of their central body.

To an unparalleled degree, the campaign of 1905 focused on issues directly related to the working class, and on an appeal for the laborer's vote. Hearst won a great tactical victory by forcing Tammany to abandon the generalities of most campaigns and to battle it out on such specific issues as municipal ownership and enforcement of the labor law. The Hall was vulnerable in these areas, but no recent opponent had made enough of an impact on Tammany's working-class supporters to force the Democrats to defend their labor record within the city. Hearst presented the positive alternative of social reform, and the voting results show his effect upon the working-class vote and upon Tammany Hall.

Although the official voting figures show that McClellan beat Hearst by a margin of 3,474 in a total vote of approximately 609,000, students of Hearst's career agree that the election was stolen from him by the Democratic machine.[24] Hearst contested the election in the courts, and from subsequent testimony it appeared that ballot boxes had been dumped into the river, and that an extraordinary number of floaters and imported men had voted the Tammany ticket. Several minor officials were imprisoned because of these frauds, but the election was not

[24] John K. Winkler, *William Randolph Hearst* (New York, 1955), p. 143; Lundberg, *Imperial Hearst*, p. 103. The final official totals were McClellan 228,397; Hearst 224,923; Ivins (Republican) 137,193; Lee (Socialist) 11,817. That the Socialist vote dropped 30 per cent below the total of 1903 indicates the effect of Hearst's campaign.

voided. The circumstances of 1905, however, led to the requirement of a personal signature on registration and voting lists to prevent the impersonation of voters by ineligible hirelings.[25]

Contemporary observers substantially agreed in their evaluation of the surprising vote for Hearst in the election of 1905. One large group of supporters came from the lower middle class.[26] A second group voted for Hearst as a protest against the political machines, and it included the persistently independent voter who in 1901 and 1903 had favored Seth Low. Finally, large numbers of working-class voters left their traditional Democratic moorings to vote for Hearst's ticket. *Harper's Weekly* noted disparagingly that "direct self-interest was at the bottom of Mr. Hearst's campaign." He offered higher wages to the street cleaners, shorter hours to the streetcar workers, and something for everybody in the "East Side horde." [27] *The Independent*, which was more sympathetic to the Municipal Ownership ticket, concluded that "Mr. Hearst's strength at present is found mainly among the workingmen." [28] A leading Republican agreed: "There is no doubt that many who voted for Mr. Hearst felt that he was trying to do something for the so-called 'common man' in whom the old parties seemed to have little interest." [29] An examination of the election figures substantiates these judgments concerning Hearst's appeal to the working-class voter.

The sixteen Assembly districts below Fourteenth Street in

[25] Winkler, *Hearst*, p. 143.

[26] George B. McClellan, Jr., *The Gentleman and the Tiger: The Autobiography of George B. McClellan, Jr.* (New York, 1956), p. 226; "Election in New York City," *The Independent*, LIX (Nov. 16, 1905), 1178.

[27] *Harper's Weekly*, XLIX (Nov. 18, 1905), 1656.

[28] "Politics in New York," *The Independent*, LXI (Aug. 9, 1906), 341.

[29] William Prendergast's comment as found in McClellan, *The Gentleman and the Tiger*, p. 226. For a discussion of Hearst's appeal to lower-middle-class and working-class voters, by two authors who believe his methods, philosophy, and political appeal were essentially fascistic, see Oliver Carlson and Ernest S. Bates, *Hearst, Lord of San Simeon* (New York, 1936), pp. 136ff.

Manhattan were a major source of Tammany's power. These teeming working-class tenement districts gave Tammany large majorities in election after election. Low had failed to carry any of these districts in 1897, and in his successful campaign of 1901 he had managed to win in only one of them. By contrast, Hearst carried five of the sixteen in 1905, polling 38,804 votes compared to McClellan's 47,459. The Republican candidate, William M. Ivins, lagged far behind with 15,961. McClellan's vote had dropped 28 per cent from the 66,418 given him by these districts in 1903, while the Republican vote fell 50 per cent from the fusion total of 1903. In some of the sixteen districts, the Republican total was 66 to 75 per cent below Low's fusion totals in 1903. McClellan's losses were spaced more evenly throughout the area.

The large vote for Hearst is the more remarkable since he did not have the benefit of fusion, which would have brought all the Republican votes into his column. The low Republican totals throughout the city indicate that many independent voters supported Hearst because of his continuation of the battle against the Tammany machine. But this is not the entire explanation for the drop in Republican votes. Although some Republicans may have supported Hearst because of the Municipal Ownership League's backing of G.O.P. candidates for assemblyman and alderman, many Republicans committed the almost inconceivable political act of voting for McClellan. Hearst's call for municipal ownership had produced frenzied conservative opposition. It was feared that such radical campaigns might lead to basic reforms in the city, something Tammany could be counted upon not to support. The thoroughly conservative and previously anti-Tammany *New York Times* thus called for Republicans to support McClellan, since it saw Tammany government as the lesser of two evils.[30] The movement of Republicans into the Democratic ranks can be best seen in the strong G.O.P. districts of upper Manhattan. Here the margin by which

[30] *New York Times*, Nov. 1, 1905, p. 8.

McClellan lost was far narrower, as compared with his totals in 1903, than in the Democratic areas of the city. Many Republicans deserted Ivins, who had no chance in the three-man race, to make certain that Hearst did not win the election.[31] The same thing undoubtedly occurred in predominantly Democratic districts as well, and thus the loss of Democratic votes to Hearst was greater than the raw figures indicate. The Tammany totals were swelled by the strange presence of conservative Republicans who under normal circumstances would have shuddered at the thought of voting the Democratic ticket. Also, it must be remembered that Hearst's totals were lower than they should have been because of the vote frauds.

It can be safely surmised that much of the Democratic total in the first through the sixteenth Assembly districts were working-class votes, and thus the loss of Democratic votes to Hearst must have meant that many workers left Tammany's ranks to support the Municipal Ownership League. McClellan's losses were not confined to a few of these districts—as they might have been if a specific immigrant group or local leader had had an unusual affinity for the independent candidate—but were consistent from district to district, revealing that the appeal of Hearst to the working class reached into all the national groups populating the area.

In other parts of the city McClellan's totals were also far below the usual Democratic vote. The Brooklyn Democratic organization, led by State Senator Patrick McCarren, was not nearly as strong as Tammany Hall. Considering the results in Tammany's Manhattan districts, it is no surprise that Hearst carried Brooklyn, while McClellan lost one-third of the total he had received in 1903. Ten of the twenty-one Assembly districts in Brooklyn gave pluralities to Hearst. Again the voters for

[31] This trend in the vote was noted, after the election, in "The Rout of the Bosses in New York," *The Outlook*, LXXXI (Nov. 18, 1905), 633; and "The New York Election," *American Monthly Review of Reviews*, XXXII (Dec. 1905), 644. The voting figures bear out this analysis.

McClellan included some Republicans who ordinarily would not favor a Democrat, and thus the percentage of Democratic voters who switched to Hearst was actually even higher. The borough of Queens also went to Hearst by a margin of 500 in a total vote of 33,000.[32] In the less homogeneous Assembly districts of Brooklyn and Queens, it is much more difficult to discover which groups of voters supported Hearst; but his winning totals in both boroughs indicate widespread support in all areas, and one can conclude that his supporters were not greatly different in kind from those in Manhattan. Hearst had appealed to the lower middle class and the working class by his attacks on the entrenched wealth and power represented in the trusts and political machines, and by his promise to return government to the people. He had truly "come, in the minds of a great mass of poor men, to stand for the rights of the poor,"[33] and they swung to his support with a vengeance.

Not since Henry George's campaign of 1886 had there been so massive a defection of working-class voters from Tammany Hall. Hearst was able to do what organized labor could not: he changed the labor vote from its traditional Tammany, straight-ticket pattern. The election indicates most clearly that trade unions in New York City, as elsewhere in the United States, were not viewed as political bodies in any sense, and their efforts to influence the workers' votes often caused as much suspicion as enthusiasm. The term "labor fakir" was used widely in this period to describe the union leader who entered politics under the guise of serving the interests of organized labor, but who soon became nothing more than another party politician, anxious for all the perquisites of political office, and often short in memory when the demands of organized labor conflicted with the dictates of party policy.

Hearst did not lay claim to the workers' votes because of his

[32] For complete, official election figures of the 1905 election see *The City Record* (Supplement, Feb. 1906).

[33] *The World's Work*, XI (April 1906), 7364.

class position; instead he emerged as the *representative* of the little man. His newspapers proved this day after day, and many voters were convinced that if he could be elected, the energy of destructive attack would be converted to constructive reform. Hearst's parties, whatever their name or program, were all one: Hearst. Without him, municipal ownership or any other program of reform meant little. He reached the working class through an emotional and sensational campaign, and his success proved how fallacious it was to regard the working-class vote as stolidly machine-bound. The worker in New York City voted for Tammany because it had given more attention to his interests, and had recognized his existence as a person more fully than any other political group. Yet the election of 1905 proved that an attractive alternative—one demanding not only honesty in government but also a more basic honesty in the social organization—could attract large numbers of workers. Fusion campaigns, guided by the wealthy; independent labor campaigns, directed by a small number of union leaders; Socialist campaigns, based on promises of a perfect society in the future —all failed to offset the traditions and everyday activities of the Tammany machine in New York. It took a Henry George or a William Randolph Hearst—a man of personal magnetism, with a positive promise of social reform implicit in himself—to arouse the worker. Anything less did not succeed.

Although Hearst originally contested the voting irregularities in the courts, he made no real effort to win a reversal of the election.[34] By early 1906, Hearst realized that greener fields might await him, since the contest for the governorship came up in a nonpresidential year. The Republican administration had been marred by a widely publicized investigation of the ties between politicians and the state's leading insurance companies. Hearst planned to make full use of his proved ability to win working-class votes, and he thus continued to support organized labor within New York City.

[34] *New York Times*, March 13, 1906, p. 3.

The Municipal Ownership League, now renamed the Independence League, supported organized labor's demands for passage of the eight-hour-day and prevailing-wage bills for public works. It also called for municipal ownership, direct nominations, ballot reform, and a pure food bill.[35] In the dispute that developed between the Workingmen's Federation and the C.F.U. over the exact form of the eight-hour-day bill, Hearst gave unqualified support to the C.F.U.[36] Clearly Hearst was relying on the continued support of New York City's labor leaders in any campaign he might make for the governorship, and thus he gave them his full support even though it might alienate the upstate labor leaders who controlled the Workingmen's Federation.

Shortly after Hearst had become interested in the race for the governorship, organized labor in New York City began to prepare for the same election. In 1906 the A.F.L. recommended that organized labor take a more active interest in electing its friends and defeating its enemies. The A.F.L. statement merely reinforced the traditional policy of the national labor federation, but New York City labor groups used it as a convenient basis for demanding independent political action within the state. The Brooklyn Central Labor Union referred specifically to the Bill of Grievances issued by the executive committee of the A.F.L. in March 1906 as the basis for its demand that organized labor set up an independent state organization to direct political action.[37] The Central Federated Union also used A.F.L. policy as justification for a June 18 resolution urging the organization of an independent political movement. The central bodies linked their call for independent political action to statements by the A.F.L. in an effort to quiet opposition to this policy. One body of delegates opposed all political efforts, while a much larger group still remembered the fiasco of 1899 and insisted that such

[35] *New York Times*, Feb. 19, 1906, p. 18.
[36] See Chapter II, p. 29.
[37] *New York Times*, March 26, 1906, p. 7.

independent action only weakened the trade unions as a political force.[38]

Hearst realized that a majority within the C.F.U. favored his candidacy, and thus he did not attempt to block an independent political movement. The C.F.U. soon announced the formation of a new political organization, again named the Independent Labor Party. This time the Party did not restrict its membership to unionists initially, as it had in 1899, or make a pretense of running a completely independent race; instead, the I.L.P. had an option to endorse other independent candidates "who fully subscribed to the platform in cases where nomination of candidates by the labor party is deemed inadvisable."[39] Labor candidates might also accept the endorsement of other political parties.[40] The provision allowing endorsement of labor candidates by other parties offered Hearst the opportunity to place unionists on his ticket in exchange for the support of the I.L.P. Thus the Independent Labor Party of 1906 was basically a workingmen's political league, like the organization of 1899. It sought to have as many labor men nominated as possible, and it was virtually committed to support of a Hearst ticket should he accept unionists.

However, the Brooklyn Central Labor Union quickly attacked this plan. Hearst's support here was even stronger than in the C.F.U., and it had been cemented by promises that important Brooklyn labor leaders would be nominated on his ticket. Thus the I.L.P.'s objective already had been secured by the Brooklyn Central Labor Union, and they saw no reason to join the new party.

Hearst had placed unionists on his Brooklyn ticket so quickly because he intended to run an independent ticket for all Assembly seats and borough offices. The Brooklyn Democratic machine already had opposed any alliance with Hearst on a state

[38] *New York Times*, June 18, 1906, p. 4.
[39] *New York Times*, Aug. 6, 1906, p. 2.
[40] *New York Times*, July 16, 1906, p. 2.

ticket. Tammany Hall, however, had said nothing. Hearst realized that a state race as an independent would mean certain defeat for the Democrats, since he would draw away much of their support; but it also offered little promise for his own success against the strong Republican Party vote upstate. Thus in an extraordinary about-face, Hearst began to negotiate with Charles Murphy and the Tammany organization he had reviled so mercilessly in 1905. Murphy faced the unpleasant choice of either accepting Hearst as candidate for governor or surely losing in a three-way race.[41]

Murphy made the choice and swallowed his pride in hopes of winning against the scandal-ridden Republican administration: Hearst would be the Democratic nominee for governor. Tammany, however, placed its trusted men on the Democratic ticket for positions such as that of state engineer, with control over 101 million dollars in barge canal expenditures, plus another 50 million dollars in road-building contracts.[42] It also seemed clear that the Hall would demand Hearst's support for its entire ticket of state senators and assemblymen in Manhattan.[43]

The probability of Hearst's nomination by the Tammany-controlled state Democratic convention produced consternation among his adherents in the Independence League, many of whom were renegade Democrats. These men demanded that Hearst also run as an independent, and they especially opposed any support of Democrats running for assemblyman and for local offices, since they expected Independence League nominations for these positions.[44] Hearst accepted the Independence League's nomination for governor, as well as that of the Democrats, and announced his intention to support a full independent ticket down to the Assembly and local levels. However, the

---

[41] "The Political Muddle in New York," *Harper's Weekly*, L (Aug. 11, 1906), 1124.

[42] *New York World*, Nov. 9, 1906, p. 2.

[43] *New York Times*, Sept. 30, 1906, p. 4.

[44] *New York Times*, Sept. 12, 1906, p. 2.

alliance with Tammany cast ominous shadows over this possibility.

The threat posed by Hearst led the Republicans to nominate Charles Evans Hughes, who had been the chief investigator in the insurance scandals.[45] Hughes's candidacy successfully divorced the gubernatorial campaign from the scandals of the Republican administration.

As it became clear that the Democrats would nominate Hearst for governor, Independent Labor Party leaders began to worry whether Hearst would include large numbers of labor men on his ticket in the face of Tammany's demands for these spots. Twice during the month of September, I.L.P. leaders indicated that the labor party's support of Hearst was not automatic, but that it was dependent on Hearst's intention to "champion the cause of organized labor." [46] As late as the first week in October, Hearst promised the leaders of the I.L.P. that he would have a substantial number of labor men on the ticket, and the Labor Party even nominated these men, expecting Hearst to have at least the Independence League, if not Tammany, follow suit. However, Hearst reneged at the last moment, turning down the labor nominees after having received full publicity value from the reports that he would accept the I.L.P. candidates.

The chairman of the Independent Labor Party made these disclosures before the October 14, 1906, meeting of the C.F.U., and he declared that Hearst had played a deceitful role from the time of his agreement with Murphy concerning the Democratic nomination for governor. He charged that a deal had been arranged in which Hearst was to scuttle his Independence League's nominations for the Assembly, the State Senate, and local offices so that Tammany's candidates could win easily.[47]

[45] *Harper's Weekly*, L (Nov. 17, 1906), 1627.
[46] *New York Times*, Sept. 7, 1906, p. 4; Sept. 24, 1906, p. 16.
[47] *New York Times*, Oct. 15, 1906, p. 2.

Organized labor had to be sacrificed—and it was. Another I.L.P. leader later asserted that Hearst originally had promised the Labor Party a judgeship and eighteen Assembly nominations.[48]

The Independent Labor Party had attempted to achieve the election of unionists by working through a Hearst ticket where labor candidates might have a chance for victory. However, Hearst clearly valued the support of Tammany Hall more than that of the I.L.P., and thus he sabotaged the plans for labor representation on his Independence League slate. The election of 1905 had revealed clearly that Hearst, and not the labor leaders, influenced a significant section of the working-class vote. Lacking anything to offer, politically, labor received nothing.

The events that followed the I.L.P.'s charges against Hearst seemed to prove the existence of the deal with Tammany. Many of the district organizations of the Independence League in Manhattan nominated candidates, including some unionists, to oppose Tammany's slate. Hearst gave these efforts no encouragement, and the Tammany-dominated Board of Elections threw out most of the Independence League's nominating petitions on technicalities. In Brooklyn, however, where Tammany favored a weakening of McCarren's Democratic organization, every Independence League candidate was approved.[49] In addition, Tammany leaders in several districts gained control of the Independence League organizations—again without Hearst's objection—and they circulated nominating petitions under the Independence League's label as well as that of the Democrats. The Board of Elections accepted most of these petitions while it ordered the truly independent candidates off the ballot.

The final result of these events was that the entire Brooklyn Independence League slate remained intact to oppose McCarren's choices for the Assembly and for local office, whereas in almost every predominantly Democratic Assembly district of

[48] *New York Times*, Nov. 1, 1906, p. 3.
[49] *New York Times*, Oct. 24, 1906, pp. 1, 3.

Manhattan the Independence League candidate was a Tammany man, or the League's choice had been invalidated.[50] By election day there was no substantial independent opposition to Tammany, and although Hearst was technically the candidate of the Democrats and the Independence League, the latter organization functioned so as not to tread on the Hall's toes. In this decimation of the Independence League's ticket, most of the men favored by the I.L.P. had fallen.

Once the prospective alliance with Hearst collapsed, the Independent Labor Party had no reason for continuing to function. At its October 13 meeting, the I.L.P. resolved that "when the unions organized as a political party they were under the impression that other independent organizations existed so that they could meet and confer with a view to harmonizing on a ticket, but finding that no 'other independent party existed' the labor unions intended to take no active part in the campaign of 1906." [51] The deal between Murphy and Hearst had ended all possibilities that the Independent Labor Party might cooperate with Hearst.

On the following night, at the C.F.U. meeting, the Labor Party's decision to disband for the year was approved after the leaders of the I.L.P. bitterly assailed Hearst's political integrity.[52] In the week following, Republicans used these events to prove that organized labor did not support Hearst, nor vice versa. Republicans announced throughout the state that the C.F.U. had condemned Hearst because of his break with the I.L.P.[53] In reality, nothing of the kind had occurred. The C.F.U. simply had approved the disbanding of the I.L.P. No resolution embodying the Labor Party's charges against Hearst had been presented, and no vote on this subject had been taken. During the week following the C.F.U.'s meeting on October 14, Hearst

[50] *New York Tribune*, Nov. 1, 1906, p. 2.

[51] *New York World*, Oct. 14, 1906, p. 3.

[52] *New York Times*, Oct. 15, 1906, p. 2.

[53] *The Labor Advocate*, Oct. 26, 1906, p. 1, and *New York Times*, Oct. 18, 1906, p. 3, are examples.

and his labor supporters unleashed a vicious attack upon the critics in the defunct Labor Party, including an unproved contention that the two most vocal opponents of Hearst were paid agents of the Republicans.[54] Despite the I.L.P.'s charges Hearst still had overwhelming support in the labor movement, and at its meeting on October 21, the C.F.U. specifically noted that no action it had taken "could be construed as antagonistic in the slightest degree to the candidacy of the nominee of the State Independence League ticket." [55] This resolution passed 67 to 30 [56]—a vote that roughly indicated the strength of the pro- and anti-Hearst groups.

The C.F.U., however, did not endorse Hearst formally. It was more important for the C.F.U. to be neutral than to endorse him, since his appeal to the workers of the state was greater than that of any candidate within memory. Thus the crucial decision was the refusal of the C.F.U. to entertain any resolutions condemning Hearst for his dealings with the I.L.P. The central body saw no reason to make a specific political commitment when the same objective could be obtained by a less definite action. Accordingly, at a meeting of the C.F.U. on October 28, a prominent supporter of Hearst ruled a motion specifically endorsing the publisher to be out of order. He declared that the central labor body had given all political responsibility for 1906 to the I.L.P., and that the disbanding of the Labor Party therefore ended all direct political involvement by the C.F.U.[57]

Clearly the breakdown of the I.L.P.'s efforts to win spots for unionists on the Hearst ticket did not end the support for him even in the central body most directly concerned. It had almost no effect on the widespread support for Hearst among labor leaders and workers elsewhere in the state. The Brooklyn Central Labor Union formally endorsed Hearst shortly after the

[54] *New York Evening Journal*, Oct. 17, 1906, p. 5; *New York World*, Oct. 21, 1906, p. 3.

[55] *New York Times*, Oct. 22, 1906, p. 1.

[56] *New York World*, Oct. 22, 1906, p. 3.

[57] *New York Times*, Oct. 29, 1906, p. 5.

Labor Party's leaders attacked him,[58] and one of Hearst's bitterest enemies admitted rather ruefully that despite his support of Tammany Hall, and his double-crossing of the I.L.P., he had overwhelming labor support.[59] The reports from upstate also indicated that Hearst was running well among working-class voters. The *New York World* reported that in Erie County "the preponderance of the vote of the workingmen will be for Hearst especially in the cities and the mill towns, but it will not be solidly Hearst." [60] In the Rochester area, Hearst was stronger in the cities and towns than any Democrat in years, despite the opposition of conservative upstate Democrats.[61] Hearst also had widespread support in other upstate cities and towns with large working-class populations, despite strenuous efforts by the Republicans to hold these areas.[62]

A pre-election poll in the strongly Democratic, predominantly working-class lower East Side of New York City gave Hearst 418 ballots and Hughes 317. Of the Hearst supporters, 182 had voted for him in 1905, 165 had voted for McClellan and 30 for Ivins, and 31 had not voted. Even this small sample indicates that Hearst needed the Democratic endorsement if he was to be more than a spoiler in the gubernatorial election. Without the 165 Democratic voters who had supported McClellan against him in 1905, Hearst could not hope to beat Hughes in New York City by a margin wide enough to offset the large rural Republican vote throughout the state. Hughes's support came from 123 voters who had supported Ivins in 1905, 52 who had voted for Hearst, 17 who had not voted, and—most significantly—125 who had supported McClellan.[63] This defec-

[58] *New York American*, Oct. 22, 1906, p. 2.

[59] *New York Times*, Nov. 1, 1906, p. 4.

[60] *New York World*, Oct. 29, 1906, p. 5.

[61] *New York World*, Oct. 30, 1906, p. 5.

[62] *New York Times*, Oct. 23, 1906, p. 5; *New York World*, Oct. 31, 1906, p. 3.

[63] *New York World*, Oct. 31, 1906, p. 4. The Hearst total also included ten voters who had supported splinter groups in 1905.

tion among Democratic voters, who should have favored Hearst, was quite unexpected. Even though the poll was small and hardly scientific in its sampling, the election figures bore out its results.

Evidence before the 1906 election thus indicated that Hearst continued to attract the working-class vote. He became very popular upstate despite open hostility from many leaders of the Workingmen's Federation. They had not forgotten Hearst's attack upon the Federation during the legislative session of 1906. At the convention of the Workingmen's Federation in September 1906, the elections for officers were contested—a rare event since this matter usually was arranged by a private caucus. Supporters of Hearst led this opposition to the incumbent leaders, but their ticket was defeated by a wide margin.[64] A resolution endorsing Hearst was presented to the resolutions committee, but was then withdrawn,[65] obviously to avoid the embarrassment of a defeat. One Federation vice president was credited with preventing the endorsement of Hearst by the Syracuse Trades Assembly. Another vice president attacked Hearst in Schenectady, where the Democratic candidate had attracted strong working-class support. Officers of the Federation organized a Workingmen's State Political League to oppose Hearst in upstate areas.[66] Thus Hearst faced the opposition of important labor leaders upstate, yet all reports indicated that workers were supporting him in unprecedented numbers.

Hearst's popularity among workers upstate made it possible for him to duplicate there his performance a year earlier in New York City. Even the alliance with the Tammany machine could not sully thus unusual personal prestige. Hearst attracted the labor voter because he was so much the exception in New York politics. He based his campaign on an appeal to the interests of the worker and the lower middle class, and there were no fail-

[64] *Workingmen's Federation of the State of New York, Proceedings,* 1906, p. 54.

[65] *Official Record,* Nov. 1906, p. 1.

[66] See *The Labor Advocate,* Oct. 26, 1906, pp. 1–8, for a description of anti-Hearst activities by labor leaders in upstate New York.

ures in execution to mar the promises of social and political reform. In upstate areas, traditional voting patterns had been least powerful in local elections when specific issues touched upon the worker's interests. In state elections the party label usually had been the important factor. Hearst changed this, for he stood above party to an unparalleled degree; and his reputation as a social reform candidate brought conservative Democrats into Hughes's camp just as it led Republican workingmen to vote the Democratic line.

The Hearst press played an important part in the campaign, just as it had in 1905. A friend of the Tammany congressman William Cockran warned that he should not discount attacks upon his record by the *New York American*. "It exerts more political power than any dozen other papers put together. . . . There is no doubt that this paper appeals very strongly to the great mass of wage earners, and to the vast mob of foreign born citizens in whom socialistic ideals are strong, and who have innate class-prejudices. The *American* has become the printed protest of the poor against the rich." [67] Hearst's papers naturally edited the news so that it would aid his campaign, and like most of the newspapers of the period, they indulged heavily in endorsements, real and faked, incomplete news articles which often completely misrepresented the facts and exaggerated accounts of political support.[68]

Hearst attained his campaign objectives, for he won the votes of many Republican workingmen upstate, and held a good part of his support in New York City—yet he lost the election by

[67] William Bourke Cockran Papers (New York Public Library): Letter file, April 10, 1906.

[68] As an example see the *New York American*'s report of the hectic October 14, 1906, meeting of the C.F.U., at which the Independent Labor Party's leaders vehemently attacked Hearst. The *American*'s readers learned nothing of this from an article which stressed only one aspect of the meeting and thus by omission produced a completely misleading account. Cf. *New York American*, Oct. 15, 1906, p. 5, with other newspapers of that date.

55,000 votes. The rest of the Democratic state ticket won. Murphy and Pat McCarren had been successful in their separate efforts to damage the official Democratic candidate. Hearst had a margin of 4,563 votes in Brooklyn while the rest of the ticket won by from 35,000 to 39,000 votes.[69] His poor showing resulted from a split ticket voted by the better-disciplined members of McCarren's machine, who supported the whole Democratic ticket with the exception of Hearst.

Murphy had swallowed much of his pride when he approved Hearst as Democratic nominee for governor after the vicious personal attacks upon him by the Hearst press in 1905. The results of the election in Manhattan and the Bronx reveal clearly why the Tammany leader accepted such humiliation. In the final days before the election, rumor had it that Hearst would have a very small margin in Tammany's districts.[70] Like the McCarren organization, the Tammany machine gave full support to the Democratic ticket, which included a great majority of the Hall's men, while knifing Hearst.[71] Thus the Democratic ticket ran up margins of from 87,000 to 90,000 in Manhattan and the Bronx, but Hearst had an edge over Hughes of only 63,312 votes. Tammany used Hearst's great popularity to attract votes for the entire Democratic slate, but by then knifing Hearst, it brought about the defeat of the only man on the ticket whom the Hall did not control. Hearst had allied himself with Tammany to gain substantial machine support; yet in effect the machine gained needed support from him.

Despite Hearst's defeat, it is evident that he had attracted working-class and lower-middle-class voters who once again broke their traditional voting patterns. Hearst won in important upstate cities and cut Republican majorities in others. He carried Buffalo, Syracuse, Rochester, and Troy. In Schenectady and Albany the Republican machine of State Senator William Barnes

[69] *New York Times*, Nov. 7, 1906, pp. 1–3.
[70] *New York World*, Nov. 4, 1906, p. 2.
[71] *The World To-Day*, XI (Dec. 1906), 1236.

spent large sums of money and held control of the vote.[72] In Troy, where Hearst won by 200 votes, as compared with a Republican victory by 4,000 in the presidential election of 1904, the stanchly Republican *New York Tribune* concluded, "The defection is due to the labor vote," [73] Thus important upstate cities turned to the Democrats, as had been predicted, and without doubt a great part of this shift was the product of Hearst's breakthrough in the Republican working-class vote. If Hearst had not been knifed by the Brooklyn and Tammany machines, he would have won the election as the rest of his ticket did.

Moreover, Hearst gained his large vote in the upstate cities against a very popular Republican candidate who also claimed to be a reformer, and who had the active support of Theodore Roosevelt. Hughes's reform program, however, was essentially another of the Mugwump variety, and unlike Theodore Roosevelt he made few public pronouncements on social reforms, even those he favored. Hughes was a strong Republican candidate who held the rural vote, and a good part of the traditional middle-class Republican support; but without the aid of the New York machines he would have been defeated.

Further evidence of Hearst's popularity appeared in Brooklyn, where he ran independent candidates against the Democratic machine. The Independence League entered candidates in five of the six congressional races, and although it won none of these, 26 per cent of the voters supported the Independence League's nominees. Out of the eighteen State Assembly races which the Independence League contested, Hearst's candidate was elected in one—with a unionist as the nominee—while in three other districts the Independence League votes produced a victory for the Republicans. In six of the eight Assembly districts carried by the Democrats, Hearst's party ran second, cutting significantly into the usual Democratic margin. The Independence League's candidates ran behind the Democrats in all but one of the nine

[72] *New York World*, Nov. 7, 1906, pp. 1–2.
[73] *New York Tribune*, Nov. 7, 1906, p. 2.

Assembly districts captured by the Republicans; but they averaged a strong 21 per cent of the vote as compared with 30 per cent for the Democrats. These totals represent Hearst's minimum strength, since many persons voted for him on the Democratic line and then continued a straight-ticket vote, thus aiding the McCarren machine at the lower levels. In all, the performance of the Independence League in these races is exceptional, and it represents further proof of the appeal of a vital social-reform alternative to the traditional parties.

The election of 1906 marked the height of Hearst's political career. In succeeding years he remained a powerful political force in New York State, though not a serious contender for any office. The years 1905 and 1906 were also the high point of political independence for the working-class voters of the state: no independent candidates, including the Progressives in 1912, changed the voting habits of workers so sharply. Hearst's honesty and sincerity as a person, the demagogic quality of his appeal, and the feasibility of his reform program, had he been able to win election, are all open to debate,[74] but his unrivaled ability to win a significant independent vote is beyond doubt.

[74] There is no complete, authoritative biography of Hearst. Carlson and Bates, in *Hearst, Lord of San Simeon*, attempt to analyze Hearst's motives and political appeal. They conclude that his career is essentially that of an American fascist. Both this volume and Lundberg, *Imperial Hearst*, were written in the 1930's, when fascism presented a serious threat to democratic ideals, and when Hearst's political activities were quite different from his actions during the Progressive years. Lundberg, in particular, writes more in the tone of a New Dealer attacking the obstructionist Hearst of the 1930's than as a candid observer of his subject's long career. At the other extreme is Mrs. Fremont Older, *William Randolph Hearst, American* (New York, 1936), a laudatory and purely descriptive account. Winkler, *William Randolph Hearst*, also lacks any real analysis of the man or his significance. W. A. Swanberg, *Citizen Hearst* (New York, 1961), is the newest biography. It is not definitive, but it does attempt to give a balanced portrait of this enigmatic figure.

X

The Continuing Political Involvement
of Organized Labor, 1907-1916

IN 1906 the A.F.L. launched an intensified campaign of political action. Its leaders hoped the final result would be more effective reward and punishment, plus an increased number of unionists in Congress. The press quickly attacked the A.F.L.'s increased emphasis on political action, and many editors predicted that this would be the first step toward a United States counterpart of the British Labour Party. A few observers, however, opposed this view; and they correctly interpreted the statements of the A.F.L. as an effort to unite labor behind its friends in the old parties, and as a restatement of the long-established policy of electing unionists to office on the major party tickets.[1] This new step merely sought to increase the effectiveness of the A.F.L.'s old policy: organized labor must be beholden to no political organization, be it an established party or an independent one; instead, labor should seek to use its voting potential in a unified manner for effective reward and punishment.

If the increased political action was not a new departure, it most certainly was a significant intensification of a basic dogma of the A.F.L., which had become inactive on the national scene. State and city labor bodies, however, had applied the principles of reward and punishment and the election of unionists much more widely, although with only limited success. It is thus not unexpected that the A.F.L.'s intensification of political action

[1] "Labor Unions in Politics," *The Independent*, LX (May 3, 1906), 1050.

should have acted as a spur to the Workingmen's Federation of New York. The increased scope of the Federation's activities became clear the very next year.

The courts of New York struck down several important labor laws as unconstitutional during the early years of this century. The state labor body's objections to these decisions reached a climax in 1907, when the New York Court of Appeals, in *Williams vs. New York*, upset the decade-old law prohibiting the employment of women during the hours between 9 P.M. and 6 A.M. The decision, like many others, was based on the violation of individual liberty as a result of the state's improper use of its police powers. The social Progressives and organized labor attacked the obstructive role of the courts in the area of social reform, and the Workingmen's Federation sought to have pro-labor men nominated by the major parties for the two places on the New York Court of Appeals that were to come up for election in 1907. After several meetings had indicated support from key central bodies, the Federation demanded that the major parties select William Gaynor and John McDonough as their candidates.[2] Gaynor had a reputation as a crusader against municipal corruption, and had spoken favorably of the need for labor reforms. In 1909 he was elected mayor of New York City on the Democratic ticket. McDonough had done legal work for the Workingmen's Federation and the social Progressive organizations. Both men had served as judges in lower New York courts.

Hearst's Independence League nominated McDonough,[3] but the Republicans and Democrats completely ignored the Federation's demands, and selected their candidates, as usual, according to the political necessities of the situation. Hearst's action continued his appeal for the working-class vote. He hoped that the inclusion of McDonough would add strength to the entire In-

[2] *Official Record*, June 1907, p. 1; Dec. 1907, p. 1.
[3] Workingmen's Federation of the State of New York, *Proceedings*, 1908 (no pagination).

dependence League slate, and maintain Hearst's personal political power in New York.

This was the first time that the Workingmen's Federation had seriously interfered in a statewide election. Previously, governors had been rebuked for failing to support labor legislation, but the honor roll and blacklist had included only assemblymen and state senators. Gubernatorial elections appealed much more strongly to the voters' sense of party responsibility. Thus workers who might support an independent effort to elect a unionist as an alderman or assemblyman, or who might ignore party labels in the election of a mayor, usually returned to their traditional voting pattern when selecting a governor or president. The Workingmen's Federation had acknowledged this voting trend by carefully avoiding any position in state or national races. Other groups of voters responded in a similar fashion: the Progressive Party discovered that its candidate for governor of New York in 1912, Oscar Straus, outran Theodore Roosevelt. Many Republicans voted as mavericks in the gubernatorial race to show their opposition to the Party machine in New York, but they refused to end their traditional support of the Republican Party in national elections. In the Assembly contests of 1912, the tendency toward party irregularity was even more marked.

When the Independence League accepted McDonough, the Federation appealed immediately for money from member unions so that it might finance a campaign. The state body's normal financial resources were inadequate for such an undertaking. The response indicated the basic opposition to political action by most local unions, and also the lack of unity in the state labor movement, which so often made decisions of the Federation worthless. Fifty member organizations, including central bodies, contributed a total of $745; and accordingly the campaign for McDonough had to be limited to a mailing to the member unions, and a few speaking tours by the officers.[4] In

4 *Ibid.*

comparison with those of other political groups, the Federation's efforts were ludicrous.

The election figures show that McDonough ran about 7,000 votes ahead of the Independence League's other nominee for the Court of Appeals. The Hearst organization polled 110,000 votes for its candidates as against 906,000 for the two incumbent judges who had been renominated by both Republicans and Democrats. This was a most creditable performance for the Independence League, but McDonough's small margin over Hearst's other judicial nominee indicates that most of his vote came from straight-ticket support given the Independence League. Not many workers specifically crossed from the major parties to support the candidate of the Federation, although a good part of the Hearst organization's total came from labor voters.

The state labor body thus found once again that the major political parties would not recognize its demands when they competed with other political necessities. Neither the Republicans nor the Democrats believed that snubbing the Federation would affect the labor vote materially. The committee of the Workingmen's Federation responsible for the campaign admitted that "the organized workingmen of the state did not do their duty to the Judge [McDonough] or to the Workingmen's Federation, and that a much larger vote should have been given for the nominee." The committee sanguinely added, "We believe that this was largely due to the feeling that running only on the League ticket that his election was impossible." [5]

The A.F.L.'s intensified political program had an even stronger influence on the New York State labor movement during the presidential campaign of 1908. Following the Danbury Hatters decision in 1908, the A.F.L. demanded the equivalent of the British Trade Disputes Act, including the exemption of labor unions from antitrust actions and legal protection for peaceful picketing.[6] The A.F.L. hinted that there would be increased

[5] *Ibid.*   [6] *American Federationist*, March 1908, p. 263.

political opposition to the Republican Party if it did not meet some of labor's demands. However, this threat had little effect: "The majority of the members of Congress, those responsible for legislation or its failure, have turned a deaf ear to both the appeal and the protest which Labor presented." The reaction to this, the A.F.L. asserted, would be that "the workers, the liberty-loving public will stand faithfully by our friends and elect them. They will oppose their enemies and defeat them." [7]

The A.F.L. then presented its demands to the Republican and Democratic conventions, and made it clear that it would support the party that accepted most of labor's program. The Democratic platform proved more satisfactory, and in August 1908 the A.F.L. endorsed the candidacy of William Jennings Bryan,[8] although on lesser levels Democrats were not always supported. The A.F.L.'s executive council denied all charges that it had pledged the labor vote, and reaffirmed the traditional policy of reward-and-punish. Bryan favored key policies of organized labor, whereas the Republican platform indicated that party's hostility to the A.F.L.'s demands. Organized labor would point this out to its members, and to the nation, and then the worker would be free to make his own decision.[9]

The A.F.L.'s endorsement of Bryan merely advanced reward-and-punishment a logical step forward, but it was called a radical move—especially by the Republicans. Following the leadership of the A.F.L., and with the destructive effects of the Danbury Hatters case all too clear, New York State central labor bodies came to the support of the Bryan ticket. Although the Workingmen's Federation and the city central labor councils had been more persistent than the A.F.L. in their political activity, they had never supported a candidate in a presidential election. However, the central labor councils of Buffalo, Utica, Schenectady, Binghamton, and Brooklyn quickly endorsed Bryan.[10] The largest city labor body in the state, the C.F.U., applauded the

[7] Ibid., July 1908, p. 528.   [8] Ibid., Aug. 1908, p. 603.
[9] Ibid., Sept. 1908, pp. 727, 746.   [10] Ibid., Oct. 1908, pp. 879–882.

decision to favor Bryan because of the Democratic convention's action "for protecting organized labor by inserting in their platform a labor recommendation and pledging its support to the same." [11] The C.F.U. also responded to the A.F.L.'s request for contributions, and it followed the national labor body's recommendation for labor rallies by organizing one in New York City during the last few days of the campaign. The Brooklyn Central Labor Union,[12] and other city bodies in the state, took similar action.

The Workingmen's Federation also broke with precedent and approved a $250 contribution to the A.F.L.'s campaign fund, declaring that "we are with him [Gompers] in this fight to oppose and defeat our enemies, whether they be candidates for President, for Congress, or other offices and we will stand faithfully by our friends." [13] Clearly the Workingmen's Federation believed that the A.F.L.'s action continued the old reward-and-punish policy, and thus its support was a logical advance from its position in state politics.

Support for the A.F.L.'s decision to favor Bryan was overwhelming among the state and city central bodies in New York. Only one delegate opposed the State Federation's action, although he asserted that at least fifty others did so privately but had hesitated to intrude on labor unity.[14] With Gompers present at the meeting of the C.F.U., only seven members voted against endorsing Bryan.[15]

The biggest handicap for organized labor's campaign in New York was not the opposition within the central labor bodies, but the lack of active participation by the national unions and their affiliated locals. Although their sympathies undoubtedly rested with Bryan, since the A.F.L. and the state and city central

[11] *New York Times*, Aug. 31, 1908, p. 3.
[12] *New York World*, Oct. 12, 1908, p. 3.
[13] Workingmen's Federation of the State of New York, *Proceedings*, 1908.
[14] *Official Record*, Nov. 1908, p. 2.
[15] *New York World*, Aug. 25, 1908, p. 4.

bodies were composed of their representatives, the national unions did not support him actively. The influence of either the A.F.L. or the C.F.U. was weak in comparison with the power of these national unions. The potentially disruptive effect of partisanship upon their basic economic functions led most national unions to continue their traditional avoidance of direct political activity. With the failure of the local unions to enter the campaign, it was hardly a surprise that Bryan did not carry New York despite the support he had received from the central labor organizations.

Taft carried most of the traditionally Republican upstate cities, and there was no evidence of a labor vote cutting into his margins. Taft even won traditionally Democratic New York City by 9,000 votes. Before the election there had been rumors that Tammany would knife Bryan in New York City,[16] and the low vote for the Democratic candidate in Manhattan seemed proof that the Hall had not worked strongly for the national ticket. Bryan also ran poorly in Democratic areas of Brooklyn. It was charged that the Democratic leader Patrick McCarren had made a deal with the Brooklyn Republican organization in which he agreed to reduce Bryan's vote if the Republicans would cut Hughes's vote in the gubernatorial race.[17] In addition, Hearst had a personal objection to Bryan, and he leveled a typically emotional and sensational attack upon the Democratic ticket. This reached the very voters who ordinarily would have voted for Bryan. Several labor leaders in New York City agreed that there had been no sign of a strong labor vote for Bryan,[18] and this situation, aggravated by the knifing of the national ticket by Tammany and McCarren, had led to his loss of the city.

Organized labor in New York also gave strong support to the

[16] *New York Evening Call,* Oct. 7, 1908, p. 1; *New York Times,* Oct. 27, 1908, p. 4. Bryan ran only 10,000 votes ahead of Taft in the Tammany strongholds of Manhattan and the Bronx.

[17] *New York Times,* Nov. 5, 1908, p. 3.

[18] *New York World,* Nov. 5, 1908, p. 6.

incumbent Democratic candidate for secretary of state, John S. Whalen, a unionist who had won election in the Democratic victory of 1906. The Workingmen's Federation thoroughly circularized the state in favor of Whalen, and he received support from city central bodies.[19] Despite these efforts, Whalen ran last on the Democratic ticket. Thus despite the increased activities by organized labor in New York, a significant labor vote did not appear in any state or national race.

After his defeat in 1906, William Randolph Hearst continued his political career, though now as a third force in state politics rather than as a serious threat for any office. Hearst continued to seek the support of the working-class voter and of organized labor. In addition to accepting McDonough in 1907, the Independence League nominated more unionists for local offices than the major parties usually did. The Independence League selected four unionists for Assembly races in Manhattan and the Bronx; and one, running with Republican support, was elected in a traditionally Democratic district. Nine unionists were offered as candidates for the Board of Aldermen from Manhattan and the Bronx. The Hearst organization in Brooklyn nominated union men for six Assembly seats, five places on the Board of Aldermen plus the borough offices of registrar and sheriff. Labor leaders composed the entire seventeen-man slate of the League in White Plains. Unionists had seven League nominations in Yonkers, four in Utica, nine in Buffalo, and six in Amsterdam. In all, at least sixty unionists ran on the Independence League tickets in 1907.[20]

Despite these nominations, Hearst's relations with the leaders of organized labor rapidly deteriorated after his unsuccessful race in 1906. His old enemies from the ranks of the Workingmen's Federation, and of the defunct Independent Labor Party, still opposed the Independence League. Other labor leaders criticized Hearst's cooperation with the Republicans in New York

[19] Workingmen's Federation of the State of New York, *Proceedings*, 1909: Secretary Bates's Report, p. 7.
[20] *New York Evening Journal*, Oct. 31, 1907, p. 2; Nov. 1, 1907, p. 3.

City in 1907. Hearst's organization received the nomination for sheriff of New York County and six of the eleven local judicial places; he then supported a majority of the Republican choices for the Assembly, the Board of Aldermen, and local offices.[21] Furthermore, several important supporters of Hearst in 1905 and 1906, including James Holland, a leader in the C.F.U. and later president of the State Federation, had grown most friendly with Tammany Hall. Holland soon received a Tammany appointment as a member of the Board of Education. The C.F.U. refused to take any stand in the election of 1907, or to contemplate any independent political action.[22]

In 1908 Hearst opposed the election of William Jennings Bryan because of the personal hostility that had developed between the two men.[23] Hearst did not hesitate to attack Gompers and other labor leaders when they supported Bryan.[24] He also organized a national ticket to run under the Independence League's name. This party could only hurt Bryan, since it would draw mainly Democratic votes. Hearst's stubborn opposition to the Democratic ticket caused a split among his supporters,[25] and his attacks on Gompers and Bryan destroyed his good relations with many labor leaders. By 1909, when Hearst once again ran for mayor of New York City, his support among labor leaders had dwindled, and even the previous stronghold of Hearstism, the Brooklyn Central Labor Union, refused to endorse him.[26]

Without the support of the labor leaders, Hearst continued to

[21] See *New York Times*, Oct. 6–11, 1907, for details.

[22] *New York Times*, Nov. 4, 1907, p. 3.

[23] *New York World*, Aug. 9, 1908, p. 3.

[24] For one prominent attack, and Gompers's reply, see *American Federationist*, Sept. 1908, p. 735.

[25] Judge Samuel Seabury had been one of Hearst's original supporters in 1905, but during the campaign of 1908 he attacked Hearst publicly for his fanatical hostility to Bryan. Seabury insisted that the hostility was based on personal malice alone. In 1909 Seabury split with Hearst for good.

[26] *New York Call*, Oct. 11, 1909, p. 1. The Brooklyn Central Labor Union endorsed the Democratic candidate, William Gaynor.

exhibit a positive appeal which centered in districts with large working-class and lower-middle-class populations. In the mayoralty election in New York City in 1909, Hearst had refused to join anti-Tammany groups in a fusion campaign because his supporters were not awarded the nominations for Manhattan district attorney and president of the Board of Aldermen.[27] However, after the nomination of Judge William Gaynor by Tammany, the Hall attempted to raid the Independence League's district conventions so that Tammany men might receive the nominations. When Tammany carried out the same maneuver in 1906 Hearst had done nothing, but this time the action infuriated him and led to a verbal duel with Gaynor. The result was a personal antagonism that never healed, and the re-entry of Hearst into the race as an independent candidate for mayor. Hearst had no supporting ticket; instead, he placed the entire fusion slate under his own name on the ballot.[28] His campaign thus aimed solely at the defeat of Tammany.

Tammany could not have nominated a stronger candidate than Gaynor. He had not been associated with the Hall before 1909, and he appealed to independent voters more strongly than any Tammany choice for mayor within memory. Organized labor trusted Gaynor, as was evident from their attempt to nominate him for a seat on the Court of Appeals in 1907. He would also draw a full machine vote in both Brooklyn and Manhattan. Nevertheless, Hearst polled 26 per cent of the popular vote as against 43 per cent for Gaynor. The rest of the fusion ticket, running with the support of Hearst, snowed under the Democrats. In the Tammany districts of Manhattan with large working-class populations, Hearst repeated his strong showing of 1905 and 1906, and in most of these he drew enough votes from the Democratic Party to outrun Otto Bannard, a Republican, who headed the fusion slate.

Hearst did not have the endorsements of labor leaders in 1909,

[27] *New York Times*, Sept. 23, 1909, p. 1.
[28] The Reminiscences of William S. Bennet (Oral History Project, Columbia University), pp. 203–211.

yet he still attracted many working-class votes. Hearst had his own methods of reaching the workers, and in doing so his newspapers were more effective than occasional pronouncements by central labor bodies. He continued to represent social reform in the minds of those who were most in need of it; he continued to represent active opposition to the political boss—and he demonstrated the appeal of these factors, once again, in 1909.

Hearst did not contest any office between 1910 and 1916, and although his Independence League continued to operate, its influence declined steadily. It was Hearst who drew the votes, and without him the Independence League became merely another faction in New York, seeking alliances with other political groups in an effort to earn some small measure of the electoral spoils.

The workingmen's political leagues, as ephemeral and partisan as ever, also reappeared in the election of 1909. The fusion ticket in New York City had the backing of a Working Men's Independent Political League, composed mainly of building trades leaders. This organization helped arrange several meetings among labor voters in support of the entire fusion slate; in return, it received several nominations for unionists.[29] In the same election another workingmen's political league appeared, and after the usual announcement of its representativeness and of its intention to work for the candidates most favorable to labor, the organization supported the Tammany ticket from top to bottom. This was not unexpected, since the leaders of the new league were unionists prominently identified with the Hall, including several who held patronage positions from Tammany's shrinking supply.[30] As in previous elections, two rival workingmen's political leagues claimed to represent the sentiments of organized labor, whereas in reality they represented only themselves.

[29] R. V. Ingersoll to Welling, Welling Papers, Sept. 9, 1909; Oct. 8, 1909; Oct. 15, 1909.
[30] *New York Call*, Aug. 28, 1909, p. 4.

The Federated Labor Party, another workingmen's political league, dutifully supported the Democrats in the successful state campaign of 1910, and in the equally successful election of 1912. The names of New York City labor leaders closely linked to Tammany once more appear as the officers of this organization. Although it made the claim to represent "100,000 voters throughout this state who were members of labor unions," [31] the Party was endorsed by no labor body, and played no prominent part in the campaigns. Similiar workingmen's leagues appeared upstate as well, for example, the Trade Union Political Alliance of Syracuse, which also claimed to represent organized labor yet did not have the endorsement of the local Trades Assembly.[32] The record of the workingmen's political leagues had been an empty one, and none of the organizations had met the expectations of Henry Streifler and the others in the late 1890's who believed they could provide an effective means of political action without the involvement of unions or central bodies.

Following the Triangle Fire in 1911, and with the heightened campaign for reform legislation in New York, the State Federation of Labor intensified its political activities. The prospects for significant labor legislation were better between 1911 and 1914 than at any time in the past, and the State Federation could look to the A.F.L.'s increased emphasis on politics, and its own expanded activities in 1907 and 1908, as precedents for a new attempt to make the voting power of organized labor a real force for reform.

In a letter to the leaders of the state legislature in 1911, the Federation threatened retaliation should the workmen's compensation and women's fifty-four-hour bills not pass at a coming special session. After passing the Assembly during the regular

[31] See *New York Times*, Sept. 19, 1910, p. 3; Oct. 22, 1910, p. 6; and Nov. 2, 1910, p. 3, for the activities of the Federated Labor Party. For its appearance in 1912, see *New York Times*, Aug. 25, 1912, p. 8, and Oct. 20, 1912, p. 11.

[32] *New York Call*, June 2, 1911, p. 3.

session, both bills had died in the State Senate. The Federation's letter demanded the passage of these measures and asserted that the state body was "determined to hold responsible the dominant influences in the Legislature of 1911, if you ignore our request. Our constituents are your constituents. Our members are voters. Feeling our responsibility to the workingmen whom we represent, we shall be compelled to adopt radical and far reaching measures, if necessary, to secure this beneficial legislation." [33] Despite this clear threat of political reprisal, the Democratic majority failed to pass either bill. The Federation did not organize a retaliatory campaign, but the Democrats lost their Assembly majority in the elections of 1911 because of the temporary cooling of the Progressive–Old Guard split within the New York Republican Party.

The statement of 1911 became the basis of action in 1912, as the Federation decided to make its traditional reward-and-punish policy more effective. The convention ordered the president and legislative chairman to visit the districts of candidates opposed by the Federation, in order to enlist the support of local unions and city central bodies in the campaign against labor's enemies. The officers also were instructed to seek the support of all candidates for the Federation's version of the compensation bill and for the constitutional amendment on compensation which was to come before the legislature in 1913.[34]

The attempt to have candidates pledge their support for organized labor's measures brought the Federation before the state nominating conventions, just as the A.F.L. had made its appearance before the national conventions in 1908. Samuel Gompers wrote a workmen's compensation plank which was presented to both state conventions. Although neither platform included the Gompers plank, the Democratic Party seemed more favorable on the issue.[35] The State Federation did not endorse the

[33] New York State Federation of Labor, *Proceedings*, 1911, p. 19.
[34] New York State Federation of Labor, *Proceedings*, 1912, p. 100.
[35] *New York Globe*, Sept. 27, 1912, p. 2; Oct. 2, 1912, p. 2.

Democrats officially, but its officers worked informally for the Party.[36] Clearly the Federation was involved in state politics more fully than before, and with an energy not often exhibited by the state body.

The blacklist issued by the State Federation in 1912 cited forty-two legislators, including only two Democrats among the seventeen state senators, and none at all among the twenty-five assemblymen.[37] Since the legislature had been divided between a Republican Assembly and a Democratic Senate, labor legislation in 1912 had to have the support of both parties, or at least not their opposition. The Republicans had voted more consistently against organized labor's bills in both Assembly and Senate, despite their support of a substantial number of reform measures, including the compromise cannery bill and the recommendations of the Factory Investigating Commission.[38] The State Federation's blacklist contained only the most consistent opponents of organized labor, and as usual in this period, they came overwhelmingly from the rural, Republican areas of New York.

In view of the past inability of the State Federation to dent the solidly Republican areas upstate in efforts to defeat its enemies, the campaign of 1912 promised little success. However, only fifteen of the forty-two men on the blacklist gained re-election, and the Federation proudly announced this result with the clear implication that the heightened activity of 1912 had achieved a memorable success.[39] An examination of the political situation, however, does not substantiate this optimism on the part of the Federation's leaders.

Most of the Republicans on the blacklist did not face the usual two-party election—with the Democrats a substantial but unvictorious minority. In 1912 the Progressive Party placed a third

[36] *Official Record*, June 1913, p. 2.
[37] *Official Record*, Dec. 1912, pp. 3–4.
[38] See the report of Legislative Chairman Fitzgerald in New York State Federation of Labor, *Proceedings*, 1912.
[39] New York State Federation of Labor, *Proceedings*, 1913, p. 19.

ticket in the field. The Progressives ran strong candidates against many of the Federation's blacklisted legislators because these men were the stoutest members of the Old Guard upstate machines, and the political enemies of the Progressive movement within the Republican organization. This split in the Republican forces led to the defeat of many Republicans in traditional G.O.P. districts. The same split won the governorship for the Democratic candidate, William Sulzer, and New York's electoral votes for Woodrow Wilson. Both men polled fewer votes than the combined total of Republican and Progressive ballots. Although not all Progressives were Republicans, a majority were, and the split in the Republican Party provided the Democrats in New York with their greatest victory of the period before World War I. The success of the State Federation's attack on its enemies was also the result of the Progressive Party's strength.

In addition to the campaign against those on the blacklist, the Federation's officers supported Homer Call, a State Federation vice president, for secretary of state on the Progressive ticket. As part of their offensive against labor's enemies, the officers of the state body boosted the candidacy of Call throughout the state, even though he did not have the official endorsement of the Federation's convention.[40] Clearly a victory for Call would fulfill the A.F.L.'s demand that unionists be elected to public office. Despite the Federation's campaign, Call had the same proportion of votes as the Progressive candidates for attorney general and state engineer, and ran behind Oscar Straus, the Progressive nominee for governor.[41] He apparently received only the straight Progressive vote, with no evidence of any shift of labor votes to him. It thus would seem that the great victory of the State Federation over its political enemies came about

[40] *Official Record*, Dec. 1912, p. 2.
[41] See totals in the *Manual for the Use of the Legislature of the State of New York*, 1913.

almost entirely because of factors beyond the control of organized labor.

Organized labor's support of Bryan in 1908 had led to charges that the labor movement was prepared to ally itself with the Democratic Party. In the years following 1906 organized labor certainly did favor the Democratic Party more than the Republicans. However, this support did not envisage an ultimate alliance. During the height of the attack on the A.F.L.'s involvement in the campaign of 1908, Gompers succinctly stated labor's position: "Labor has been and will be accused of partisanship, but in performing a solemn duty at this time in support of a political party Labor does not become partisan to a political party but partisan to a principle." [42] Organized labor viewed its endorsement of Bryan or Wilson or Tammany Hall as a commitment not to the party but to the policies the party stood for at that particular time. Labor would support those who supported it, regardless of their affiliation. If the Democrats presented the most favorable platforms and candidates, organized labor would aid them; and it could end its support should another party meet its demands more fully. Thus Hearst had attracted many labor leaders in 1905 and 1906, yet because of his subsequent policies, and the apparent inability of his Independence League to be anything more than a permanent splinter group, he had lost the greatest part of that support by 1909. Undoubtedly certain labor leaders favored Hearst because of the possibilities his movement offered for securing office, just as other union leaders had sought to gain office and preferment through the two major parties. Most labor leaders, however, followed Hearst because he promised to execute important demands of the trade unions; and in subsequent years Hearst lost these leaders' support because he no longer could offer anything substantial. Like other groups in New York, the labor movement sought to secure whatever it could through political action

[42] *American Federationist*, Nov. 1908, p. 957.

—but among such efforts, those of organized labor received particular attention. The true nature of New York labor's support of the Democrats was revealed clearly in the events of 1913.

The Democratic state convention of 1912 had written a plank broadly supporting the demands of organized labor for compensation legislation. In addition, both Samuel Gompers and Daniel Harris, president of the State Federation, insisted that the Democratic leaders had promised them informally that the state labor organization's version of the compensation bill would be enacted. Yet the Democrat-controlled legislature of 1913 refused to honor these pledges, and after much controversy and compromise finally enacted compensation legislation which the State Federation opposed. Governor Sulzer vetoed this bill. By the time the Federation's convention opened in September 1913, Sulzer had been impeached by the Assembly and was awaiting trial. The compensation bill had not been a prime factor in the Democrats' impeachment of their own nominee for governor, but the State Federation clearly took sides by passing a resolution in support of Sulzer which included these barbs at Tammany Hall:

We also wish to extoll you [Sulzer] for the valiant fight you have waged against corrupt, unscrupulous and greedy political bosses. . . . And we wish to pledge to you our hearty support and cooperation and express our willingness to assist you in any way possible to exonerate you from the charges that are trying to be proven against you, and in your fight to rid this State from the most disgraceful political outfit that exists in this great Republic.[43]

The Federation's attack on Tammany was much more a reaction to the failure of the state body's compensation bill than it was an expression of support for Governor Sulzer in his battle with Charles Murphy. The convention then castigated those Democrats who had followed Party orders and had refused to support the Federation's compensation bill. All assemblymen

[43] New York State Federation of Labor, *Proceedings*, 1913, p. 147.

who had opposed the Federation's bill were declared unfair to labor, and "a vigorous campaign was instituted throughout the State against the re-election of these men to the Legislature." [44] Almost two-thirds of the men on the blacklist were Democrats, including many from New York City. The decision to base the Federation's unfair list on this one bill placed the Democrats on record as enemies of labor, although more labor legislation had been passed in 1913 than in any other year of the Progressive period. Yet the all-important issue to the State Federation was its version of workmen's compensation, and the failure of the Democrats to provide such a law led the state labor organization to oppose them.

In the years from 1907 to 1910, the Democrats had a consistently better voting record than the Republicans on labor bills. Of course, the Democrats were the minority, but much had been expected of them after they captured the legislature and the governor's chair in 1910 for the first time since the 1890's. The defeat of the cannery bill in 1911 and of the Federation's compensation bill in 1913 indicated how carefully Tammany Hall weighed all the political consequences before passing controversial labor bills. Yet the record proved that the Democrats in New York would offer—and pass—more labor legislation than the Republicans, even though this meant much less than organized labor demanded. Thus the Democrats had continued to form the great majority of the Federation's honor roll, while the Republicans filled most of the places on the blacklist. The quick, determined opposition to the Democrats in 1913 proved that organized labor in New York was not committed permanently to the Democratic Party, any more than the A.F.L.'s support of Bryan made the latter organization an adjunct of the Democrats nationally.

The Federation's political campaign in 1913 was conducted once again by its executive committee. In addition to circulars and visits by the officers to local districts, a special issue of *Leg-*

[44] New York State Federation of Labor, *Proceedings*, 1914, p. 27.

islative Labor News was distributed to labor organizations throughout the state. However, grass roots support for the Federation once more failed to develop, and the campaign effort had to be limited. The Federation spent only $815 for its attack upon labor's enemies.[45]

The split within organized labor caused by the compensation issue had not healed by election time. Thus the United Board of Business Agents of New York supported the Democratic assemblyman John Kelly even though he was opposed by the Federation. In this instance, the Federation triumphed: Kelley lost his bid for re-election.[46] The Central Federated Union had provided little support for the Federation's legislative efforts in 1913, and it gave no concerted aid to the state body's election campaign. As usual, the Federation had no way to unify labor's political efforts, or to ensure the cooperation of all labor organizations in the state. Despite these weaknesses, the election campaign again was labeled a success because fifty-five black-listed assemblymen were defeated for re-election. Once more, however, the main factor in the Federation's success had little to do with the efforts of organized labor.

Governor Sulzer had been convicted and removed from office, and Lieutenant Governor Martin H. Glynn had replaced him. The reaction of the press to these proceedings had been overwhelmingly hostile, and even when editors admitted that Sulzer might have been guilty of the charges concerning improper financial contributions to his campaign in 1912, they continued to attack the impeachment. For Tammany Hall to indict its own choice for governor on charges of improper electoral practice clearly was ludicrous. Other portions of the indictment concerned Sulzer's activities after taking office, and the press asserted that these charges were evidence of Tammany Hall's vengeance against the Governor. Sulzer's real "crimes" had been his refusal to appoint Tammany men to all the key posts, his investigations of corruption during the previous Democratic

[45] *Ibid.*, p. 92.   [46] Ibid., p. 28. Also see pp. 31–32 above.

administration, and his opposition to certain features of the Hall's legislative program. He soon emerged as a martyr to the cause of clean, honest, unbossed government. In the election of 1913, Sulzer had run for the Assembly from a New York City district, but his speeches against Tammany Hall became ammunition for Republican guns throughout the state, and those who had supported his impeachment in the Assembly discovered that their support of Tammany against William Sulzer had become the main issue of the campaign. As it happened, most of these same assemblymen had voted the Tammany line on the compensation bill, and thus were on the State Federation's blacklist as well.

The election results clearly reveal the comparative effect of the Federation's blacklist and the impeachment of Sulzer in producing the defeat of the Democrats. Of those assemblymen blacklisted by the Federation, forty-eight also had voted for the impeachment of Sulzer. Eighteen of these forty-eight did not run, as Tammany attempted to reduce the effect of the Sulzer issue. Of the remaining thirty assemblymen, twenty-eight were Democrats. Only twelve of these Democrats gained re-election, and both anti-Sulzer Republicans lost. Of those assemblymen who had supported impeachment, but were not on the Federation's blacklist, six won re-election, and nine lost. Thus the percentage of anti-Sulzer assemblymen defeated was the same regardless of whether or not their names appeared on the blacklist.

Among the ranks of those who had voted against impeachment, three Democrats and seven Republicans on the Federation's blacklist gained re-election, while only two Democrats lost. Of the assemblymen not on the blacklist, who had opposed Sulzer's impeachment, the score stood as eight Democrats elected with three defeated, and three Republicans re-elected with none defeated. Once again the percentage of those elected was not affected by the blacklist. The significant difference appears in comparison of the pro- and anti-impeachment groups:

the percentage of those elected varies directly with the opposition to Sulzer's impeachment. Finally, there were fourteen
blacklisted assemblymen who had managed to dodge the impeachment vote entirely. Twelve of the fourteen ran for re-
election, and nine won their campaigns. The blacklist thus had
little effect in these races where the Sulzer issue was minor.[47]

There is no doubt the Democrats suffered because of Sulzer's
impeachment, especially in the Republican districts they had
carried in 1912. The reaction against the impeachment, and the
decline in the Progressive Party's vote, defeated many of the
assemblymen elected from these upstate districts and restored a
Republican majority in the Assembly.

One of the most crucial races for the State Federation in 1913
involved a unionist Democratic assemblyman, Edward Jackson
of Buffalo. He had been the Federation's major spokesman in the
Assembly, and the leader in the unsuccessful fight for the Federation's compensation bill. However, Jackson had voted with
the Democratic majority to impeach Sulzer, and despite his
popularity with organized labor, and the active support of the
State Federation, he was narrowly defeated by a Republican-
Progressive opponent in a strong Democratic district. Clearly
Jackson's support of the impeachment had been the decisive factor in his defeat. Thus, in the campaigns of 1912 and 1913, the
State Federation benefited from the coincidence of its blacklist
with other, more decisive political factors.

Just as the influence of Sulzer's impeachment had aided the
Federation in 1913, so the same factor worked against organized

[47] The roll call vote on the impeachment of Sulzer by the Assembly
can be found in the *New York Times*, Aug. 14, 1913, p. 3. The *Manual
for the Use of the Legislature of the State of New York* for 1913 and
1914 provides complete election results for the Assembly. The New York
State Federation of Labor, *Proceedings*, 1913, provides the roll call vote
on the Foley-Walker compensation bill. Those who supported this bill
in preference to the Federation-sponsored bill (Jackson-Murtaugh) became the enemies of the state body in the 1913 election. The State Senate
was elected for a two-year term in 1912, and thus it remained in Democratic hands.

labor's choice in the gubernatorial election of 1914. A compromise workmen's compensation bill had passed in December 1913, with the active aid of Governor Glynn, and although organized labor considered the new law far from perfect, it was realized that nothing better could have been secured under existing conditions. Furthermore, the effects of the recession of 1914 had stiffened business opposition to further labor reform, and thus much less reform legislation was enacted in 1914 than in 1913. After considering these factors, organized labor decided to support Governor Glynn for re-election. At the State Federation's convention in 1914, President Harris praised him as a governor "who on every occasion, is ready to assist us in every matter that would be helpful to labor," and as the man who secured the final passage of the compensation bill.[48] Samuel Gompers also commended Glynn in a letter to John O'Hanlon, editor of the *Legislative Labor News*.[49] On the other hand, the Republicans had increased their opposition to labor legislation, especially in the Republican-controlled Assembly. Old Guard leaders demanded a halt to social reform, which they declared had contributed to the business recession. Thus organized labor renewed its support of the Democrats after the hostilities of 1913.

Governor Glynn lost the election badly and the Democrats gave up control of the Senate to the Republicans, thus ending their four-year tenure in Albany. Glynn had the strongest support from organized labor, yet he ran far behind the rest of his ticket. The figures indicate that the Democratic ticket polled its normal number of votes: in the first popular election for United States Senator the Republican candidate won by only 54,000 votes. Glynn, however, lost the gubernatorial election by 136,000 votes. The key to this discrepancy is Sulzer's entrance

[48] New York State Federation of Labor, *Proceedings*, 1914, p. 39.

[49] *New York Times*, Oct. 24, 1914, p. 9. Ernest Bohm, corresponding secretary of the C.F.U., and a Democrat, blamed some of the hostility of the 1915 Republican legislature on "the union endorsement of Governor Glynn when he was running for re-election." See *New York Times*, April 15, 1915, p. 18.

into the campaign as the gubernatorial candidate of the American Party and the Prohibitionists. Glynn most probably would have lost in any event since the decline of the Progressive Party restored the Republican vote to near the pre-1910 totals. Sulzer, though, polled 119,000 votes. Many Democrats voted the rest of the ticket while striking out Glynn in favor of the martyred Sulzer.[50] Thus despite the support of organized labor and the Tammany machine, Glynn ran far behind the rest of the ticket in New York City and in upstate areas. It was not until 1917 that Tammany Hall once more gained control over a major source of power through its victory in New York City. The impeachment of Governor Sulzer had been a victory of the kind Tammany could not afford.

The Republican Party in New York became openly hostile to organized labor, and to social reform in general, as the Progressive spirit cooled during 1915 and 1916. The State Federation reacted by renewing its attempts to retaliate upon antilabor forces at the polls. As early as April 1915, the Federation announced plans for a $100,000 fund to be used against the Republican onslaught on recent labor reforms.[51] Member organizations were to provide the money. Although this fund never materialized, the announcement was meant to warn the Republican leaders that they would face strenuous opposition if they pushed their antilabor activities. In the midst of the fight to block the antireform bills, Daniel Harris died. Following his death, Legislative Chairman John Henley attacked the Republicans in a statement marked by an unusual display of emotion and partisanship. Henley praised the Democrats for "putting up one of the greatest fights for organized labor that has ever been fought by any political party in the history of the State of New York." He urged all central labor bodies to begin work in May

[50] *New York Times*, Nov. 4, 1914, p. 1. In some traditional Democratic areas upstate, Sulzer cut into Glynn's vote drastically. In normally Democratic Schoharie County, Sulzer actually polled more votes than Glynn.
[51] *New York Times*, April 5, 1915, p. 18.

1915 to defeat the Republicans at the election so as to "avenge the death of our late President Daniel Harris." Henley linked Harris's death to his insistence upon working against the reactionary labor bills despite doctors' orders. "The death of him who we all loved is on the heads of the Republican majority." [52] The Federation's convention then set up a special committee to publicize the antilabor records of legislators and work for their defeat.[53]

Despite the emotionalism brought forth by the situation, and the unabashed hostility of the Republicans to social reform, there is no evidence of a coordinated statewide labor campaign to oppose the G.O.P. assemblymen. A comparison of the efforts of organized labor in the elections for the Assembly and in the campaign to defeat the proposed state constitution at the same November elections, clearly illustrates the weakness of the Federation's retaliatory campaign. A few speeches by members of its executive council, and the distribution of blacklists, could not break the traditional Republican voting habits of many upstate workers—even if the workers had access to such material. Without the cooperation of the local central labor councils and local unions, the average unionist would have little opportunity to learn the Federation's views. A concerted drive did not materialize at the local level, and the election of 1915 returned a Republican majority, with no discernible revolt among working-class voters.

The opposition to the proposed state constitution of 1915, however, revealed the possibilities for coordinated political action by the labor movement. In 1913 the Democrats had passed a bill calling for a referendum on a constitutional convention, and the voters had approved the proposition in November 1913. The members of the constitutional convention were selected in the general election of 1914, and the Republicans swept the voting for these delegates just as they dominated the balloting for the

[52] *Official Record*, May 1915, pp. 2–3.
[53] *Auburn Labor Weekly*, Sept. 10, 1915, p. 1.

legislature. Organized labor had asked the major parties to select prominent unionists as convention delegates, and the Progressive and Democratic parties did place two union leaders each on their slates of delegates-at-large. Gompers and Labor Commissioner Lynch received the Democratic nominations, while Homer Call and John Mitchell ran on the Progressive ticket. The Republican Party selected no unionist for its list of delegates-at-large, although a few union men were nominated in upstate districts.

The Federation supported these unionists, and urged all workers to cross party lines and vote for the four labor candidates.[54] As in previous elections, the results indicated that the union leaders ran at the level of their tickets without any apparent labor vote. The convention met with only two or three recognized unionists in its ranks, and all of them had been selected in the district balloting. In accordance with their usual policy in other elections, none of the parties had placed very many labor men on their local tickets.

The constitutional convention closely resembled the legislature of 1915 in its unfriendly attitude toward the labor movement. Organized labor submitted a list of twenty-four demands, and only two received the convention's approval. In addition, the proposed constitution contained new provisions which produced strenuous opposition from labor.[55] It was the view of organized labor that a new convention, elected in 1916, might be more amenable to its demands but that if the document of 1915 were accepted, constitutional reform would be dead for another twenty years.[56]

Organized labor was not alone in opposing the convention's work. It became evident that Tammany Hall would oppose the constitution because it had not changed the apportionment for New York City in the legislature, nor granted the city any greater home rule—both perennial demands of the under-

[54] *Auburn Labor Weekly*, Oct. 23, 1914, p. 1.
[55] *Legislative Labor News*, Oct. 1915, p. 4.
[56] *New York Call*, Nov. 1, 1915, p. 6.

represented Democratic minority. In addition, some Progressives disliked the increase in the power of the executive at the expense of the legislature. They particularly disliked a clause that allowed the governor to prepare the budget instead of the legislature's committees. Old Guard Republican leaders also opposed the increase in the governor's budget powers, and the clause allowing the governor to appoint officials without the approval of the State Senate. Both changes would reduce the legislature's power, and it was there that the upstate Republican leaders had their greatest influence. Thus the defeat of the proposed constitution was assured with or without organized labor's opposition, and the Federation's campaign is significant simply as an illustration of united action by labor, not because it played the decisive role in the ultimate defeat of the proposed new charter.

The executive council of the Federation congratulated the state's labor organizations on their united campaign against the constitution: "The result demonstrated labor's solidarity as it never was demonstrated before. It is proof of the strength of labor when united. The New York State Federation of Labor takes credit for the uniting of the forces." [57] This pat on the back by the Federation was justified. The state body had taken the lead in formulating a labor program to place before the convention, and it had done so once again in opposing the constitution. However, the key to the success of the campaign was not in the Federation's activities, for it had taken the initiative many times in the past, but in the unparalleled cooperation of the city central labor councils and local unions. This time no important group in New York City clashed with the Federation, as had happened in 1899, 1906, and 1913. City central bodies throughout the state cooperated fully by distributing Federation material as well as their own. Committees were organized to visit local union meetings and explain to the rank-and-file members why the proposed constitution should not be approved. The officers of the city central bodies used their personal influence to gain

[57] *Labor Herald* (Rochester), Nov. 12, 1915, p. 2.

the cooperation of local unions.[58] The Federation's campaign thus reached the local areas, and became the activity of organized labor in the true sense of the term.

The local and national unions cooperated with the Federation wholeheartedly. National unions wrote urging their members to oppose the constitution; [59] local unions converted their meetings into forums to discuss the issue, and they distributed the material received from city and state central bodies. The Federation reported that $2,392 had been expended on the campaign by the state body, and that most of this money had come from special contributions.[60] Ernest Bohm of the Central Federated Union pointed out that most of the money for the campaign in New York City came from the funds of local unions,[61] and thus the State Federation's expenditures represented only the base of labor's total, not its apex. It should be recalled that the Federation spent only $815 in the election campaign of 1913. Most local unions had refused to support the campaign of 1913 actively, and important elements in New York City had opposed it.

The Federation also distributed literature to unorganized workers, especially in the larger cities of the state. In these cities, the newspapers generally supported the new constitution as they followed the lead of an influential group of Republicans led by Governor Whitman, Elihu Root, and Seth Low.[62] In most past campaigns, the Federation had lacked the resources to reach its own membership, let alone influence the great mass of unorganized workers.

Two major factors account for this exceptional unity. First, the constitution was not technically a political issue. The Repub-

[58] See *New York Call*, Oct. 9, 1915, p. 1; *Official Record*, Oct. 1915, p. 1; *Legislative Labor News*, Dec. 1915, p. 5, for details of the activities of city central bodies.

[59] *New York Call*, Oct. 18, 1915, p. 4.

[60] New York State Federation of Labor, *Proceedings*, 1916, p. 135.

[61] *New York Call*, Oct. 22, 1915, p. 2.

[62] *Legislative Labor News*, Dec. 1915, p. 5.

licans who supported the new constitution asserted continually that if Tammany opposed the document, it would destroy the very basis of the convention's existence. They argued that although the convention had been elected by parties, it was a nonpolitical body; and to ensure that this rested on more than theory, the convention made the controversial apportionment clause of the constitution a separate item. The main body of the constitution, however, had to be supported or rejected as a whole, and this take-it-or-leave-it choice had led many Progressives to oppose the document rather than accept some of the objectionable features. Tammany did not oppose the constitution officially until October 21, and then only by private letter to its membership, not by public announcement.[63] It was not until the last days before the election, when the newspapers publicized Tammany's opposition, that the Hall ended the fiction of nonpartisanship and attacked the proposed constitution.

However, both the Republicans and Progressives split over the issue which was thus not squarely a party one. Organized labor could enter the battle without becoming involved in party politics. The issues were fought out without reference to party labels, and the diversity of opinion within the Republican organization made it clear that the local unions need not discuss politics in order to discuss the constitution. Thus the constitution was artificially labeled nonpolitical although it was clearly inseparable from the politics of the state. The local and national unions, and many of the city central bodies, failed to support the Federation's Assembly campaign of 1915, which clearly involved an attack upon the Republican Party. Only the peculiar political status of the constitution allowed united labor support for the state body to develop.

Secondly, the constitutional fight provided an opportunity for organized labor to show its opposition to the reactionary policies of the legislature. The constitutional convention disregarded labor's program just as the legislature had done. The New York

[63] *New York Times*, Nov. 1, 1915, p. 1.

labor movement had supported the Federation's lobbying activities in 1915, for the reforms achieved since 1911 appeared to be in jeopardy. The constitutional campaign thus provided an appropriate area in which organized labor could display its potential unity and strength.

In the state and national elections of 1916, organized labor's central bodies participated in electoral battles for posts from assemblyman to President of the United States. In the gubernatorial race, the Central Federated Union did not await the lead of the A.F.L. or the State Federation. As early as February 1916, the labor group began boosting Judge Samuel Seabury for governor, and by June it had endorsed him formally. The C.F.U. then asked for the aid of other central bodies.[64] Clearly this campaign was aimed at the Democratic nomination, since the Republican incumbent, Charles Whitman, stood for reelection, and the Progressive Party's strength had deteriorated badly. Tammany Hall, however, had no desire for Seabury, since he had been a Hearst supporter in 1905 and a Progressive in 1913, even though he now claimed to be an independent Democrat.

The C.F.U.'s campaign for Seabury received encouragement from several other city labor councils,[65] but important upstate city labor organizations did not support the movement actively. It became apparent at once that the split in the state labor movement over political policy would hamper this effort as it had others in the past. The campaign to nominate Seabury, however, was a high point in New York labor's political action: it marked the first time in the Progressive period that an important labor body had sought to influence the choice of gubernatorial nominees.

The campaign for Seabury also received strong support from Progressive and independent groups in the state, and by the time of the Democratic state convention he was the leading contender

[64] *New York Times*, June 26, 1916, p. 6.
[65] *Legislative Labor News*, Sept. 1916, p. 5.

for the top place on the ticket.[66] Even though he was sure to be an independent if elected, the Tammany-dominated convention nominated Seabury. Charles Murphy seemed ready to pass up a serious attempt at the Statehouse, which the Democrats had won only twice in twenty years, in favor of building the strength of the Hall among Progressive and independent voters. By supporting Seabury, he hoped to prepare for the crucial mayoralty election in New York City in 1917, which Tammany had a good chance to sweep.[67]

The State Federation concentrated on attacking Governor Whitman and the Republican legislature. Its committee on the legislative report pointed out to the convention in 1916 that the legislature had seemed eager to wipe out all of labor's legislative gains; "and the legislature was not alone responsible for they were ably assisted and encouraged by Governor Whitman in all their raids upon organized labor's legislation." The committee labeled the session as "the BLACKEST PAGE ever written in the history of this State by any Governor and his co-operating legislative body." Because of the "outrages perpetrated upon the working people of this State," the committee urged the Federation to accept the challenge by punishing Governor Whitman and the Republican legislators accordingly.[68]

On the national scene, the A.F.L.'s leaders supported Wilson for a second term, but not in the same way they had supported Bryan in 1908. Instead, the leadership suggested that all labor groups discuss the issues during the final weeks of the campaign. However, Gompers, Frank Morrison, and James O'Connell, who composed the labor representation committee of the A.F.L., made it clear through letters and speeches before these

[66] Theodore Roosevelt had promised Seabury the support of New York's Progressive Party; but when Seabury endorsed Wilson, T.R. induced the Progressive convention to nominate Whitman. See Herbert Mitgang, *The Man Who Rode the Tiger: The Life and Times of Judge Samuel Seabury*, (Philadelphia, 1963), pp. 112–118.

[67] *New York Times*, Aug. 5, 1916, p. 4; Aug. 8, 1916, p. 4.

[68] New York State Federation of Labor, *Proceedings*, 1916, p. 158.

meetings that their choice in 1916 was Wilson.[69] The A.F.L.'s leaders received important support in New York from officers of the State Federation who also supported the President.[70] Like the national labor body, the state organization refrained from a formal endorsement. Thus in major state and national races, important elements in organized labor supported the Democratic candidates.

Organized labor in New York, however, was hardly unanimous in its support of Wilson and Seabury. In areas where the city labor council favored the Republicans, the campaign of the state or national officers for the Democratic candidates received no publicity. Thus in Auburn and Rochester, the labor papers made absolutely no mention of the C.F.U.'s support of Seabury, of the State Federation's condemnation of Whitman and the Republican legislature, or of the support of the A.F.L.'s labor representation committee for Wilson. Neither paper even printed the statement in which the A.F.L.'s committee called for labor meetings to discuss the pending election, since the letter containing it also included favorable comments about the Wilson administration.[71] The editors of both these official labor papers had been associated with the Republican Party in the past, and the G.O.P. had support among local labor leaders and the rank and file. Neutrality, of course, aided the Republicans in areas where they normally could expect a good share of the labor vote. In addition, most of the national unions, and their New York locals, stayed clear of political involvements, so that it was once more a case of the central bodies seeking to influence

[69] *Albany Federationist (Official Record)*, Nov. 1, 1916, p. 1; *New York Times*, Nov. 6, 1916, p. 4.

[70] *Legislative Labor News*, Nov. 1916, p. 1.

[71] See the *Labor Herald* (Rochester), Sept.–Nov. 1916, and the *Auburn Labor Weekly* for the same period. The *Auburn Labor Weekly* did print paid advertisements by supporters of Wilson and Hughes. Cf. the *Albany Federationist*, whose editor was Thomas Fitzgerald, a Democrat. The Albany paper printed the October 14 letter of the labor representation committee of the A.F.L. calling for local meetings, and the Albany Central Federation of Labor arranged such a meeting, at which O'Connell spoke.

the labor vote, but without the support of the organizations most closely associated with the individual worker.

The results of the election in 1916 indicated most decisively the general ineffectiveness of organized labor's political campaigns. The State Federation's attack on the Republicans was no more successful than in the past, and the new Legislature contained the same antilabor Republican majority. Samuel Seabury lost his race for governor. He won only a 22,000-vote victory in Democratic New York City, and thus was swamped by a predominantly Republican upstate vote. The low vote for Seabury in New York City, despite the nine-month campaign by the C.F.U. for his nomination and election, could not be explained as the result of knifing by the machine, for the Tammany nominee for United States Senator had only a 29,000-vote advantage in the city. The leaders of the A.F.L. and the C.F.U. worked on behalf of Wilson, but his margin in New York City was a slight one of 40,000. The secretary of the C.F.U. had predicted that from 80 to 85 per cent of the labor vote in New York City would be counted in the Democratic column; [72] but he was forced to admit after the election, "While we can't tell exactly how the working man voted, it seems that at least in this city they did not give the Democratic ticket the help that had been expected." [73]

In several upstate cities, including the strong Republican centers of Rochester, Syracuse, and Albany, the Democrats did make small gains, but normally Democratic Utica went to the Republicans. Wilson had more votes than in 1912, but most of the increase came from the rural areas, not from strong labor centers. With the Progressive Party vote of little consequence, and with Hughes's wide popularity in New York, the state went to the Republicans by a healthy margin.

Wilson's German policy had produced much bitterness

[72] Ernest Bohm of the C.F.U. in the *New York Times,* Oct. 23, 1916, p. 3.
[73] *New York Times,* Nov. 9, 1916, p. 4. For the official State Federation view, which stressed labor's support of Wilson in the election, see the *Legislative Labor News,* Nov. 1916, p. 1.

among the sizable German-American population of New York City, and this hurt the entire Democratic ticket.[74] His opposition to the Irish Republicans' attempts to take advantage of British involvement in the war reduced his popularity with the Irish voters in New York City.[75] Naturalized citizens of Russian background opposed the President's increasing support of the Allies, including the Czar, and they expressed their feelings by bolting the Democratic ticket.[76] These influences lowered Seabury's vote as well, and in addition he faced the personal opposition of his former political ally, William Randolph Hearst. Clearly these noneconomic factors had proved strong enough to offset the work of the labor leaders, and to overcome the traditional voting pattern of many Democratic voters. The New York worker once again failed to follow a class-conscious voting pattern; instead, he responded to national, cultural, and traditional factors against which organized labor's efforts could have little effect.

The central bodies of the city and state had increased their political efforts considerably during the years 1907 to 1916. They recognized more than ever that effective political retaliation was the key to a better legislative record. However, organized labor failed to influence the vote significantly, and thus the major parties made few changes in their attitude toward the trade union movement. Organized labor attempted political action without adequate financial resources, without the cooperation of all the labor elements in the state, and without a tradition of class-conscious voting by workers; and its failure to produce greater results must be measured against the overwhelming obstacles it had to face.

[74] *New York Times*, Nov. 9, 1916, p. 6.   [75] *Ibid.*
[76] *Albany Federationist*, Dec. 6, 1916, p. 2.

Bibliography

UNPUBLISHED SOURCES

UNPUBLISHED sources were not important for the study of organized labor in New York State. The files of central labor organizations, such as the New York State Federation of Labor, have disappeared as a result of fire, lack of space, and/or a lack of concern about the future value of correspondence and official records. Thus the student of labor's political activity must depend upon the printed materials of state and city central bodies, and upon sources outside the trade union movement.

Unpublished material is a more important complement to published sources in the study of the social Progressive organizations. Major manuscript collections, such as the Andrews Papers and the files of the New York Women's Trade Union League, contain valuable material, but the social Progressive movement can be well understood from published sources. Since the reform societies were public organizations, their published materials explain the objectives, methods, and philosophy of the movement, and unpublished sources are particularly important for financial arrangements, for personal relations within the social Progressive group and in those areas where the public record is weak.

Of the unpublished sources consulted, the following were most significant.

Andrews, John B. Papers, American Association for Labor Legislation (School of Industrial and Labor Relations, Cornell University).

A large and valuable collection, which consists of more than eighty boxes that contain the correspondence and press releases of the Association, drafts and final copies of articles and other material prepared by the A.A.L.L. or by Andrews, and a wealth of material on all aspects of the organization's activities. This collection is not catalogued beyond rudimentary divisions of the correspondence into years, and some labeling of types of material to be found in a particular box.

Bennet, William S. The Reminiscences of William S. Bennet (Oral History Project, Columbia University, 1950).

Contains much material on political conditions in New York during the first decade of the twentieth century, including valuable comments on the method of Republican Party nominations, Hearst's role in the 1909 mayoralty race, and the influence of William Sulzer following his impeachment.

Bernheimer, Charles L. Papers (New-York Historical Society).

Includes some valuable material on the 1913 Fusion campaign, in which Bernheimer was a member of the finance committee.

City Club of New York. Papers (New York Public Library).

Cockran, William Bourke. Papers (New York Public Library).

Consumers' League of New York. Papers (School of Industrial and Labor Relations, Cornell University).

A small collection which does not include records or correspondence for the period before 1916. It does contain some valuable pamphlets and leaflets issued by the State League and several of the city leagues in New York.

Dubofsky, Melvyn. New York City Labor in the Progressive Era, 1910–1918 (unpublished doctoral dissertation, University of Rochester, 1960).

Fein, Albert. New York City Politics from 1899 to 1903 (master's essay, Columbia University, 1954).

Greene, Francis Vinton. Papers (New York Public Library).

Low, Seth. Papers (Columbia University).

Valuable material can be found in this voluminous collection on Low's unsuccessful race for mayor in 1897. Also included is considerable material on his activities in the National Civic Federation, but almost all of this concerns events outside New York.

Rosenthal, Herbert H. The Progressive Movement in New York State, 1906–1914 (unpublished doctoral dissertation, Harvard University, 1955).

This fine study provides a detailed and perceptive analysis of the growth of the Progressive Party in New York and the links between New York and national politics. It has little on the social Progressive movement.

Social Reform Club of New York. Leaflets and cards to membership, 1896–1901, with gaps; 1902–1903, scattered (New York Public Library).

These materials were mailed weekly to the membership to inform them of the Club's activities. They indicate the scope of the Club's work and summarize some of the important discussions.

Veiller, Lawrence. Papers (Microfilm, Columbia University).

Veiller was a leader in the fight for tenement reform, and an important member of the City Club. This collection, though not very large, provides some important insights into the problems of reform.

——. The Reminiscences of Lawrence Veiller (Oral History Project, Columbia University, 1949).

Wald, Lillian. Papers (New York Public Library).

This collection has some interesting material on the involvement of social Progressives in the national campaign of 1912, and in the peace movement during 1915 and 1916. Material on events in New York is limited.

Welling, Richard W. G. Papers (New York Public Library).

Contains some material on the Citizens Union and the fusion campaigns of 1897, 1903, 1905, and 1909, in which Welling played a prominent role.

Women's Trade Union League of New York. Papers (New York State Department of Labor Library, New York City).

These important files lack the correspondence of the New York League and its officers. However, they do contain the valuable executive board meeting minutes, 1906–1916, the general monthly meeting minutes, 1907–1916, and the secretary's monthly reports, 1906–1916, among other items. Until 1913, Helen Marot was secretary, and her reports expound her ideas on the labor movement and its proper relation to the social Progressive allies.

PUBLISHED SOURCES

Organized Labor

The New York Public Library holds the richest collection for New York labor, in large measure as a result of the library's acquisition of the extensive labor materials collected by the Social Reform Club. The instability of labor newspapers, a disastrous fire in the library of the New York State Department of Labor in 1911, and the general disregard of labor materials by public and private libraries during the Progressive era, help explain the spotty character of many labor sources.

American Federationist (American Federation of Labor), Washington, 1897–1916.
> Although specific references to events in New York are not common, New York labor was influenced greatly by the decisions of the A.F.L., with which most central labor bodies were affiliated.

Auburn Labor Weekly, Auburn, N.Y., Vols. 4–7, 1914–1916.
> This official weekly of the Auburn Central Labor Union devoted little space to the central body's meetings. Union strength was slight in the Auburn area, and the labor newspaper emphasized discussions of the principles of trade unionism.

Central Labor Union of New York City. *Handbook*, 1897.

Farm and Factory. See *Independent*, Binghamton.

Garment Worker, The (United Garment Workers Union), New York, 1898–1903.
> The editorials were written by Henry White during his most active years in the Social Reform Club and in the anti-Tammany political movements.

Independent, Binghamton, N.Y., Vols. 6–8 (with gaps), 1899–1901.
> This official weekly paper of the Binghamton Central Labor Union was printed by an independent publisher. After May 1901 the paper stopped printing labor news, undoubtedly because of a split between the central body and the publisher, Fred S. Kennedy, a supporter of the single tax. The title was changed to *Farm and Factory* early in 1900; to *Independent and Farm and*

Factory in June 1900; and back to *Independent* in May 1901. It contains fuller reports of the meetings of the local central body than was usual in other official labor papers.

International Ladies' Garment Workers' Union. *Proceedings*, 1904–1916.

——. *Report of General Secretary-Treasurer*, June 3, 1900–June 1, 1901; June 1, 1901–June 1, 1902.

Knights of Labor, District Assembly 49, New York, *Annual Official Handbook*, Nov. 15, 1897.

Labor Advocate, The (formerly *The Troy Advocate*), 1903–1905 (with gaps); Oct. 26, 1906.

Reprints portions of the reports of the *Labor Legislative News* on the legislative work of the Workingmen's Federation. The editor, John O'Hanlon, was a Republican at the time, and he actively encouraged labor to support the G.O.P. It is thus no surprise that the *Labor Advocate* was not the official paper of the local central bodies during these years.

Labor Herald, Rochester, N.Y., Vols. 3–4 (with gaps), 1915–1916.

The Rochester Trades and Labor Council published this weekly as its official organ. It devoted most of its space to general labor news.

Labor Legislative News, Albany, N.Y., Vol. 1, Nos. 1–20, 1903.

This paper was supported by the executive board of the Workingmen's Federation, although it was not the official organ. It is an excellent source for the legislative activities of the Federation.

Ladies' Garment Worker (International Ladies' Garment Workers' Union), New York, Vols. 1–6, 1910–1916.

Legislative Labor News and Labor Advocate, Albany, N.Y., Vols. 4–5 (four issues missing), 1915–1916.

This valuable publication was the official paper of the New York State Federation of Labor. Issued weekly during the legislative session, and monthly thereafter, it provides valuable information about the activities of the state body during the period of reaction following the election of 1914.

New York State Federation of Labor (Workingmen's Federation of the State of New York, 1897–1911). *Proceedings*, 1899, 1901, 1904–1914, 1916.

These increasingly lengthy Proceedings are the best source for the activities of the state body. Reports of the president, secretary-treasurer, and legislative chairman are included in full.

New York Union Printer, 1905–1906 (with gaps).

Not the official paper of any union despite the deceptive title. The publisher actively supported Hearst in his race in 1905.

Official Record, Albany, N.Y., Vols. 12–27, 1900–1916.

Published monthly as the official paper of the Albany Central Federation of Labor. After May 1916 the title was changed to *Albany Federationist*. Despite the occasional gaps, the newspaper provides a valuable account of the activities of this central labor council.

Saturday Critic, The, Oneonta, N.Y., 1897–April 1898.

Published as the official weekly of the Oneonta Trades and Labor Council. The copies of this newspaper in the New York Public Library are badly worn and can be used only with great difficulty.

Troy Advocate. See *Labor Advocate*.

Union Labor Advocate, Chicago, Ill., 1906–1908.

This monthly publication features the official material of the Chicago Federation of Labor and the Illinois State Federation of Labor. Of major interest for the present study were the occasional reports of the activities of the National Women's Trade Union League during its years of formation.

Unionist, The, Vols. 24–31, 1899–1907 (with gaps).

This semimonthly newspaper was primarily concerned with the printing trades, although matters affecting organized labor generally were also included.

Utica Advocate, The, Vols. 6–19, 1898–1912 (some gaps).

This independently published weekly was the official organ of the Utica Trades Assembly until 1901. As a result of some controversy the editor and the central labor body split permanently, and after 1901 the paper's coverage of labor news declined sharply. Throughout the period the editor vigorously supported the Republican Party in local, state, and national races.

Workingmen's Federation of the State of New York. See *New York State Federation of Labor*.

Social Progressives

The printed materials for the study of the social Progressive organizations are extensive, and more widely available than the labor publications.

American Association for Labor Legislation. *Proceedings*, 1907–1909.
American Labor Legislation Review (American Association for Labor Legislation), Vols. 1–6, 1911–1916.
  Contains a wealth of information on the reforms demanded by the social Progressives. Also includes the Proceedings of the annual meeting of the Association beginning with 1910.
Citizens Municipal Committee of the City of New York. *Treasurer's Report for the Campaign of 1913*, New York, 1913.
Citizens Union, The. *The Work of the Citizens Union*, 1909–1916.
Consumers' League of Buffalo. *Annual Report*, 1911, 1912.
Consumers' League of the City of New York. *Annual Report*, 1895–1916.
  The policies and personnel of the New York City League are clearly revealed in this important source.
Consumers' League of the State of New York. *Bulletin*, Nos. 1–4, 1911–1912.
  State League activities, and those of leagues in upstate cities, are summmarized.
Consumers' League of the State of New York. *Report for the Year Ending February 27, 1907; Report for the Year Ending February 27, 1909; Report for June 1910–February 26, 1913*.
Hammer and Pen (Church Association for the Advancement of the Interests of Labor), 1898–1908; May 1910; June 1912; June 1916.
  After April 1908 the journal was published only fitfully because of lack of funds.
League for Political Education. *Yearbook*, New York, 1902.
Life and Labor (National Women's Trade Union League of America), Vols. 1–6, 1911–1916.
  Alice Henry edited this official monthly journal.
National Child Labor Committee. *Proceedings*, 1905–1911.
  The meetings were mainly opportunities for the presentation of

papers on important aspects of child labor reform. All the annual meetings to 1911 were reprinted in full in *The Annals of the American Academy of Political and Social Science*. After 1912 the Proceedings are found in *The Child Labor Bulletin*.

National Conference of Charities and Correction. *Proceedings*, 1895–1916.

As the charity societies became more interested in social reform after 1906, these annual meetings produced some significant statements of the social Progressives' philosophy and program.

National Consumers' League. *Report*, 1901–1913.

Reports the activities of the National League, and also provides summaries of local league activity throughout the nation. Florence Kelley was secretary of the organization, and the *Reports* served as forums for her views.

National Women's Trade Union League of America. *Convention Handbook*, 1909, 1911.

Discusses industrial conditions in trades employing female labor.

National Women's Trade Union League of America. *Proceedings, Biennial Convention*, 1909–1915.

This is a major source for the policies of the National League. For the constitution and first convention of the National League, see the account in the *Union Labor Advocate* of December 1907 and January 1908.

National Women's Trade Union League of America. *Report of Interstate Conference Held September 26–28, 1908 in New York*.

New York Branch, American Association for Labor Legislation. *Report*, 1910–1911.

The name was changed to New York Association for Labor Legislation in 1911. Contains some important comments on the efforts to secure labor legislation in New York.

Social Reform Club of New York. *Annual Report*, 1897–1900.

Provides valuable information, especially on the membership of the club.

The Child Labor Bulletin (National Child Labor Committee), Vols. 1–4, 1912–1916.

Contains full information on the activities of the Committee, and the best of the material used in the campaign against child labor.

University Settlement Society. *Annual Report,* 1894–1916.
——. *University Settlement Bulletin,* Fall and Winter, 1902–1903.
Women's Trade Union League of New York. *Annual Report,* 1906–1917.
    Provides valuable material about the policies and composition of this important organization.
Women's Trade Union League of New York. *Bulletin,* Vols. 1–2, 1911–1913.
    Includes a calendar of the monthly League activities.

Newspapers

In general, most newspapers in New York City ignored the activities of organized labor, except when there was sensational news such as a major strike, overt violence, or labor racketeering. Organized labor never solved the problem of how to present its views to possible supporters in the middle class who ordinarily would learn almost nothing about the labor movement from the daily newspapers. In addition, the press often was biased in its reporting of labor news, following the common practice of printing unsubstantiated opinion as fact. In editorial policy, most New York City newspapers were open enemies not only of the strike and boycott, but often of the very principle of unionism and collective agreements. Very few of the many New York City newspapers added anything significant to the information on organized labor's activities, and even in these few dailies the quality and reliability of the reporting frequently varied from month to month, and always did so from year to year.

The reporting of the work of social Progressive organizations was more complete, and less biased. However, only the highlights of the social Progressives' activities reached the news columns. Most of their lobbying received scant attention, except when an individual newspaper had taken up the cause of a specific social reform. The dailies were extremely valuable for their reporting of the political activities of the reformers, especially the work of the Citizens Union and other anti-Tammany reform societies.

New York American, 1905–1906.
    The Hearst press was an active campaign vehicle. On the whole,

the *Evening Journal* provides fuller coverage of labor news than does this Hearst morning daily.

New York Call, 1908–1916.

From May 30, 1908, to June 26, 1909, the paper was titled the *Evening Call.* It constitutes an unusually rich source because the publishers and editors were socialists. The *Call* was fully as biased in favor of the labor movement as the majority of the press was biased against organized labor. It also tended to exaggerate the role of the socialists in the New York labor movement. Until September 1912, when the *Call's* reporter was barred from the meetings of the Central Federated Union of New York, the paper provided the fullest reports of the activities of this important labor body. Unfortunately, the C.F.U. did not publish a newspaper at any time during these two decades.

New York Daily News, 1900–1905.

One of the few newspapers that expressed a pro-labor view in its reporting and editorials. It staunchly supported Tammany and seemed to be a propagandist for the claim that the Hall was the workingman's advocate. In 1904–1905 a daily column, "Trade Union Notes," carried local union news of interest to the rank and file.

New York Evening Journal.

From 1897 until the break between Hearst and the leaders of New York labor in the years after 1907, the *Evening Journal* led all New York papers in the amount of labor news it carried, and in its support of union objectives. During 1905–1906 this paper became a propaganda organ, with major emphasis on Hearst's friendship for the worker. The *Evening Journal* featured a special labor column during most of the decade after 1897. Although there were gaps in the appearance of this column, and though it tended at times to offer Hearst's views rather than those of organized labor, it did present much valuable material.

New York Herald, 1905–1906.

The *Herald* was one of the bitterest opponents of Hearst.

New York Times.

The *Times* is the best single general news source for the entire period, although in its reporting of the activities of organized labor and of the social Progressives it does not rank with the

Evening Journal or *Call*. From 1897 to 1904, the *Times*'s accounts of the C.F.U.'s weekly meetings were the fullest in any newspaper. However, these reports were often patently anti-labor, stressing frivolous and unimportant disputes between individual delegates, and/or ungentlemanly conduct by less polished union delegates. Despite this, the *Times* constitutes an important source for the C.F.U.'s activities to 1904. The *Times*, like other dailies, ignored the political efforts of labor unless they were in support of candidates favored by the editor, as happened in 1899, 1906, and 1907.

New York Tribune.

The *Tribune* reported most of the C.F.U.'s meetings through 1904, and its accounts also tended to stress the petty or ludicrous wherever possible. The *Tribune*'s editorials were even more sharply antiunion than those of the *Times*.

New York World.

The *World* was an excellent source for city and state politics. As a source for the activities of organized labor and the social Progressives, it ranked considerably below the *Times*, the *Evening Journal*, and the *Call*. An exception was its intensive coverage of Hearst's campaign for governor in 1906, including assessments of the importance and direction of the labor vote.

Pamphlets

The social Progressives placed great reliance on pamphlet propaganda. In the campaigns for the various reform bills, large numbers of pamphlets and simpler leaflets of all sorts were distributed. This material constituted a major expense of the individual societies. Any study of the social Progressives' methods and ideas must take into account this popular literature (see pp. 84–85, above).

Brooklyn Central Labor Union. *Why New York State Should Enact a Legal Minimum Wage for Women and Minors*, New York, 1915.
    The publication of this pamphlet was one important indication that the anti-minimum-wage position of organized labor in New York was crumbling.

Brooks, John Graham. *The Consumers' League*, New York, 1900.
    An excellent discussion of the League's social reform philos-

ophy. Brooks was president of the National Consumers' League from 1900 to 1915.

Citizens Union, The. *Tammany's Million Dollar Fraud on the Workingmen*, New York, 1897.

——. *Workingmen as Citizens*, New York, 1897.

Issued to aid in Seth Low's campaign for mayor.

Consumers' League of the City of New York. *Historical Sketch of the Pioneer Consumers' Leagues*, 1908.

——. *Laws Every Woman Should Know*, 1918.

——. *The Consumers' League: The Why and the Wherefore* [1919].

——. *The Menace to the Home from Sweatshop and Tenement Made Clothes: Testimony from Prominent Physicians, Nurses and Inspectors before the Tenement Commission of the State of New York*, New York, 1901.

——. *White Facts about Retail Stores*, New York, 1911.

Consumers' League of the State of New York. *Consumers' League of New York State* [1915].

Dorr, Rheta Childe. *Women's Demand for Humane Treatment of Women Workers in Shop and Factory*, New York, 1910.

Eastman, Crystal. "Employers' Liability: A Criticism on Facts," *Publications of the New York Branch of American Association for Labor Legislation*, No. 1, New York, 1909.

Goldmark, Pauline. *Do Children Work in Canneries?*, New York, 1909.

Gompers, Samuel. *Organized Labor's Attitude toward Child Labor*, New York, 1906.

Published by the National Child Labor Committee.

National Child Labor Committee. *Bulletin*, Nos. 1–2, 1909, No. 3, 1911.

——. *Leaflets*, Nos. 1–75, 1905–1919.

——. *Pamphlets*, Nos. 1–50, 1905–1907.

The speeches and papers delivered at the annual meetings of the Committee were reprinted as separate pieces and widely distributed.

New York Branch, American Association for Labor Legislation. *Labor Legislation*, New York, 1910.

——. *Workmen's Compensation Constitutional Amendment*, New York, 1912.

Written to gain conservative support for moderate Bayne-Phillips Compensation Amendment supported by the Association but opposed by the State Federation of Labor.

——. *Workmen's Compensation Versus Employers' Liability*, New York, 1910.

New York Child Labor Committee. *A Report to Governor Frank W. Higgins upon the Failure of Commissioner John McMackin to Enforce the Labor Laws*, New York, 1905.

The campaign against McMackin was led by Robert Hunter, later a socialist, but at this time a leading social Progressive.

——. *1903–1908: A Five Years' Fight for New York's Children*, New York, 1908.

——. *Child Labor—Factories and Stores*, New York, 1903.

——. *Summary of the Child Labor Laws of New York State*, New York, 1903.

——. *What the Newspapers Are Saying about Child Labor in New York State*, New York, 1903.

The wide range of support, even among conservatives, for child labor legislation of some kind becomes evident from this piece.

New York State Federation of Labor. *Achievements of a Progressive Up-to-Date Labor Organization*, 1918.

The State Federation claims credit for almost every major labor law passed in the period 1864–1918.

——. *Historical*, 1923.

A brief sketch of the major legislative battles of the Progressive era, written by John O'Hanlon.

Pike, Violet. *New World Lessons for Old World People*, New York, 1909.

Published by the Women's Trade Union League of New York. Written in simple English, this pamphlet served a dual purpose: not only did it support unions for women, but it could be used to teach English to the foreign-born, who were the main objective of the League's organizational campaign. Violet Pike, a Vassar graduate, was one of the leading "socialite" supporters of the Shirtwaist strike of 1909–1910.

Poole, Ernest. *The Street—Its Child Workers*, New York, 1903.

Published by the University Settlement to aid in the fight for the child labor bills of 1903.

Sergeant, Elizabeth S. *Toilers of the Tenements*, New York, 1910.

Social Reform Club of New York. *Union Label Leaflets*, Nos. 1–3, New York, 1897.

    A fine statement of the Club's support for the principles of trade unionism.

——. *In Memory of Charles B. Spahr*, New York, 1905.

    Spahr was a leading social Progressive, and one of the founders of the Club.

Socialist Party, The. *Facts for the Election*, New York, 1908.

——. *Should Wage-Earners Vote for Hearst?*, New York, 1905.

    Other pamphlets issued by the Socialist Party during the 1905 campaign reiterated the theme of this one: Hearst is a fraud, and he will only disappoint the workers; whereas Socialist candidates truly represent the working class.

Van Kleeck, Mary. *Child Labor in New York City Tenements*, New York, 1908.

    Sponsored by the New York City Consumers' League and the New York Child Labor Committee, and prepared by a professional social worker.

Women's Trade Union League of New York. *The Story of a Waitress*, New York, 1907.

All of the above pamphlets, with the exception of those published by the Socialist Party and the State Federation of Labor, may be found in the collections of the New York Public Library. The Socialist pamphlets are at the Tamiment Institute Library in New York City. The two State Federation pieces may be seen at the office of the New York State A.F.L.–C.I.O. in New York City.

Government Publications

"Administration of Labor Laws and Factory Inspection in Certain European Countries," U.S. Department of Labor, Bureau of Labor Statistics, *Bulletin* No. 142 (Feb. 1914), 9–300.

    This account was written by Dr. George M. Price, who had held important positions in the New York factory inspector's office. He was a member of the American Association for Labor Legislation, and his views had a significant impact upon the thinking of the social Progressives.

Clark, Victor S. "Labor Conditions in Australia," U.S. Department of Commerce and Labor, Bureau of Labor, *Bulletin* X (1905), 9–243.

——. "Labor Conditions in New Zealand," U.S. Department of Commerce and Labor, Bureau of Labor, *Bulletin* VIII (1903), 1142–1311.

This piece and the companion work on Australia were the most comprehensive discussions of the operation of the arbitration and minimum wage boards available to American reformers. Clark's own views about the effectiveness of these boards and the applicability of this reform to the United States are also interesting.

——. "Women and Child Wage-Earners in Great Britain," U.S. Department of Commerce and Labor, Bureau of Labor, *Bulletin* XVIII (Jan. 1909), 1–85.

"Comparison of Workmen's Compensation Laws of the United States up to December 31, 1917," U.S. Department of Labor, Bureau of Labor Statistics, *Bulletin* No. 240 (May 1918), 5–101.

New York City. *The City Record*, 1897–1916.

Of chief interest for this study were the official city election statistics contained in an issue which appeared shortly after the election.

New York State Bureau of Labor Statistics. *Annual Report*, 1897–1900.

Contains special reports concerning proposed legislation, for example on employers' liability and a more effective eight-hour day for public works, in addition to statistical material.

New York State Department of Labor. *Annual Report*, 1901–1914.

In 1901 the bureaus of Factory Inspection, Labor Statistics, and Mediation and Arbitration were combined into the Department of Labor. The reports of the Commissioner of Labor provide valuable material on the problems of enforcement.

——. *Bulletin*, 1899–1916.

Issued as the *Bulletin* of the Bureau of Labor Statistics before 1901, and by the Industrial Commission in 1915 and 1916. Until 1914 it was a quarterly and contained important material on the labor laws of each year and major court decisions, plus special articles on labor problems. After 1914 the *Bulletin* was issued as needed, and each number covered a special subject.

New York State Factory Investigating Commission.

Preliminary Report, 1912.

Second Report, 4 vols., 1913.

Third Report, 1914.

Fourth Report, 5 vols., 1915.

An invaluable source on industrial conditions within New York, and all aspects of reform opinion—both Progressive and labor.

New York State Industrial Commission. *Annual Report*, 1915–1916.

Continues the form and content of the Department of Labor's *Annual Report*.

——. *The Bulletin*, 1915–1916.

Information on the administrative activities of the Commission can be found in this monthly bulletin.

New York State Secretary of State. *Manual for the Use of the Legislature of the State of New York*, 1897–1916.

Election results for all state races, the full membership of the Legislature, etc., are conveniently presented in this annual volume.

Veditz, C. W. A. "Child-Labor Legislation in Europe," U.S. Department of Commerce and Labor, Bureau of Labor, *Bulletin* XXI (July 1910), 1–413.

Willoughby, William. "Foreign Labor Laws," *Bulletin of the* [*U.S.*] *Department of Labor*, IV–VI (1899–1901).

The author provided intensive summaries of the labor laws of the European states, Australia, and New Zealand.

"Workmen's Compensation Laws of the United States and Foreign Countries," U.S. Department of Labor, Bureau of Labor Statistics, *Bulletin* No. 126 (Dec. 1913), 1–464, and No. 203 (Jan. 1917), 9–939.

Contemporary Periodicals and Books

As might be expected, the nationally distributed magazines, including the muckraking journals, did not cover New York affairs very intensively. However, certain specific events in the state did attract national attention. Hearst's political activities brought significant comment from the national magazines. The constitutional struggle of 1915 also attracted attention outside the state. Tammany Hall came under periodic examination as part of the continuous Progressive attack on political institutions that curtailed the free operation of democracy. Magazines such as *Charities* (and its successors) were edited by men closely associated with the social Progressives and thus devoted more space to reform efforts in New York and other states than was usual in the national periodicals.

For comment in the national magazines concerning the sources of Hearst's vote in the election of 1905, see *Harper's Weekly*, XLIX (Nov. 18, 1905), 1656–1657; "New York City Vote Analyzed," *The Nation*, LXXXI (Nov. 16, 1905), 394–395; "The Rout of the Bosses in New York," *The Outlook*, LXXXI (Nov. 18, 1905), 633; and "The New York Election," *American Monthly Review of Reviews*, XXXII (Dec. 1905), 644.

The Independent, which favored municipal ownership of key public utilities, stressed Hearst's call for public ownership in "New York's Municipal Campaign," LIX (Oct. 19, 1905), 936–937, and "Election in New York City," LIX (Nov. 16, 1905), 1177–1178. Also see "The New York Mayoralty Contest," *The Outlook*, LXXXI (Oct. 21, 1905), 387–388.

Hearst's race against Hughes in 1906 occasioned further comment. *The Independent* evaluated some of the factors favoring Hearst in "Politics in New York," LXI (Aug. 9, 1906), 340–341, and "Campaign Influences in New York," LXI (Nov. 1, 1906), 1062–1063. Despite its support of Hearst in 1905, *The Independent* favored Hughes in 1906, having concluded that Hearst was irresponsible. Other views of Hearst's backers and program may be found in "A Man or a Programme," *The Outlook*, LXXXIV (Sept. 22, 1906), 155–157; "The Political Muddle in New York," *Harper's Weekly*, L (Aug. 11, Nov. 17, 1906), 1124–1125, 1626–1627; *The Nation*, LXXXIII (Oct. 4, Nov. 8, 1906), 276, 383; *The World To-Day*, XI (Dec. 1906), 1235–1237; and *The World's Work*, XI (April 1906), 7364–7366.

Hearst attracted much less attention in his campaign for mayor in 1909; but see *Current Literature*, XLVII (Dec. 1909), 587–589, 616–618; and *The Outlook*, XCIII (Nov. 13, 1909), 572–573.

The increased activity of the A.F.L. in the elections of 1906 and 1908 evoked considerable comment. Conservative sources generally opposed the purported introduction of class issues into elections, but sizable support for organized labor's political efforts appeared, in many cases tempered by the warning that to found a labor party, or a labor voting bloc, was most difficult under American circumstances.

See Thomas S. Adams, "The Trade Union in Politics," *The World To-Day*, XI (Oct. 1906). 1085–1087; John G. Brooks, "Trade Unions and Politics," *The Outlook*, LXXXV (Jan. 5, 1907), 25–29; Sydney Brooks, "Is an American Labor Party a Likelihood?" *Harper's Weekly*, LII (Nov. 14, 1908), 13; "Labor in National Politics," *Chautauquan*, XLIV (Oct. 1906), 147–149; "Labor Unions in Politics," *The Independent*, LX (May 3, 1906), 1050–1051, and LXV (July 9, 1908), 108–110; and Graham Taylor, "Organized Labor's Political Front Unbroken," *Charities and The Commons*, XXI (Oct. 31, 1908), 149–150.

Important comments on the battle for the constitution of 1915 may be found in articles by three leading social Progressives, Abram Elkus and John B. Andrews of the American Association for Labor Legislation and Owen Lovejoy of the National Child Labor Committee, in the *Proceedings*, Academy of Political Science in the City of New York, V (Jan. 1915), 392–405. See also Henry Jones Ford, "The Revised Constitution of New York," *The New Republic*, IV (Oct. 9, 1915), 257–259; Gilbert G. Benjamin, "The Attempted Revision of the State Constitution of New York," *American Political Science Review*, X (Feb. 1916), 20–43, and "Labor Opposition to the New York Constitution," *The Survey*, XXXV (Oct. 23, 1915), 81.

The newspapers of New York City provide a record of the recurrent attacks on Tammany by various reform and fusion groups. For examples of the attempt to indicate the sources of Tammany's power, see Gustavus Myers, "The Secrets of Tammany's Success," *The Forum*, XXXI (June 1901), 488–500; Walter L. Hawley, "The Strength and Weaknesses of Tammany Hall," *North American Review*, CLXXIII (Oct. 1901), 481–486; "The Sources of Tammany's Power," *The Outlook*, LXXIII (Feb. 21, 1903), 419–421; Sydney Brooks, "Tammany," *The English Review*, III (Nov. 1909), 716–723; Everett P. Wheeler, "Tammany Hall," *The Outlook*, CV (Sept. 13, 1913), 73–81 and Burton J. Hendrick, "The Twilight of Tammany Hall," *The World's Work*, XXVII (Feb. 1914), 432–440.

Hawley's article linked the Roman Catholic Church with Tammany and brought a specific rebuttal from M. P. Curran, "Tammany Hall and the Catholic Church," in *Donahoe's Magazine*, XLVI (Nov. 1901).

In other areas of investigation, the following books and articles proved to be most useful.

Abbott, Edith. *Women in Industry*, New York, 1910.

Adams, Thomas S. and Helen L. Sumner. *Labor Problems*, New York, 1913.

Addams, Jane. "The Function of the Social Settlement," *The Annals, American Academy of Political and Social Science*, XIII (May 1899), 323–345.

Addresses Delivered at Members' Council Luncheon of the Merchants Association of New York on the Subject of "Unemployment in New York" by William Breed, Esq., Hon. John Purroy Mitchel, Hon. Elbert H. Gary, Hon. Henry Bruere [1915].

Andrews, John B. *Labor Problems and Labor Legislation*, New York, 1919.

This volume, published by the A.A.L.L., is valuable not only for its discussion of past gains but for its many samples of the publicity materials used by the reformers in their campaigns.

Anthony, Katharine. *Labor Laws of New York, A Handbook* (The Brooklyn Auxiliary of the Consumers' League of the City of New York), New York, 1917.

"Bad Housing Bills in New York," *Charities and The Commons*, XV (Feb. 10, 1906), 661–663.

Baldwin, W. H., Jr. "Publicity as a Means of Social Reform," *North American Review*, CLXXIII (Dec. 1901), 845–853.

The chairman of the New York Committee of Fifteen, which carried out an antivice campaign in 1900–1901, makes some perceptive remarks.

Bauer, John. "New York Workmen's Compensation Act Unconstitutional," *American Economic Review*, I (Sept. 1911), 634–637.

Bernheimer, Charles S. *The Shirt Waist Strike*, New York, 1910.

Quickly written at the time of the strike and most valuable for its distinctive point of view. Bernheimer was assistant head worker of the University Settlement at the time, and this short piece was published by the Settlement.

Best, Harry. *The Men's Garment Industry of New York and the Strike of 1913*, New York, 1913.

Breen, Matthew P. *Thirty Years of New York Politics Up-to-Date,* New York, 1899.

Burke, William M. *History and Functions of Central Labor Unions,* New York, 1899.

A complete study which includes valuable comments on the political activities of the central bodies.

Carlton, Frank T. "Political Weakness of American Labor Organizations," *The Survey,* XXXV (March 25, 1916), 759–760.

Cease, D. L. "The Labor Vote and What Controls It," *Gunton's Magazine,* XXVII (Oct. 1904), 349–356.

The author was editor of the journal of the Brotherhood of Railroad Trainmen. Compare with Gunton's own article, "The Labor Vote," in the same issue, pp. 238–245.

Chamberlain, Mary. "The Tammany Tiger's Paw on Labor Laws In New York State," *The Survey,* XXXII (Aug. 15, 1914), 499–504, 514.

A leading social Progressive attacks the appointment of politicians and labor leaders to the top posts in the Labor Department, in preference to choice by civil service procedures.

Chapin, Robert C. *The Standard of Living among Workingmen's Families in New York City,* New York, 1909.

Despite the possibilities of error noted by the author, and by reviewers, this study had wide influence. It was quoted extensively by the reformers.

Charities, X (March 7 and March 14, 1903), 209–215, 250–252.

Charities and The Commons, XVII [Feb. 1907], 856.

——. XIX (Nov. 2, 1907), 947–948.

Accepts the view that social work must reflect an interest in social reform as well as charity and individual betterment.

Cipperly, John A. *Labor Laws and Decisions of the State of New York* (2d ed. revised to March 1908), Albany, 1908.

Clews, Henry. *Financial, Economic and Miscellaneous Speeches and Essays,* New York, 1910.

Colvin, David L. *The Bicameral Principle in the New York Legislature,* New York, 1913.

Contains some interesting material on voting trends in New York from 1909 to 1912.

Commons, John R. *Labor and Administration,* New York, 1913.

Cope, Francis R., Jr. "Tenement House Reform: Its Practical Results in the 'Battle Row' District, New York," *American Journal of Sociology*, VII (Nov. 1901), 331–358.

Daily Trade Record, 1905–1909.
The trade publication of the textile industry, issued daily in this period. Contains occasional labor items.

Dawson, William H. *Social Insurance in Germany, 1883–1911*, London, 1912.

Deming, Seymour. "From Doomsday to Kingdom Come," *Everybody's Magazine*, XXXIV (March 1916), 309–327.
Presents some provocative ideas about the importance of the lower middle class in the Progressive movement.

Devine, Edward T. "Compensation Bills at Albany," *The Survey*, XXIX (Feb. 22, 1913), 722–724.

——. *Misery and Its Causes*, New York, 1909.
An interesting blend of the traditional ideas of the charity societies and the new reform plans of the social Progressives.

De Witt, Benjamin P. *The Progressive Movement: A Non-Partisan Comprehensive Discussion of Current Tendencies in American Politics*, New York, 1915.

Dinwiddie, Emily W. "The Work of New York's Tenement House Department," *Charities and The Commons*, XVII (Oct. 6, 1906), 11–12.

Elkus, Abram. "New York's New Labor Legislation," *The Survey*, XXX (June 21, 1913), 399–400.

Fairchild, Fred. "The Factory Legislation of the State of New York," *Publications of the American Economic Association*, Third Series, VI, No. 4 (Nov. 1905).

Foerster, Robert F. "The British National Insurance Act," *Quarterly Journal of Economics*, XXVI (Feb. 1912), 275–312.

Forrest, Jay W., and James Malcolm. *Tammany's Treason: Impeachment of Governor William Sulzer*, Albany, 1913.

Gompers, Samuel. "Australasian Labor Regulation Schemes," *American Federationist*, XXII (April 1915), 253–263.

Groat, George G. *An Introduction to the Study of Organized Labor in America*, New York, 1916.

——. "The Eight Hour and Prevailing Rate Movement in New York State," *Political Science Quarterly*, XXI (Sept. 1906), 414–433.

——. *Trade Unions and the Law in New York*, New York, 1905.

Gunton's Institute Bulletin, New York, 1899–1903.

Provides a forum for the views of George Gunton, who identifies himself as a supporter of trade unionism. Gunton's views on labor resemble those of the business members of the National Civic Federation, and despite his claims of support for organized labor, he was attacked in the labor press on several occasions. For an excellent discussion of Gunton's views, see Jack Blicksilver, "George Gunton: Pioneer Spokesman for a Labor–Big Business Entente," *Business History Review*, XXXI (Spring 1957), 1-22.

Hall, George A. "New York Child Labor Legislation," *Charities and The Commons*, XVIII (July 20, 1907), 434–436.

Hall, James Parker. "The New York Workmen's Compensation Act Decision," *Journal of Political Economy*, XIX (Oct. 1911), 694–700.

Haynes, George E. *The Negro at Work in New York City* (Studies in History, Economics and Public Law Edited by the Faculty of Political Science of Columbia University, Whole No. 124), New York, 1912.

Hodder, Alfred. *A Fight for the City*, New York, 1903.

Describes some of the problems in an independent anti-Tammany campaign.

Hoxie, Robert F. "Trade Unionism in the United States: General Character and Types," *Journal of Political Economy*, XXII (March, May 1914), 201–217, 464–481.

——. *Trade Unionism in the United States*, New York, 1917.

"How Labor Voted," *Literary Digest*, LIII (Nov. 25, 1916), 1391.

Hunter, Robert. *Labor in Politics*, New York, 1915.

"Industrialized Politics," *The World's Work*, XI (March 1906), 7342–7346.

The struggle between Odell and Platt for control of the New York Republican Party is analyzed quite well.

Ingersoll, Raymond V. "Labor Clauses in Franchise Grants," *Municipal Affairs*, VI (Fall 1902), 774–780.

Kelley, Florence. "An Effective Child Labor Law," *The Annals, American Academy of Political and Social Science* (May 1903).

——. *Some Ethical Gains through Legislation*, New York, 1905.

Summarizes the major ideas of this central figure in social Progressivism.

Kingsbury, Mary M. "Women in New York Settlements," *Municipal Affairs*, II (Sept. 1898), 458–462.

Lowe, Boutelle E. *Representative Industry and Trade Unionism*, New York, 1912.

Studies the Rochester, N.Y. clothing industry, and concludes that working conditions were considerably better than in New York City.

Lowell, Josephine Shaw. *Consumers' Leagues* (Publications, The Christian Social Union, No. 46, Feb. 15, 1898).

Macarthur, W. "Political Action and Trade Unionism," *Publications of the American Academy of Political and Social Science*, No. 434, 1904.

A fine statement of the A.F.L.'s position that permanent, basic improvements in the conditions of labor must proceed from union action.

McVey, Frank L. "The Work and Problems of The Consumers' League," *American Journal of Sociology*, VI (May 1901), 764–777.

Malkiel, Theresa S. *The Diary of a Shirtwaist Striker*, New York, 1910.

The "Diary" was written by socialists after the strike had ended.

More, Louise B. *Wage-Earners' Budgets: A Study of Standards and Cost of Living in New York City*, New York, 1907.

Myers, Gustavus. *The History of Tammany Hall* (2d ed.), New York, 1917.

National Association of Manufacturers of the United States of America. *Report of the American Trade Commission on Industrial Conditions in Australasia*, New York, 1914.

New Republic, The, I (Nov. 7, 1914), 3.

Offers some interesting reasons for the apparent reaction against Progressivism in the elections of 1914.

"New York Council for Civic Cooperation," *Charities*, X (Jan. 31, 1903), 113–114.

Parmelee, Maurice F. "The Bakeries of the East Side," *University Settlement Studies*, I, Nos. 3–4 (Oct. 1905–Jan. 1906).

Contends that the legislation upset by the Lochner case was already ineffective in practice.

Pink, Louis H. "Old Tenements and New Law," *University Settlement Studies*, III, No. 2, Supplement (June 1907).

Platt, Thomas C. *The Autobiography of Thomas Collier Platt*, New York, 1910.

Pope, Jesse. *The Clothing Industry in New York* (University of Missouri Studies, I), 1905.

A careful monograph that discusses all phases of the industry.

Porritt, Edward. "The British National Insurance Act," *Political Science Quarterly*, XXVII (June 1912), 260–280.

"Proposed Changes in the New York Labor Laws," *Charities and The Commons*, XV (Feb. 17, 1906), 684–685.

Reynolds, James B. "Eight Years at the University Settlement," *University Settlement Studies*, II, No. 2 (July 1906).

Riordan, William L. *Plunkitt of Tammany Hall*, New York, 1905.

Ross, J. Elliot. *Consumers and Wage Earners*, New York, 1912.

Supports the Consumers' League philosophy that consumers have a responsibility to ensure fair working and living conditions for labor through direct economic action and by legislation. Some specific discussion of League policy is included.

Seager, Henry R. *Labor and Other Economic Essays*, New York, 1931.

Includes a collection of Seager's writings during the Progressive period. He was a leading publicist for a program of comprehensive legislative reform.

——. *Social Insurance*, New York, 1910.

"Social Bodies Ask Removal of Commissioners," *The Survey*, XXXV (Jan. 1, 1916), 369–370.

Speed, John G. "The Purchase of Votes—New York City and New York State," *Harper's Weekly*, XLIX (March 25, 1905), 422–424.

For another description of vote frauds in New York City see Charles Edward Russell, "At the Throat of the Republic: Postscript—The Election of 1907," *Cosmopolitan*, XLIV (April 1908), 475–480.

Steffens, Lincoln. *The Shame of the Cities*, New York, 1957 ed.

——. *The Struggle for Self Government*, New York, 1906.

Stelzle, Charles. *Letters From a Workingman*, New York, 1908.

The pseudonym "An American Mechanic" appears on the title page. The book is a complete statement of the reform philosophy which had its roots in American Protestantism. Stelzle worked extensively with laborers in New York City.

Stevens, George. *New York Typographical Union No. 6*, Albany, 1913.

An exhaustive study written from original sources by the senior statistician of the New York Department of Labor. Unfortunately these sources are poorly noted.

Taylor, Graham. "Where There's Common Ground in Civic Progress," *Charities and The Commons*, XVII (1906), 188–189.

"The Minimum Wage Board and the Union," *The Unpopular Review*, IV (Oct. 1915), 397–411.

"By a Trade Unionist" is the only designation of the author. Effectively presents the view that minimum wage legislation, even for women, is a threat to the union movement.

The Redemption of New York (Milo T. Bogard, ed.), New York, 1902.

"The Tammany Victory," *The Spectator*, LXXIX (Nov. 6, 1897), 637–638.

See also "The Next Mayor of New York," in the October 9, 1897, issue. Both articles present a keen analysis of the election.

"Tinkering with New York's Tenement House Law," *Charities*, X (Feb. 7, 1903), 168–170.

Also see March 14, 1903, issue, pp. 250–252, for further material on the reformers' campaign to prevent the wrecking of the tenement reform laws of 1901.

Veiller, Lawrence. "Attacks on New York's Tenement House Law," *Charities and The Commons*, XVIII (1907), 8–9.

——. "The City Club of New York," *Charities and The Commons*, XVII (1906), 212–213.

Walling, William E. "Why American Labor Unions Keep Out of Politics," *The Outlook*, LXXX (May 20, 1905), 183–186.

Waring, George. "The Labor Question in the Department of Street Cleaning," *Municipal Affairs*, I (Sept. 1897), 515–524.

White, Henry. "The City's Health—Working Conditions," *Municipal Affairs*, II (June 1898), 237–246.

——. "Effects of New York Sweatshop Law," *Gunton's Magazine,* XVIII (April 1900), 348–354.

"Why Municipal Reform Succeeds in Chicago and Fails in New York," *The Independent,* LVI (April 14, 1904), 829–835.

Wolman, Leo. "The Extent of Labor Organization in the United States in 1910," *Quarterly Journal of Economics,* XXX (May 1916), 486–518.

Noncontemporary Books and Articles

Abell, Aaron I. *American Catholicism and Social Action: A Search for Social Justice, 1865–1950,* New York, 1960.

——. "Labor Legislation in the United States: The Background and Growth of Newer Trends," *Review of Politics,* X (Jan. 1948), 35–60.

——. *The Urban Impact on American Protestantism, 1865–1900,* Cambridge, Mass., 1943.

   The author concludes that the social gospel was growing in importance within Protestant religious opinion. However, in New York churchmen of all denominations played only a small role in the social Progressive movement.

Adamic, Louis. *Dynamite, The Story of Class Violence in America* (rev. ed.), New York, 1934.

Baker, Mrs. Elizabeth Faulkner. *Protective Labor Legislation with Special Reference to Women in the State of New York* (Studies in History, Economics and Public Law Edited by the Faculty of Political Science of Columbia University, Whole No. 259), New York, 1925.

Barker, Charles A. *Henry George,* New York, 1955.

Bean, Walton. *Boss Ruef's San Francisco: The Story of the Union Labor Party, Big Business and the Graft Prosecution,* Berkeley, 1952.

   This account of San Francisco under the administrations of a supposed labor party indicates how class-conscious voting can develop among unionists, and how quickly they can lose control over their own party.

Beyer, Clara M. "History of Labor Legislation for Women in Three States," U.S. Department of Labor, Women's Bureau, *Bulletin,* No. 66, Washington, 1929.

An excellent treatment of the subject for New York is found in this monograph. California and Massachusetts are the other states discussed.

Bimba, Anthony. *The History of the American Working Class*, New York, 1927.

Boone, Gladys. *The Women's Trade Union Leagues in Great Britain and the United States of America*, New York, 1942.

A favorable account which concentrates mainly on the National League in the United States.

Boyer, Richard O., and Herbert M. Morais. *Labor's Untold Story*, New York, 1955.

Stresses the accomplishments of the radical labor groups. Of major interest is the extensive bibliography.

Bremner, Robert H. *From the Depths: The Discovery of Poverty in America*, New York, 1956.

Brown, Ira V. *Lyman Abbott, Christian Evolutionist: A Study in Religious Liberalism*, Cambridge, Mass., 1953.

Carlson, Oliver and Ernest S. Bates. *Hearst, Lord of San Simeon*, New York, 1936.

Presents interesting ideas concerning Hearst's motivations, political ideology, and appeal to social class-consciousness.

Carroll, Mollie Ray. *Labor and Politics: The Attitude of the American Federation of Labor toward Legislation and Politics*, Boston, 1923.

Chamberlain, John. *Farewell to Reform: Being a History of the Rise, Life and Decay of the Progressive Mind in America*, New York, 1932.

Coben, Stanley. "Northeastern Business and Radical Reconstruction: A Re-examination," *Mississippi Valley Historical Review*, XLVI (June 1959), 67–90.

Commager, Henry Steele. *The American Mind: An Interpretation of American Thought and Character since the 1880's*, New Haven, 1950.

Davis, Allen F. "The Social Workers and the Progressive Party, 1912–1916," *American Historical Review*, LXIX (April 1964), 671–688.

Douglas, Paul H. *Real Wages in the United States, 1890–1926*, Boston, 1930.

Dreier, Mary E. *Margaret Dreier Robins: Her Life, Letters and Work*, New York, 1950.

Does not focus on any one issue long enough to do more than describe. The book is valuable, however, as an exploration of the reformer's psyche by a writer who was herself the prototype of the wealthy and socially prominent social Progressive.

Dulles, Foster R. *Labor in America*, New York, 1955.

Ellis, David, James Frost, Harold Syrett, and Henry Carman. *A Short History of New York State*, Ithaca, N.Y., 1957.

Epstein, Melech. *Jewish Labor in the United States of America: An Industrial, Political and Cultural History of the Jewish Labor Movement, 1882–1914*, New York, 1950.

The author supports no faction in the schismatic Jewish labor movement, and the book is a most readable survey of a complex subject.

Faulkner, Harold U. *The Quest for Social Justice, 1898–1914*, New York, 1931.

Fine, Sidney. *Laissez-Faire and the General Welfare State: A Study of Conflict in American Thought, 1865–1901*, Ann Arbor, Mich., 1956.

Flint, Winston A. *The Progressive Movement in Vermont*, Washington, 1941.

Friedman, Jacob A. *The Impeachment of Governor William Sulzer* (Studies in History, Economics and Public Law Edited by the Faculty of Political Science of Columbia University, Whole No. 447), New York, 1939.

This well-written monograph is the best work on the subject.

Geiger, Louis. *Joseph W. Folk of Missouri* (University of Missouri Studies, XXV, No. 2), 1953.

Glaab, Charles N. "The Failure of North Dakota Progressivism," *Mid-America*, XXXIX (Oct. 1957), 195–209.

Glad, Paul W. "Bryan and the Urban Progressives," *Mid-America*, XXXIX (July 1957), 169–179.

Goldman, Eric F. *Rendezvous with Destiny*, New York, 1952.

Goldmark, Josephine. *Impatient Crusader: Florence Kelley's Life Story*, Urbana, Ill., 1953.

A sympathetic biography written by a long-time associate.

Gosnell, H. F. *Boss Platt and His New York Machine: A Study of the Political Leadership of Thomas C. Platt, Theodore Roosevelt and Others,* Chicago, 1924.

A complete, detailed study of the Platt machine.

Grantham, Dewey W. *Hoke Smith and the Politics of the New South,* Baton Rouge, La., 1958.

Green, Marguerite. *The National Civic Federation and the American Labor Movement, 1900–1925,* Washington, 1956.

A good monograph which includes an exhaustive bibliography.

Greenwood, Gordon, ed. *Australia: A Social and Political History,* Sydney, 1955.

Hall, Frederick Smith. *Forty Years, 1902–1942: The Work of the New York Child Labor Committee,* New York, 1942.

This brief account presents the Committee's view of its major accomplishments.

Handy, Robert T. "Christianity and Socialism in America, 1900–1920," *Church History,* XXI (March 1952), 39–54.

A clear, concise account of the activities and thought of the small group of Christian Socialists who were active during the Progressive period.

Hansen, Alvin H. "Factors Affecting the Trend of Real Wages," *American Economic Review,* XV (March 1925), 27–42.

——. "Industrial Class Alignments in the United States," *Quarterly Publication of the American Statistical Association,* XVII (Dec. 1920), 417–425.

Hartz, Louis. *The Liberal Tradition in America,* New York, 1955.

History of Labor in the United States, 1896–1932, New York, 1935. Vol. 3: Don Lescohier, "Working Conditions," and Elizabeth Brandeis, "Labor Legislation."

History of the State of New York (Alexander C. Flick, ed.), 10 vols., New York, 1933–1937.

Hofstadter, Richard. *The Age of Reform from Bryan to F.D.R.,* New York, 1955.

Hopkins, Charles H. *The Rise of the Social Gospel in American Protestantism, 1865–1915,* New Haven, 1940.

Hurwitz, H. L. *Theodore Roosevelt and Labor in New York State, 1880–1900* (Studies in History, Economics and Public Law Edited by the Faculty of Political Science of Columbia University, Whole No. 500), New York, 1943.

A careful discussion which accords organized labor some influence over T.R., but concludes that political ends determined most of his positions on social reform legislation.

Huthmacher, J. Joseph. "Urban Liberalism and the Age of Reform," *Mississippi Valley Historical Review*, XLIX (Sept. 1962), 231–241.

Karson, Marc. *American Labor Unions and Politics, 1900–1918*, Carbondale, Ill., 1958.

Kipnis, Ira. *The American Socialist Movement, 1897–1912*, New York, 1952.

Knight, Robert E. L. *Industrial Relations in the San Francisco Bay Area, 1900–1918*, Berkeley, 1960.

Kovaleski, Emanuel. *Illustrated History of the Central Trades and Labor Council, Rochester, New York*, Rochester, 1927.

By a former vice president of the New York State Federation of Labor.

Link, Arthur. *Woodrow Wilson and the Progressive Era, 1910–1917*, New York, 1954.

Lubove, Roy M. *The Progressives and the Slums: Tenement House Reform in New York City, 1890–1917*, Pittsburgh, 1962.

Lundberg, Ferdinand. *Imperial Hearst: A Social Biography*, New York, 1936.

An extremely critical account which appears to be a product more of the author's political opposition to Hearst in the thirties than of any other factor.

McClellan, George B., Jr. *The Gentleman and the Tiger: The Autobiography of George B. McClellan, Jr.*, Philadelphia, 1956.

Contains some interesting comments on New York politics. It is well edited by Harold C. Syrett.

McGinley, James J. *Labor Relations in the New York Rapid Transit Systems, 1904–1944*, New York, 1949.

Margulies, Herbert. "The Decline of Wisconsin Progressivism, 1911–1914," *Mid-America*, XXXIX (July 1957), 131–155.

——. "Political Weaknesses in Wisconsin Progressivism, 1905–1908," *Mid-America*, XLI (July 1959), 154–172.

These two articles provide an excellent analysis of the structure of Progressivism in Wisconsin and of the stresses and disunity within the movement.

Maxwell, Robert S. *La Follette and the Rise of the Progressives in Wisconsin*, Madison, 1956.

May, Henry. *Protestant Churches and Industrial America*, New York, 1949.

Miller, Spencer, Jr., and Joseph F. Fletcher. *The Church and Industry*, New York, 1930.

    An uninspired text, but with an invaluable bibliography of materials on the relation between the churches and organized labor during the Progressive era.

Millis, Harry A., and Royal E. Montgomery. *Labor's Progress and Some Basic Labor Problems*, New York, 1938.

Mitgang, Herbert. *The Man Who Rode the Tiger: The Life and Times of Judge Samuel Seabury*, Philadelphia, 1963.

Mowry, George E. *The California Progressives, 1900–1920*, Berkeley, 1951.

——. *The Era of Theodore Roosevelt, 1900–1912*, New York, 1958.

Nash, Gerald D. "The Influence of Labor on State Policy, 1860–1920: The Experience of California," *California Historical Quarterly*, XLII (Sept. 1963), 241–257.

Nathan, Maud. *The Story of an Epoch Making Movement*, Garden City, N.Y., 1926.

    Mrs. Nathan was a leading figure in the New York City Consumers' League for three decades. She discusses the activities of the organization especially such nonlegislative work as the White List.

National Consumers' League. *The National Consumers' League: First Quarter Century, 1899–1924*, New York, 1924.

Nestor, Agnes. *Woman's Labor Leader*, Rockford, Ill., 1954.

    More anecdotal than analytical, but does provide some information about the early days of the National Women's Trade Union League and the International Glove Workers Union, of which the author was a leader.

Noble, Ransom E., Jr. *New Jersey Progressivism before Wilson*, Princeton, 1946.

Nye, Russel B. *Midwestern Progressive Politics: A Historical Study of Its Origins and Development, 1870–1950*, East Lansing, Mich., 1951.

Older, Mrs. Fremont. *William Randolph Hearst, American*, New York, 1936.

Perlman, Selig. *A History of Trade Unionism in the United States*, New York, 1922.

——. *A Theory of the Labor Movement*, New York, 1928.

——, and Philip Taft. *History of Labor in the United States, 1896–1932*, Vol. 4 (*Labor Movements*), New York, 1935.

Pink, Louis H. *Gaynor*, New York, 1931.

An undocumented biography written by a social Progressive who had been active in New York during Gaynor's most important years of public service.

Pipkin, Charles. *The Idea of Social Justice: A Study of Legislation and Administration and the Labour Movement in England and France between 1900 and 1926*, New York, 1927.

Pusey, Merlo J. *Charles Evans Hughes*, 2 vols., New York, 1951.

Reed, Louis S. *The Labor Philosophy of Samuel Gompers* (Studies in History, Economics and Public Law Edited by the Faculty of Political Science of Columbia University, Whole No. 327), New York, 1930.

Rees, Albert, *Real Wages in Manufacturing, 1890–1914*, Princeton, 1961.

Rischin, Moses. "From Gompers to Hillman: Labor Goes Middle Class," *Antioch Review*, XIII (June 1953), 191–201.

Scott, Andrew M. "The Progressive Era in Perspective," *Journal of Politics*, XXI (Nov. 1959), 685–701.

Seidman, Joel. *The Needle Trades*, New York, 1942.

Contains a complete bibliography and exhaustive footnotes.

Shannon, David A. *The Socialist Party of America: A History*, New York, 1955.

Sharkey, Robert P. *Money, Class and Party: An Economic Study of Civil War and Reconstruction*, Baltimore, 1959.

Stimson, Grace H. *Rise of the Labor Movement in Los Angeles*, Berkeley, 1955.

Stoddard, Lothrop. *Master of Manhattan: The Life of Richard Croker*, New York, 1931.

Sutch, W. B. *The Quest for Security in New Zealand*, London, 1942.

Swanberg, W. A. *Citizen Hearst*, New York, 1961.

Swett, Steven C. "The Test of a Reformer: A Study of Seth Low,

New York City Mayor, 1902–1903," *New-York Historical Society Quarterly*, XLIV (Jan. 1960), 5–41.

Taft, Philip. "Labor History and the Labor Issues of Today," *Proceedings of the American Philosophical Society*, CVI (Aug. 1962), 304–309.

——. *The A.F. of L. in the Time of Gompers*, New York, 1957.

Wiebe, Robert. "Business Disunity and the Progressive Movement, 1901–1914," *Mississippi Valley Historical Review*, XLIV (March 1958), 664–685.

Winkler, John K. *William Randolph Hearst*, New York, 1955.

Woodroofe, Kathleen. *From Charity to Social Work in England and the United States*, London, 1962.

Index

American Association for Labor Legislation: and organized labor, 55–56, 62; policies of, 55–58; membership and finances of, 72–74; cooperation with other reform groups, 80; formation of, 81–82; and workmen's compensation, 109–118; opposition to New York State Federation of Labor, 112–115, 120–121; and New York Industrial Commission, 120–121; support of European system of labor law enforcement, 147; *see also* Social Progressives

American Federation of Labor: and Social Reform Club, 52, 54; and Women's Trade Union League, 63–66; support of workmen's compensation in New York, 108; and labor legislation, 132–136; and political action, 159–160, 203, 216, 219–222, 231, 245–247; *see also* Gompers, Samuel, *and* Labor, organized

Arbitration, compulsory, 142–143

Astor, Mrs. Madeline, 73

Bannard, Otto, 225

Barnes, William, 213–214

Bates, Edward, 133

Bliss, Rev. W. D. P., 59, 62, 79

Bohm, Ernest, 242, 247

Brooklyn Central Labor Union: opposes New York State Federation of Labor, 124; supports minimum wage laws for women, 135; and Hearst, 203–204, 209–210, 224; support of Bryan in 1908, 220

Brotherhoods, railroad, *see* Railroad brotherhoods

Brown, Elon, 119, 122

Bryan, William Jennings, 220–222, 224, 231, 245

C.A.I.L., *see* Church Association for the Advancement of the Interests of Labor

Call, Homer, 135, 230, 240

Central Federated Union of New York City: disagreements with New York State Federation of Labor, 28–33, 124–125, 176; and *New York Call*, 37; and child labor laws, 90–91; and compulsory arbitration, 142–143; attempts to secure enforcement of the labor laws, 148–149, 171, 175; and political action to 1904, 161–163, 171–178, 186–187; disputes with Low Administration, 162, 185; and Henry George, 186–187; and Hearst, 197, 203–204, 208–209; support of Bryan in 1908, 220–221; opposition to political action in 1907, 224; and Seabury, 244, 247; *see also* Labor, organized

Charities, 40–41

Child Labor Committee, National, 76, 84–85; *see also* Social Progressives

Child Labor Committee, New York, and organized labor, 49, 53; activities of, 49, 84–85, 90–95, 119–121; *see also* Social Progressives

Child labor laws, New York, 88–89, 94–95